American River College Library
4700 College Oak Drive
Sacramento, California 95841

The Practice of Reading

ALSO BY DENIS DONOGHUE

The Third Voice: Modern British and American Verse Drama
An Honoured Guest: New Essays on W. B. Yeats (editor, with J. R. Mulryne)
The Ordinary Universe: Soundings in Modern Literature
Swift Revisited (editor)
Emily Dickinson
Jonathan Swift: A Critical Introduction
Yeats
Jonathan Swift: A Critical Anthology (editor)
Thieves of Fire
Memoirs, by W. B. Yeats (editor)
The Sovereign Ghost
Ferocious Alphabets
Connoisseurs of Chaos: Ideas of Order in Modern American Poetry
The Arts Without Mystery
Selected Essays of R. P. Blackmur (editor)
England, Their England
We Irish
Reading America
Warrenpoint
The Pure Good of Theory
The Old Moderns
Walter Pater: Lover of Strange Souls

DENIS DONOGHUE

The Practice of Reading

YALE UNIVERSITY PRESS

NEW HAVEN & LONDON

Published with assistance from the Kingsley Trust Association Publication Fund established by the Scroll and Key Society of Yale College.

Copyright © 1998 by Denis Donoghue. All rights reserved. This book may not be reproduced, in whole or in part, including illustrations, in any form (beyond that copying permitted by Sections 107 and 108 of the U.S. Copyright Law and except by reviewers for the public press), without written permission from the publishers.

Designed by Nancy Ovedovitz and set in Minion type by Keystone Typesetting, Inc. Printed in the United States of America by Thomson-Shore, Dexter, Michigan.

Library of Congress Cataloging-in-Publication Data
Donoghue, Denis.
The practice of reading / Denis Donoghue.
p.   cm.
Includes bibliographical references (p.   ) and index.
ISBN 0-300-07466-2 (alk. paper)
1. English literature—History and criticism—Theory, etc.   2. Reader-response criticism.   3. Books and reading.   I. Title.
PR21.D66   1998
820.9—dc21   97-42549

A catalogue record for this book is available from the British Library.

The paper in this book meets the guidelines for permanence and durability of the Committee on Production Guidelines for Book Longevity of the Council on Library Resources.

10   9   8   7   6   5   4   3   2   1

For Frances and the children

Contents

Acknowledgments

I did much of the reading for this book while I was a fellow of the Woodrow Wilson Center for International Scholars, in Washington D.C., and, later, while I was a senior Mellon fellow at the National Humanities Center, in North Carolina. I am grateful to the staff of these centers for their help and to the fellows in both places with whom I had lively discussions.

I have tried to indicate, in each chapter, the context of the debate—so far as I have access to it—and the critical occasions that I have found most instructive. I wish to acknowledge the scholars and critics who have pointed the debate. The kind of reading that I advocate is best done in such a context of agreement, dissent, and clarification.

In rereading this book, I have come upon pages in which my debts to particular friends and colleagues are especially clear. So I thank Stephen Bann, Ralph Cohen, John Coleman, Geoffrey Hill, Lisa Jardine, Richard Lehan, Melissa Malouf, and Eugene Vance. The customary exemption is appropriate: none of these friends and colleagues is to be blamed for my errors.

Some chapters or parts of chapters appeared earlier in

the *Times Literary Supplement, New York Review of Books, Sewanee Review, Southern Review, New Literary History,* and *Comparative Criticism.* A shorter version of Chapter 3 appears in Alvin Kernan, editor, *What's Happened to the Humanities?* (Princeton University Press, 1996). I am grateful to the publisher for permission to reprint that material. Chapter 8 was given as the Hilda Hulme Memorial Lecture at the University of London on December 6, 1993, and published by that university.

Reading is the easiest thing in the world, it is freedom
without work, a pure Yes blossoming in the immediate.
—Maurice Blanchot, *The Gaze of Orpheus*

It is the peculiar business of poetry and the other arts to
qualify with form and order so much of experience as can
be made intelligible.
—R. P. Blackmur, *Outsider at the Heart of Things*

Part I

Curriculum Vitae

The first book of criticism that I recall reading, pencil in hand and taking notes, was T. S. Eliot's *The Sacred Wood*. Many of its sentences have lodged with me for so long that I have stopped thinking of them as quotations; I recite them as if they were my own. "When we are considering poetry, we must consider it primarily as poetry and not as another thing." "Poetry is not the inculcation of morals or the direction of politics; and no more is it religion or an equivalent of religion, except by some monstrous abuse of words." "The progress of an artist is a continual self-sacrifice, a continual extinction of personality."[1] These sentences are as close to me as lines from "The Waste Land": "In the mountains, there you feel free." "I will show you fear in a handful of dust." But what I found most edifying in *The Sacred Wood* was Eliot's concern for language, his sense of the relation between the quality of language and the quality of the feeling it inhabited, his conviction that a particular language was an indication of the quality of the society in which it was spoken. I admired, too, in Eliot's later critical writings, his responsiveness to differences of tone and style; as in "Poetry and Drama," where he comments on the first scene

3

of *Hamlet* and notes the anticipation of the plot in Horatio's word "usurp'st" when he addresses the Ghost—"What art thou that usurp'st this time of night?" Eliot quotes the great speech by Horatio with which the scene ends:

> But, look, the morn, in russet mantle clad,
> Walks o'er the dew of yon high eastward hill.
> Break we our watch up. . .

—and comments:

> This is great poetry, and it is dramatic; but besides being poetic and dra-
> matic, it is something more. There emerges, when we analyse it, a kind of
> musical design also which reinforces and is one with the dramatic move-
> ment. It has checked and accelerated the pulse of our emotion without our
> knowing it. Note that in these last words of Marcellus—
>
> It faded on the crowing of the cock.
> Some say that ever 'gainst that season comes
> Wherein our Saviour's birth is celebrated,
> The bird of dawning singeth all night long,
>
> —there is a deliberate brief emergence of the poetic into consciousness.
> When we hear the lines
>
> But, look, the morn, in russet mantle clad,
> Walks o'er the dew of yon high eastward hill.
>
> we are lifted for a moment beyond character, but with no sense of unfitness
> of the words coming, and at this moment, from the lips of Horatio. The
> transitions in the scene obey laws of the music of dramatic poetry.[2]

During those years I was a student at University College, Dublin, and at the Royal Irish Academy of Music, having recently arrived from Warrenpoint, a small town in Northern Ireland where my father was the local police sergeant. For financial and other reasons, we were not a bookish family. I had access to a few shelves of books in the home of my local elementary teacher, Sean Crawford, but the range of reading matter was small. At UCD I read for a B.A. in Latin and English; at the academy—where my tuition for the first year was paid by a well-wishing donor, Alan Boydell, cousin of my music teacher, Brian Boydell—I studied harmony, counterpoint, and lieder. I worked as hard trying to sing Schumann's *Dichterliebe* as I did coping with Shakespeare's plays and poems. I don't recall feeling the need of a theory to get me started in reading literature or listening to music. In those days one learned a few rudimentary skills by practice or, as in my case, by apprenticing oneself to a master or several masters. If I gave any thought to theory, I'm sure I wanted a theory of the arts to be equally responsive to literature and music. It meant a good deal to me to know that Kenneth Burke's earliest essays were on music, that Eliot's Quartets were written in some relation to the last quartets of Beethoven, and that Theodor Adorno, the author of *Negative Dialectics,* also wrote *The Philosophy of Modern Music.* I read this latter book in the library of Trinity College, Dublin, without quite understanding why Stravinsky came out so badly from a comparison with Schoenberg. I didn't read *Negative Dialectics* till much later.

Meanwhile, I was trying to break into print, starting with book reviews for the *Irish Independent,* little essays on music for a weekly magazine, the *Leader,* and later, music criticism for the *Irish Times.* The Irish Jesuit quarterly, *Studies,* published some of my essays and reviews. But I wanted a larger context. It was my ambition to publish literary essays in the American quarterlies, so I kept up with the *Sewanee Review,* the *Kenyon Review,* and the *Hudson Review* even more assiduously than with their English counterparts, *Scrutiny* and *Essays in Criticism.* I read every new essay I could find by Cleanth Brooks, Allen Tate, John Crowe Ransom, William Empson, Yvor Winters, Lionel Trilling, Robert Penn Warren, Kenneth Burke, R. P. Blackmur, and Francis Fergusson. It was a glorious day for me when Ransom, in a handwritten letter, accepted my essay on Yeats's "Words for Music Perhaps" for the *Kenyon Review.* A few months later an essay of mine on Joyce appeared, my first name misspelled, in the *Sewanee Review.* Soon I was trying to write sentences of my own, not entirely purloined from those of Eliot, Burke, and Blackmur.

We may as well continue to call these writers the New Critics, though none of them liked the label and Trilling and Fergusson went their different ways. I admired the New Critics first because they were good writers. Some of them were poets or novelists first and critics only betimes. Each had his particular style, instances of which I transcribed on request forms in the National Library of Ireland. I was also impressed by the fact that these writers so evidently and powerfully read the literature they wrote about. At least to begin with, each of them submitted his mind to the book he was reading. He might assert himself later and keep his distance. When Eliot compared a few lines of Philip Massinger with their putative origin in Shakespeare, his judgment came with the authority of immense reading and the providential method of criticism he recommended, that of being highly intelligent. To compare Burke's essay on Marianne Moore with Blackmur's on the same subject was to be struck by the possible variety of literary criticism and the scale of the merit entailed. Blackmur spoke of criticism as bringing the work of art to the condition of performance. That was what these critics were doing. They didn't avoid generalizing, but their general statements always issued from a sufficient phalanx of particulars, local perceptions in the act of reading. Blackmur especially took care not to let his mind capitulate to a formula, a pattern set in advance of need. In "A Critic's Job of Work," he said that poetry is life at the remove of form and meaning: "not life lived but life framed and identified." But he was alive to the difference between a form and a formula—which he sometimes called a doctrine or a code. Thinking of Henry James, he argued that William Dean Howells and Edith Wharton sank by comparison "because their moral codes very often prohibited feeling, made whole classes of feeling impossible."[3] Like Brooks and Tate, Blackmur acted upon Eliot's distinction between writers who think and feel in turns and writers who "feel their thought as immediately as the odour of a rose."[4] Thought, Blackmur said, "defines relationships as formulae and makes a shorthand, a blueprint of its subject matter."[5] More generally: "For most minds, once doctrine is sighted and is held to be the completion of insight, the doctrinal mode of thinking seems the only one possible. When doctrine totters it seems it can fall only into the gulf of bewilderment; few minds risk the fall; most seize the remnants and swear the edifice remains, when doctrine becomes intolerable dogma."[6] It makes no difference to the case if the dogma is religious, political, social, or psychological, or if the formula is applied on behalf of one cause or another. Either way is death to critical intelligence and the experience of reading a poem or a novel. A formula is a form congealed.

Blackmur kept this emphasis in play. He proposed a distinction between Henry Adams and Henry James, with *The Education of Henry Adams* and James's *Notes of a Son and Brother* as the relevant books:

> Both men were concerned with experience as education, and to both the judgment of education called for a specialized form of autobiography in which the individual was suppressed in the act, only to be caught in the style. James imagined human reality always through dramatizing the bris-

tling sensual record of the instance—almost any instance that had a story in it—and let the pattern, the type, the *vis à tergo*, take care of itself, which under the stress of the imaginative process it commonly did. Adams, on the other hand, tended in a given case to depend on his feeling for human type and pattern—for history and lines of force—as the source of drama, and hence saw the individual as generalized *first:* so that whatever happened would fall into the pattern, if you only had the wit to see how—which Adams by the strength of his conceptual imagination did commonly see. To put it another way, Adams's set of intellectual instruments more or less *predicted* what he would discover; James resorted to instruments only to ascertain what his sensibility had *already* discovered.[7]

I was pleased, too, that the New Critics spoke of culture as if it did not coincide at every point with the interests of the state. It has been alleged that the pedagogical method they employed—practical criticism, close work on texts—is inherently conservative and that it is designed to imply that social harmony has the force of natural law. David Lloyd and Paul Thomas argue that the politics of "culture" is always conservative: "Culture is, to a civil society conceived as the site of the war of all against all, a domain of reconciliation precisely as is the state. But while the function of the state is to mediate conflicts among interest groups, it is the function of culture to interpellate individuals into the disposition to disinterested reflection that makes the state's mediations possible. . . . The importance of the discourse on culture lies in its theorization of an extrapolitical, extraeconomic space in which 'freedom' and 'the harmonious development of the whole person' can be pursued as the very ground on which representational politics can be practised."[8] But literature and music can be attended to only in such a space. If I am listening to a quartet by Bartók or reading *Nostromo,* I should not be using the occasion to plan my next move in the class struggle or the war of all against all. If I were teaching one of those works, I would assume that I was in that extrapolitical, extraeconomic space at least for the time being. Besides, close reading was practiced equally by critics on the Right—Ransom, Brooks, and Tate—and by those on the Left—Empson and Burke. It was Burke who wrote a book called *Counter-Statement* and who formulated there a motto for the workings of the literary imagination: when in Rome, do as the Greeks. His first work of fiction was a grim comedy called *Towards a Better Life.* He always thought of the arts as bohemian counterstatements to the statements made by society and other institutions. Blackmur held that the civil purpose of literature was to remind the powers that be, simple and corrupt as they are, of the forces they have to control. It is an error to claim that the New Critics were in league with the White House and Wall Street or that those who were also Agrarians wanted to effect a strategic retreat south of the Mason-Dixon Line.

To cite a small piece of evidence: what is irony—the trope so much favored by Eliot, Brooks, Ransom, Burke, and Blackmur—but an act of the mind that refuses the destiny of official thought? In his essay on Andrew Marvell, Eliot chose to call irony "wit" and to say that "it involves, probably, a recognition, implicit in the expression of every experience, of other kinds of experience which are possible."[9] I don't find a sinister "politics of culture" at work in that sentence. Or in Adorno's statement that art is art because it is not nature. One doesn't need to look far into *Aesthetic Theory* to find Adorno saying that "aesthetic identity seeks to aid the nonidentical, which in reality is repressed by reality's compulsion to identity" and later that "art allies itself with repressed and dominated nature in the progressively rationalized and integrated society."[10] I don't claim that these few citations make the case, but they should discourage the current habit among intellectuals of trying to make bourgeois liberals feel ashamed of themselves.

In Dublin I eventually looked for an aesthetic theory among the New Critics, but with little success. Philip Blair Rice, Ransom's colleague at Kenyon College, published a few helpful essays in the *Kenyon Review*. Ransom turned Kant's third Critique to his own purposes. W. K. Wimsatt, Jr., and Monroe Beardsley wrote of literature in relation to philosophic and aesthetic issues. But none of these was decisive. Reading further afield, I was much taken with Philip Wheelwright's *The Burning Fountain* and, when I belatedly came to it, Northrop Frye's *Anatomy of Criticism*. But these didn't quite satisfy. They seemed to be theories of myth rather than of literature. I knew that myth was important, but I couldn't be convinced that literature and myth were, in effect as well as in nature, one and the same. When Frye read a poem or a novel he seemed to survey it from an immense height and to discern mainly the pattern he was looking for, a seasonal myth that evidently accounted for everything by making it predictable. But he didn't see much detail. He was like Henry Adams in Blackmur's comparison of Adams with James. Wheelwright, too, wrote of literature as if he were mainly interested in rites, myths, and rituals. *The*

Burning Fountain was instructive on the different kinds of imagination, but I wanted something more or something else.

I don't know when I first read Susanne K. Langer's *Philosophy in a New Key,* but I recall that Donald Davie recommended it to me. He taught at the University of Dublin, Trinity College. We were friends, though we quarreled in later years when I reviewed in *Partisan Review* his book on Ezra Pound in the Modern Masters series. While it lasted and now again in sad retrospect, our friendship was a vivid part of my life in Dublin. I remember with special warmth being with him one day in his rooms at Trinity when he took down from the shelf a slim volume of Yvor Winters's poems and read "On Teaching the Young." In subsequent years when I have read the poem aloud and come to the last line, "Laurel, archaic, rude," I find myself trying to speak it in Davie's rigorous Yorkshire accent. Well, too late now. We shared books, articles, and the poems he wrote; though on the one occasion when I suggested a minor change in a poem, he declined the suggestion. Why he urged *Philosophy in a New Key* on me, I can't recall: in the event, it meant more to me than to him. I went on to read Langer's *Feeling and Form* and to be convinced that I had found the aesthetic theory I needed. Davie wrote about Langer in his *Articulate Energy,* but he didn't concern himself with the aesthetic questions that preoccupied me.

Feeling and Form satisfied me because it was predicated on music and therefore attentive to form, rhythm, cadence, and the texture of sounds. But the chapter I found most suggestive was the one in which Langer explained the fundamental concept of virtuality. It was not—or so I gather—virtuality as computer scientists use that term. Langer's virtuality is the quality of something that is created only to be perceived. The thing created exists in the ordinary world and may be put to ordinary purposes, but those purposes occlude its artistic or virtual character. Music is virtual time, architecture is virtual space, dance is virtual movement. The mode of existence of every work of art is virtual. If we approach it in another spirit, we deal with it opportunistically. The cathedral at Chartres is a place of worship; we enter its space to attend Mass, but when we look at it as a work of architecture, we observe its virtual character, its aesthetic relation to possibilities of spatial form, rhythm, contrast, and so forth. It has been created as a church, but as a work of architecture it exists only for perception. Music, to Langer as to Walter Pater, is the art that is most completely art, because its materials—sounds, sequences, forms—do not readily allow themselves to be diverted into other considerations. Sounds are used as advertising jingles, pop songs, noises in the street, but a symphony performed in a concert hall holds its force as music, virtual time. Literature is to a far greater degree at the mercy of ordinary speech, conversation, gossip, the newspapers, advertisements, TV. The poetic use of the word "light," as Valéry remarked, has to clear a space for itself against the intrusion of its mundane employments.

With the virtuality of literature in mind, reading entails perceiving the pattern in the bristling sensual record of the instance, to recur to Blackmur's phrasing. The pattern is to be found in the same space as the words, neither above nor below them, neither to one side nor the other. Far from predicting the detail, it is seen as if in the split second after the detail. Here is an example from *Feeling and Form,* in which Langer reads a passage of Oliver Goldsmith's "The Deserted Village":

> How often have I blessed the coming day,
> When toil remitting lent its turn to play,
> And all the village train, from labour free,
> Led up their sports beneath the spreading tree,
> While many a pastime circled in the shade,
> The young contending as the old surveyed.

Langer reads this passage as a "created virtual history" that has the intricacy of a group dance.[11] The pattern is deployed mainly through the verbs and the participles that act as adjectives. Society and the natural world appear to join in the dance: "the coming day," "toil remitting," "lent its turn"—that is, give play its turn or chance, to be yielded up again the following morning. The train "led up their sports" as a man leads a woman in a folk dance, "While many a pastime circled in the shade," as in the circles and entwinings of a dance. The harmony of the folk dance is then amplified to include young and old, contending and surveying, the distance of the survey marking the innocence of the games surveyed. This passage, near the beginning of the poem, presents a scene from childhood, recalled from years in which the village, "Sweet Auburn," was not deserted. The later part of the poem shows different formal patterns, most of them dismaying: "Thy sports are fled, and all thy charms withdrawn." But the virtuality of the poem persists: it is what saves it from drifting into social history and losing itself there. "Created for perception," Langer says, not to be used, so long as we read it as a poem, merely to annotate a history of enclosures in seventeenth- and eighteenth-century England, the flight to the cities, the dominance of wealthy men, and other ills. Raymond Williams concedes, in *The Country and the City*, that "what is novel in 'The Deserted Village' is the sense of observation: of a precise and visible social location." But he also maintains that for Goldsmith "to be a poet is, ironically, to be a pastoral poet: the social condition of poetry—it is as far as Goldsmith gets—is the idealised pastoral economy."[12] But the phrase "pastoral poet" implies constraints and limits that aren't there. In *Some Versions of Pastoral*, William Empson shows how much diverse material, how much feeling of many kinds, can get into a pastoral poem before it closes upon the ideal reconciliation. If someone were to argue—as Williams doesn't quite—that Goldsmith's poem achieves the poise of virtual history at the expense of real or material history, or that Auburn in 1769—when he wrote the poem—was a village of poverty, disease, and dispossession, I would not deny this, but I would claim that, even in the nostalgic lines quoted, Goldsmith hasn't forgotten or transcended the "toil," and that in the word "remitting" we hear, as a token of the material life behind it, the word more commonly applied to toil, "unremitting."

I can imagine another objection to Langer's idea of virtuality. Isn't it just the theory of "aesthetic distance" under another name? Not quite. Ransom gives the tone of this theory as vividly as anyone: "Art always sets out to create an 'aesthetic distance' between the object and the subject, and art takes pains to announce that it is not history. The situation treated is not quite an actual situation, for science is likely to have claimed that field, and exiled art; but a fictive or hypothetical one, so that science is less greedy and perception may take hold of it."[13] But the difference between the theory of aesthetic distance and the theory of virtuality is that the first simply removes the artist from the scene he contemplates or imagines: it doesn't say what he does then. The spatial figure is misleading, since it doesn't hold for each of the arts. Langer's theory keeps the artist within the relevant existential mode—time, space, movement, history, voice—and shows him acting there in behalf of perception alone. It has the further merit of acknowledging the tension between the "ordinary" behavior in the relevant mode and the distinctive artistic way of negotiating that mode; between history and virtual history, for instance.

For a while I thought that Langer's theory of art was all I needed, but I found that it didn't provide a theory of reading with adequate recognition of detail. It gave me a feasible sense of art and cautioned me against thinking of a work of art as a mere reflection of life or a transcript of an instance of life. I held to an aesthetic sense of literature, but as if by natural or acquired inclination. I couldn't expound that sense except as a prejudice respecting the formal character of a poem or novel. During those years it was becoming more difficult to recommend an aesthetic reading of a book: negative associations hung upon the words "aesthete" and "aestheticism" and upon the phrase "art for art's sake." "Decadence" was just around the corner. But I was unwilling to submit to those colleagues who wanted literature to be something else: spilt religion or spilt politics. Or to those who had grown to dislike literature and wanted to set up Theory as an independent artifact. I contrived to do without an adequate understanding of reading for many years, and to read literature as I might play billiards, doing the best I could on each occasion. But at some point I came across an essay by Louise M. Rosenblatt called "On the Aesthetic as the Basic Model of the Reading Process." The audacity of the title caught my interest.

Now that I have read Rosenblatt's books I see that they depend on two related sources. The first is a theory in favor of aesthetics that starts with Kant and reaches full stretch in Friedrich Schiller's *Letters on the Aesthetic Education of Man.* The theory holds that an aesthetic sense of life is not the marginal or eccentric attitude it has often been deemed to be, but the most comprehensive attitude available. Every other sense of life—moral, economic, and so forth—is subsidiary to the aesthetic sense. Schiller defends this position by grounding it on a theory of human freedom. Of this freedom, the distinctive mark is play. We are most human when we are at play. The second source of Rosenblatt's work is the distinction between "sense" and "meaning" that she finds in L. S. Vygotsky's *Thought and Language.* According to Vygotsky, sense is the comprehensive word, meaning merely one of its capacities. I quote this passage from *Thought and Language:* "The sense of a word . . . is the sum of all the psychological events aroused in our consciousness by the word. It is a dynamic, fluid, complex whole, which has several zones of unequal stability. Meaning is only one of the zones of sense, the most stable and precise zone. A word acquires its sense from the context in which it appears; in different contexts, it changes its sense. The dictionary meaning of a word is no more than a stone in the edifice of sense, no more than a potentiality that finds diversified realization in speech."[14] Staying within Schiller's tradition and acting on Vygotsky's claim for the "preponderance of the *sense* of a word over its *meaning*" (emphasis in original), Rosenblatt distinguishes between efferent reading, in which "the reader's attention is focused on what he will take away from the transaction," and aesthetic reading, in which the reader's attention is concentrated on "what he is living through during the reading event." If you are reading the directions on a bottle of medicine, an efferent reading is enough. It is enough, too, if you are flicking the pages of a newspaper in search of a piece of information. Efferent reading is often called Practical English or Business English. But where a new experience is offered, only an aesthetic reading is adequate. Rosenblatt says, "The actual lived-through reading process is, of course, not a word-by-word summation of meaning, but rather a process of tentative organizations of meaning, the creation of a framework into which the reader incorporates ensuing words and phrases. The notion that 'literal' reading should come first (to make sure the text is 'understood') is the result of the very assumption I am challenging: namely, that literal, or efferent, meaning has a priority. . . . [Aesthetic reading] is not efferent reading plus aesthetic elements, but a distinct kind of reading, requiring an initially different stance, a different focus of attention, a concentration on lived-through experience, on the part of the reader."[15] Rosenblatt doesn't associate her aesthetic reading with Speech Act theory, but the two work well together, emphasizing what words and sentences do, and the reader's experience of following them. Her theory is compatible, too, with Empson's emphasis on "complex words" and the diverse experiences they offer. Her argument for making aesthetic reading the basic model of reading seems convincing. Such an approach would transform expository writing programs in our schools, colleges, and universities: it would show how reductive and demeaning the current fixation on the literal, cognitive, and referential aspects of language really is.

Does aesthetic reading apply only to literature? Yes, but with this qualification: that we turn the standard definition of literature around and say that a work of literature is a work that calls for an aesthetic reading and gratifies it. If it doesn't, it isn't. Let me give an example, a stanza from George Herbert's "The Pearl":

> I know the ways of Pleasure, the sweet strains,
> The lullings and the relishes of it;
> The propositions of hot blood and brains;
> What mirth and music mean; what love and wit
> Have done these twenty hundred years, and more:
> I know the projects of unbridled store:
> My stuff is flesh, not brass; my senses live,
> And grumble oft, that they have more in me
> Than he that curbs them, being but one to five:
>   Yet I love thee.

I can't bring myself to say what an efferent reading of these lines would be. It might be nothing more than: I know what pleasure is, and how diversely tempting it is, but the conclusive fact is that I love you (God). An aesthetic reading would seek the experience of imagining what it would be to love God in that way. Such an experience would be just as readily available to an agnostic or an atheist as to a Jesuit. A reader would follow the words, swaying with the rhythm of each phrase, responding to every change of pace and emphasis—the quickening in the grumble of the last two lines, for instance. To give a little detail: lullings and relishes are on the scale of pleasure, but at opposite ends of it, the one soothing, the other pungent. The relation between them is emphasized by the "l" in "relishes" that chimes with the run of "l's" in "lullings." The startling difference of tone between "propositions" and "hot blood and brains" is echoed in that between "projects" and "unbridled store," especially as the whole poem is an act of bridling. The rhetorical flourish in "my senses live," the challenging verb coming at the end of the metrical line, and the sudden contrast with the domestic grumble that follows: these are the constituents of the experience—itself an act of imaginative participation and sympathy—to which the stanza incites us.

Or take this passage from James's "The Private Life," in which the woman described is an actress, Blanche Adney: "It is difficult to be cursory over this charming woman, who was beautiful without beauty and complete with a dozen deficiencies. The perspective of the stage made her over, and in society she was like the model off the pedestal. She was the picture walking about, which to the artless social mind was a perpetual surprise—a miracle. People thought she told them the secrets of the pictorial nature, in return for which they gave her relaxation and tea. She told them nothing and she drank the tea; but they had all the same the best of the bargain."[16] The oscillation between "difficult" and "cursory" comes to a misleading rest upon the distinctly cursory phrase "this charming woman," but the paradoxes that conclude the sentence make an efferent reading absurd. To read the passage at all, we have to read it aesthetically as a lived-through experience, assenting to every change in rhythm and tone. In Vygotsky's terms, we engage in the sense rather than the meaning. The sense is an experience, corresponding to the movement of the sentences: it is not a static block of meaning waiting to be translated or otherwise construed. The wit of the passage is the play of feeling between Blanche's force of presence—her stage presence extended into social life—and the system of exchange in which she plays her charismatic role. The measured decorum of "in return for" and "the best of the bargain" keeps the economy of the exchange in force. We read these sentences as if, listening to Alfred Brendel playing a Beethoven sonata, we were also following the score.

For all I know, readers all over the world may be engaged in aesthetic reading, but I doubt it. For one thing, it is slow reading; it takes time and patience. Our students are short of time if not of patience. I have taught English, Irish, and American literature now for many years, at University College, Dublin, later at Cambridge, and for the past nearly twenty years at New York University. This is not the occasion to make comparisons or general comments on my years as a teacher. But I will mention one consideration. I am surprised to find so many students reluctant to release their imaginations. I have met students who refuse to read Yeats's "Leda and the Swan" because— they have heard—it deals with rape. A year or two ago at New York University, I taught a graduate course called Aesthetics and Aesthetic Ideology. Stimulated by a remarkably fine essay by Karsten Harries on metaphor, I asked students in one class to read three poems: Thomas Campion's "There Is a Garden in Her Face," William Carlos Williams's "Queen-Ann's-Lace," and Ransom's "The Equilibrists." In the event, one student said that she could not take part in a discussion of those poems. Why not? Because each of them, she said, is based on the metaphor of a woman's face or body being cultivated by a man. The poems were politically unacceptable. I then had one of my few brainwaves. I suggested to the student that she take her refusal as the theme of her term paper and ponder it as carefully as possible. A few weeks later she submitted one of the most cogent, intelligent papers I have read. I won't rehearse her arguments. It is sufficient to say that she indeed read the poems and set her imagination to transcend her natural or socially constituted reluctance.

But I recognize that the social current is strong and is moving for the most part the other way. I take the imagination to be the capacity to imagine being different; to enter notionally and experimentally upon experiences we have not had, ways of life other than our own. Imagination in that respect is the means of sympathy. I can sympathize with someone only to the extent to which I can imagine being that person. Emmanuel Levinas's *Totality and Infinity* and *Otherwise Than Being* are the most persuasive treatises on this faculty, but we don't need to theorize the Other to acknowledge what an act of imagination entails. We know it in the rush of sympathy and sorrow and anger we feel at the sight of someone's pain. "O to have seen what I have seen, see what I see," Ophelia says. Imagination is the seeing of difference. But there are forces at large in society that urge on us not the imagination of difference but the repetitive recital of the same. These forces are probably innate to societies as such: they want to persist in their being. Some of them are constituents of "identity politics." On all sides we are urged to define ourselves, and to do so by assembling the nearest categories and stereotypes to hand: I am female or male, white or colored, gay or heterosexual, Occidental or Oriental. If I am what I am, then you can't imagine what I am. Surely I can't be the only person who resents being told that I can't understand what it means to be a woman because I'm not one, can't understand being gay because I'm not, can't imagine being African-American because I'm Irish and white?

The bearing of these forces on the reading of literature is clear. It follows from the logic of "identity politics" that literature is compelled to confirm my prejudice—or my socially constituted identity—or be denounced for not doing so. If I'm a woman, I won't read "Leda and the Swan," because it's allegedly a man's poem, not only written by a man but written for men who enjoy the fantasy of raping a woman. If I'm white, I can't read Richard Wright, James Baldwin, or Toni Morrison. If I'm middle-class, I can't make anything of *Invisible Man*. If I'm a Christian, I can't imagine what a Jew feels about Shylock and *The Merchant of Venice*. If I'm an Indian, I can only feel patronized by *A Passage to India*. Each of these attitudes is by now a stereotype, available to anyone whose conditions of life are fulfilled in it. As a stereotype, each is a superficially helpful category, comforting to those who have been instructed to need it, but beyond that each imposes a lethal constraint on the possibilities of one's life. I wonder why we allow ourselves to be dictated to by the politicians of identity. The waltzes indeed have ended, in these days of disinheritance, if we think we need an identity according to that insulting formula. What is identity politics but the enforced repetition of the same, masquerading as the supreme declaration of difference?

I am aware of the difficulties. The destiny of men and women presents its meanings, unfortunately, in mostly political terms, as Thomas Mann said. The emergence of the managerial class as the dominant one is a crucial factor. There has been a shift of interest, especially among young people, from the written word to film and TV and tape. Reading a book is not a social or communal act, it is a private matter. There is also a widespread belief that books are a going or a gone medium; the future is the World Wide Web. Certainly it is hard to imagine a time when enthusiasm for books will be as vigorous as it was forty or fifty years ago. I have been reading *Kafka Was the Rage*, Anatole Broyard's memoir of his postwar years in Greenwich Village: "I realize that people still read books now and some people actually love them, but in 1946 in the Village our feelings about books—I'm talking about my friends and myself—went beyond love. It was as if we didn't know where we ended and books began. Books were our weather, our environment, our clothing. We didn't simply read books; we became them. We took them into ourselves and made them into our histories. . . . We had been living with whatever was close at hand, and books took us great distances."[17] I don't know what has happened to those great distances.

Still, the imagination is not idle or redundant. If you go to see a film, you read it aesthetically, not efferently, if it's worth reading. If not, not. If you watch a TV program worth watching, you read it aesthetically. The same applies to books, for those who read them slowly and patiently. So I don't think the ways of reading that I have been recommending are archaic. It is still as desirable as ever to attend to the first act of *Hamlet* as Eliot and Kenneth Burke attended to it. I began with Eliot, so I'll end with Burke. I'll quote a good deal of the commentary for the pleasure of writing it out:

> It is not until the fourth scene of the first act that Hamlet confronts the ghost of his father. As soon as the situation has been made clear, the audience has

been, consciously or unconsciously, waiting for this ghost to appear, while in the fourth scene this moment has been definitely promised. For earlier in the play Hamlet had arranged to come to the platform at night with Horatio to meet the ghost, and it is now night, he is with Horatio and Marcellus, and they are standing on the platform. Hamlet asks Horatio the hour.

HORATIO: "I think it lacks of twelve."

MARCELLUS: "No, it is struck."

HORATIO: "Indeed? I heard it not: then it draws near the season
Wherein the spirit held his wont to walk."

Promptly hereafter there is a sound off-stage. "A flourish of trumpets, and ordnance shot off within." Hamlet's friends have established the hour as twelve. It is time for the ghost. Sounds off-stage, and of course it is not the ghost. It is, rather, the sound of the king's carousal, for the king "keeps wassail." A tricky, and useful, detail. We have been waiting for a ghost, and get, startlingly, a blare of trumpets. And, once the trumpets are silent, we feel how desolate are these three men waiting for a ghost, on a bare "platform," feel it by this sudden juxtaposition of an imagined scene of lights and merriment. But the trumpets announcing a carousal have suggested a subject of conversation. In the darkness Hamlet discusses the excessive drinking of his countrymen. He points out that it tends to harm their reputation abroad, since, he argues, this one showy vice makes their virtues "in the general censure take corruption." And for this reason, although he himself is a native of this place, he does not approve of the custom. Indeed, there in the gloom he is talking very intelligently on these matters, and Horatio answers, "Look, my Lord, it comes." All this time we had been waiting for a ghost, and it comes at the one moment which was not pointing towards it. This ghost, so assiduously prepared for, is yet a surprise. And now that the ghost has come, we are waiting for something further. Program: a speech from Hamlet. Hamlet must confront the ghost. Here again Shakespeare can feed well upon the use of contrast for his effects. Hamlet has just been talking in a sober, rather argumentative manner—but now the flood-gates are unloosed:

Angels and ministers of grace defend us!
Be thou a spirit of health or goblin damn'd,
Bring with thee airs from heaven or blasts from hell . . .

And the transition from the matter-of-fact to the grandiose, the full-throated and full-voweled, is a second burst of trumpets, perhaps even more effective than the first, since it is the rich fulfilment of a promise.[18]

There is more of this in *Counter-Statement*, I am happy to report.

The moral of the story is not: Back to the New Criticism. I wish it were. For one thing, those critics had the incitement of a new and demanding literature to deal with. New methods were required. Imagine being one of the first readers of (Blackmur lists them in *Anni Mirabiles*) Pirandello's *Six Characters in Search of an Author* and *Henry IV*, Ortega y Gasset's *Invertebrate Spain* and *Revolt of the Masses*, Valéry's *Charmes*, Yeats's *The Tower*, Proust's *Sodome et Gomorrhe*, Pound's early *Cantos* and "Hugh Selwyn Mauberly," Eliot's "The Waste Land," Joyce's *Ulysses*, Stevens's *Harmonium*, Mann's *The Magic Mountain*, Gide's *Counterfeiters*. Add to the list Empson's early poems and, a few years later, William Carlos Williams's *Paterson* and Wallace Stevens's *Notes Toward a Supreme Fiction*. Then think of forms of reading adequate to each and to the sum. The moral is interrogative: Are we quite sure that we have devised methods of reading responsive to our own needs and to the literature we have still to read? Or that we haven't merely transcended the need and forgotten the incitement?

TWO

Theory, Theories, and Principles

In 1912 the philosopher Ralph Barton Perry published a
book called *Present Philosophical Tendencies;* it was subtitled
*A Critical Survey of Naturalism, Idealism, Pragmatism and
Realism, Together with a Synopsis of the Philosophy of William James.* In the first chapter Perry distinguished between
belief and theory, evidently because he thought his colleagues were confusing those terms in the zeal with which
they pursued them. Perry deemed belief, or rather "established belief," to denote faith, in the sense of "conviction
favorable to action." He regarded theory as an altogether
smaller consideration, mainly because it should not—or at
least not immediately—issue in action or otherwise change
one's life. He deemed a theory to be experimental, a notion
to be taken up or put down as it proved useful or not to a
particular task. The theorist, he said, can enjoy the experiences of doubt, interrogation, conjecture, irresponsibility,
"a certain oscillation of mind between hypothetical alternatives." But it is wise, Perry maintained, "to surrender belief
reluctantly," and it is a grave matter "to substitute one's own
theory, however well reasoned, for another man's belief."
While theories "may be changed with little cost and with

certain gain, that is not true of beliefs." Here "the cost is more certain than the gain."[1]

I have referred to Perry's book because it points to a certain distinction that we would do well to recall or to propose afresh. There is a good deal of evidence that Theory as an institution in our profession is being advanced as if it amounted to a belief, and with the insistence that normally accompanies the expression of a belief. There is no merit in being for or against Theory unless we know what it is we are for or against. It makes a difference if we are for or against an activity of mind for the most part speculative or conjectural; or, alternatively, if we are for or against an activity of mind as a result of which it is suggested that we should change our beliefs and thereby change our lives. If a theory is merely experimental or, as we say, heuristic, we do well to take it to mind if not to heart, and give it a run for whatever money we risk on it. But if it is offered to us as a creed or a vision or a doctrine, we should approach it much more skeptically and estimate the consequence of taking it to heart and soul.

It may be prudent to distinguish between Theory as an institution, which comes armed with the coercive force of a capital letter, and theories, which are more modest plays of mind, local notions. There are hundreds of theories, and they appear to do useful work. Svetlana Alpers has a theory of seventeenth- and eighteenth-century Dutch painting: or rather, she has an explanation for our relative failure to see such paintings properly; she thinks we are excessively impressed by the Italian notion that a painting should tell or imply a story. Many Dutch paintings don't. Alpers's theory helps to rid our minds of irrelevant expectations when we look at Dutch paintings. Northrop Frye had a theory of fiction: he thought that there were four forms of fiction—five if you included *Finnegans Wake*—and that we should not confuse them. While reading a romance or an anatomy, we shouldn't become tetchy because the book doesn't fulfill our expectations of reading a realistic novel. Schoenberg had a theory about twelve-tone music, the rules of its composition, and why it doesn't sound like a sonata by Beethoven. Kierkegaard had a theory of irony, the kind of stance an ironist would take up, and why he would hold that ground, if he could. J. L. Austin had a theory about felicitous and infelicitous uses of language. Conor Cruise O'Brien has a theory about nationalism, which he applies to every country except Israel. Gilles Deleuze and Félix Guattari developed a theory of "minor literature," works written from a marginal position in relation to a major language: Kafka writing in German, Prague's German; Mangan writing in English, Ireland's English. These are local theories that refer to particular forms of life, particular activities; they don't claim to be universally applicable. If you challenge such a theory you ask for immediate verification, you appeal to a specific body of evidence. It wouldn't be damaging to Alpers's theory of Dutch painting if you showed that it didn't work well for Japanese line drawing or Italian Renaissance sculpture. It wouldn't harm our lives if we discarded the theory.

We are moving toward Theory as an institution when the considerations we're offered are supposed to refer to large-scale entities and perhaps to life itself. But there are degrees of scale before we reach that extreme position. T. S. Eliot's theory of the "dissociation of sensibility" claims that something happened in the seventeenth century in England—it probably had to do with the Civil War—as a result of which the English language from the later seventeenth to the nineteenth century no longer facilitated thinking as a development of feeling. Thinking became one activity, and feeling another. If that were true, it would be a point of great interest to many people, but to more than those many it would make little or no difference. William Empson had a notion about poetic language, that it was all the better for being ambiguous, since in that respect it testified to the incorrigibly ambiguous character of life itself. There is no need to estimate the number of people who would find that notion worth losing sleep over. I. A. Richards had a theory about the neutralization of Nature in the middle of the nineteenth century: he claimed that writers who continued to think of Nature in neo-Wordsworthian terms were at best bizarre creatures, perhaps geniuses—like Lawrence and Yeats—but daft nonetheless. Jean-François Lyotard had a theory about postmodernism—whatever that might be—that it was chiefly characterized by a general incredulity toward metanarratives, large-scale stories that claimed total explanatory power. Ferdinand de Saussure had a theory that enabled him to distinguish in language between *langue* and *parole*. Bourdieu has a theory to explain the social provenance of taste, how one work is appreciated rather than another. Stanley Fish has held a theory that meaning can't be established intrinsically but only by agreement among the members of an interpretive community. I don't think he still holds to that view, but that's another issue: if he has abandoned it—as in *Academic Correctness*—no matter. These ideas are theoretical, but none of them constitutes Theory because none of them claims total explanatory force.

This is the main distinction between a theory of something—Dutch painting, twelve-tone music—and Theory as an institution. Theory as an institution is like Theology in one respect: it makes foundational claims, it starts from a posited ground and works up and out from that source. It differs from Theology mainly because it hasn't anything to say of first and last things. Theory is related to Philosophy, but the relation is juridical rather than discursive: it doesn't take part in a conversation. Instead, it aspires to the condition of a system, a metadiscourse, and longs to have the attributes of a science or a myth. If reality is widely thought to be political, Theory sets itself up as a critique of ideology. It seeks evidence wherever it chooses, often in texts of metaphysics, philosophy, literature, and politics. That is to say, Theory aspires to universal application.

The theories that claim to constitute Theory in the past two centuries include Kant's Third Critique, Hegel's *Aesthetic*, Nietzsche's *Beyond Good and Evil*, Marx's *Capital*, Freud's *Civilization and Its Discontents*, Heidegger's *Being and Time*, Sartre's *Being and Nothingness*, Derrida's *Grammatology*, and de Man's *Allegories of Reading*. The list is not exhaustive. Even if one of these works seems to refer only to local considerations, as *Capital* does, it claims endlessly allusive power of explanation and prophecy; it sets no limit on its rhetorical scale.

The main arguments we hear against Theory, as distinct from local theories, are these. It is maintained that Theory is arrogant in claiming that not to think theoretically is not to think at all. Theory is chiefly interested in spinning larger and larger webs of its own vocabulary. Christopher Ricks has argued that Theory is characterized "by its degree of elaboration, concatenation, completeness, abstraction, self-consciousness, explicitness, regression, recession and technicality."[2] In this respect, while not amounting to a philosophy, it mimes philosophy. It does not accommodate contradiction or allow for the different view a rival might take of the matter at hand. It feels no misgiving about the mode of autonomy it claims. A further argument might be mentioned, which I find in Geoffrey Hill's *Lords of Limit*. In an essay on T. H. Green, Hill quotes H. J. Laski remarking that "Green and his followers emphasized not the individual over against the process of government, but the individual in the significant totality of his relations with it." Laski's sentence prompted Hill to this development: "There is a case to be made for the suggestion that one of the major discoveries of modern criticism has been the method of transferring 'significant totality of relations' to a contextual plane and of conferring a consequent distinction upon those authors or individual works which fulfil most completely that kind of expectation: Keats, in the Odes, George Eliot in *Middlemarch,* or the poems of Green's sometime pupil Gerard Manley Hopkins."[3] It would be difficult to claim for Theory, as distinct from literary criticism, that it has worked to transfer significant totality of relations to a contextual plane. It has worked rather to limit such relations and to isolate, as far as possible, the constituents of attention that might form relations. The very fact that we can so easily think of Theory as a body rather than as a set of mutually invigorating relations speaks to this charge.

But there is a further consideration that seems to me at least as cogent as those I have mentioned: that is, the claim of Theory—at least in its most insistent forms—to act juridically in relation to knowledge. I find such a claim in Derrida's essay on Kant's *Conflict of the Faculties* (1799). Kant wrote the book under the following circumstances. In 1793 he committed the misdemeanor of publishing *Religion Within the Limits of Reason Alone.* He was free to hold whatever religious convictions he wished, provided he kept them to himself, but he was not free to spread uncertainty and dissension among the citizens by publishing those convictions. Several theologians protested that he had invaded their territory. In June 1794, Kant wrote, but did not publish, a partial reply in the form of an essay, "The Conflict of the Philosophy Faculty with the Theology Faculty." Not surprisingly, Minister of Justice Wöllner sent him a Cabinet Order, dated October 1, 1794, accusing him of having misused his philosophy in publishing *Religion Within the Limits of Reason Alone* and of having distorted and disparaged "many of the cardinal and basic teachings of the Holy Scriptures and of Christianity."[4] Kant didn't answer these charges till 1799, when he published as *The Conflict of the Faculties* three essays, the long one on the conflict of the philosophy faculty with the theology faculty, and two short ones on the conflict of the philosophy faculty with the faculties of law and medicine.

In his reply, Kant concealed the fact that his ultimate motive was to establish philosophy as superior to theology, law, and medicine. He pretended to concede that those three faculties deserved the power they exerted as instruments for the government of the citizens. They should stick to their practical, bureaucratic jobs; they should continue to be supervised by the government they served; and the criteria applied to their teachings should be civic, not philosophical. But the government should guarantee to the philosophy faculty the right to pronounce freely upon the true and the false. Philosophy would have no executive power—nor should it seek it—but it should have the right to pronounce on all matters of truth and falsehood: it would enjoy the right of free judgment on questions of theory and discourse. "The Philosophy Faculty . . . must be conceived as free and subject only to laws given by reason, not by the government."[5] Besides, Kant claimed that he had written *Religion Within the Limits of Mere Reason* as a treatise for his colleagues. The public would find it unintelligible, a closed book. His only interest was to arrange that proper or what he called legal conflicts among the faculties of the university should be adjudicated, so far as they pertained to true and false, right and wrong, moral and immoral, by the philosophy faculty. As Derrida notes, "The first examples that Kant gives—the ones that visibly preoccupy him the most—pertain to the sacred, to faith and revelation; it is the responsibility of the philosophy faculty, as Kant claims, 'to examine and judge publicly, with cool reason, the origin and content of a certain supposed basis of the doctrine, unintimidated by the sanctity of the object.'"[6]

Kant's aim was to propose a rational religious faith, as Ian Hunter has noted, "by developing a purely moral exegesis of the scriptures."[7] The only part of the scriptures that Kant valued was the part that could be turned to moral use; the rest was sensuous narrative, historical accretion, interesting, no doubt, but inessential. Besides: "The Biblical theologian says: 'Search the Scriptures, where you think you find eternal life.' But since our moral improvement is the sole condition of eternal life, the only way we can find eternal life in any Scripture whatsoever is by putting it there. For the concepts and principles required for eternal life cannot really be learned from anyone else: the teacher's exposition is only the occasion for him to develop them out of his own reason."[8] In effect, Kant wanted to use philosophy to remove from Christianity every trace of its doctrines. The Christian narrative must be expounded only in the interests of morality, "and yet"—as he wrote in *Religion Within the Limits of Reason Alone*—"(because the common man has an enduring propensity within him to sink into passive belief) it must be inculcated painstakingly and repeatedly that true religion is to consist not in the knowing or considering of what God does or has done for our salvation but in what we must do to become worthy of it."[9] The Bible deserves to be read, "put to moral use, and assigned to religion as its guide, *just as if it is a divine revelation*" (emphasis in original).[10]

Ian Hunter concludes his analysis of *The Conflict of the Faculties* by arguing that "the Kantian image of 'man' as a pure mind encumbered by an impure sensibility is . . . an anthropology for a caste defined by a practice of intellectual self-purification-clarification." Might we also suggest, he wonders, that "this practice can count among its offspring the intellectual exercises of critical theory and deconstructive criticism?": "Certainly, in framing the problem of the university in terms of an idea whose object has been delayed by history or occluded by representation, these discourses set the 'task' of an exemplary self-decipherment of this object."[11] And so it appears, on the evidence of Derrida's essay on *The Conflict of the Faculties*, except that he presents his commentary not in terms of self-purification-clarification but in terms of juridical privilege and moral responsibility.

My synopsis of Kant's essay, and of Derrida's commentary on it, must be brief and in other respects partial. Only an approximate account is possible here. My concern is not with the detail of Derrida's commentary but with the claim that it makes for Deconstruction. Derrida repeats, in favor of Deconstruction, the claim Kant made for the faculty of philosophy on all questions of true and false, right and wrong, moral and immoral. Derrida says:

> If, then, it lays claim to any consequence, what is hastily called deconstruction *as such* is never a technical set of discursive procedures, still less a new hermeneutic method operating on archives or utterances in the shelter of a given and stable institution; it is also, and at the least, the taking of a position, in work itself, toward the politico-institutional structures that constitute and regulate our practice, our competencies, and our performances. Precisely because deconstruction has never been concerned with the contents alone of meaning, it must not be separable from this politico-institutional problematic, and has to require a new questioning about responsibility, an inquiry that should no longer necessarily rely on codes inherited from politics or ethics.[12]

I construe this last claim, remarkable indeed, as corresponding to Kant's claim to rise above the specious prerogatives of theology and the merely mundane uses of law and medicine. Just as Kant hoped that one fine day the last would be first and the lowest faculty, philosophy, would be granted such privilege in the jurisdiction of truth and falsehood that it would exercise power by the sheer force and truth of its pronouncements, so Derrida claims for Deconstruction the unique privilege of pronouncing on questions of true and false, right and wrong, moral and immoral. Further, he insists on making these pronouncements by prescribing responsibility, in practice, and without relying on codes inherited from politics or ethics. Deconstruction, he maintains, "is limited neither to a methodological reform that would reassure the given organization, nor, inversely, to a parade of irresponsible or irresponsibilizing destruction, whose surest effect would be to leave everything as is, consolidating the most immobile forces of the university."[13] As if that program were not enough, Derrida asserts that the boundary between legal and illegal conflicts among the faculties that Kant spoke of is no longer tenable: there is no longer a feasible distinction between "war" and "conflict," as Kant still hoped there might be. So we must appeal—or rather, Derrida appeals—"to a *surplus* of responsibility" (emphasis in original): "This surplus of responsibility—for me, the very experience of deconstruction—leads to interrogating, suspecting and displacing those tranquil assurances in whose name so many moralisms, today more than ever, organize their courts, their trials and their censures. So long as those assurances are not interrogated or put to the test of a vigilant deconstruction, these moralisms will signify above all else a repressive violence, dogmatism and irresponsibility: the very irresponsibility that claims to speak in the name of responsibility, the well-known immorality of edifying moralism."[14] It seems strange to me that Derrida, speaking in the name of Deconstruction, should prejudge the values and motives of other people to the extent of writing off their consciences as "tranquil," their acts of mind as "assurances," their moral concerns as "moralisms," their professional activities as "the most immobile forces of the university." Who are these dreadful people? And while we're engaged in rooting them out, we are to give Deconstruction the right of becoming metapolitics, metaethics, metalaw, indeed metadiscourse. Is it impertinent to recall that Levinas insisted that ethics precedes ontology and becomes, in effect, a new and better metaphysics; and that he showed no sign of despising the codes of ethics he inherited?

I find it surprising, too, that Derrida quotes Friedrich Schelling's objection to Kant's high claim for the faculty of philosophy but doesn't take it as seriously as it deserves. Derrida admits that it is a serious problem—that the "essence of the university, namely philosophy, should also occupy a particular place and a faculty within the university topology, or that philosophy in and of itself should represent a special competence." He then quotes Schelling's objection:

> To the extent that the sciences obtain, through and in the state, an effectively objective existence, and to the extent that they become a power, the associations formed by each in particular are called faculties. As for their mutual relations—and a comment here is particularly necessary since Kant, in his work on *The Conflict of the Faculties*, strikes us as having treated the issue from an altogether unilateral point of view—it is clear that theology, as a science where the heart of philosophy is found to be objectified, should occupy the first and highest place; and to the extent that an ideal power is higher than a real one, it follows that the faculty of law precedes the faculty of medicine. As for a faculty of philosophy, however, it is our thesis that there is not, nor can there be, any such thing, the proof lying in the simple fact that something which is everything cannot, for that very reason, be anything in particular.[15]

This objection seems far more cogent to me than it evidently does to Derrida. Schelling is not objecting to the existence of a faculty of philosophy but to the hubris of such a faculty as Kant has called for, and to Kant's claims for it. If Derrida proposes to make the same claim for Deconstruction, as a faculty deserving to act in a superior relation to all forms of discourse, legal and illegal, one might transpose Schelling's objection and say that Deconstruction, as something which is everything, cannot, for that very reason, be anything in particular.

Of course it is something in particular; but what is it, if we don't concede its claim to be the modern form of the Kantian faculty of philosophy, with the moral privilege that such a claim would entail? This question may be answered in various tones, and I would prefer to be urbane, if that is possible. Instead of answering in my own perhaps truculent behalf, I prefer to quote from a recent essay by Ian Hunter that seems to me notably just and civil. His theme is the relation between Theory, in its institutional sense, and politics. He says:

> Similarly, in recognising that literary theory relates to empirical politics not as a positive knowledge or intervention but as a counter-political defense of

a particular spiritual deportment, we have effectively reframed the debate around literature and politics. Arguments over which variant of literary theory will best decipher and liberate the divided energies of an ideal political community therefore become idle, while the important question becomes why every variant assumes that politics entails deciphering man's occluded ethical being and dialectically reconciling the fragments of a once and future humanity. The answer, it seems to us, is that literary theory's "political" discourse is actually a means of converting political situations into hermeneutic occasions.[16]

The aim of these hermeneutic occasions, according to Hunter, is not to discover what is in the text but to form a "certain spiritual or intellectual comportment of the subject." If this is the case, and Hunter's evidence is impressive, there are two possible consequences. One is that literary discourse is bound to suffer from the weightlessness of which Edward Said complained, in *Culture and Imperialism,* when he said that "policy-oriented intellectuals who have internalised the norms of the state" find their mirror-image in academic "cults"—"post-modernism, discourse analysis, New Historicism, deconstruction, neo-pragmatism." The self-interested and self-enclosed jargon of these cults—as Hunter, too, puts the case—cuts them off from the political world and induces what Said calls "an astonishing sense of weightlessness with regard to the gravity of history and individual responsibility."[17] Another consequence is that Deconstruction, far from enforcing the claims that Derrida has made by appeal to Kant's faculty of philosophy, must take its chances along with other worldly forms of discourse. If, as Hunter maintains, Deconstruction converts political situations into hermeneutic occasions, it cannot claim any ex officio privilege in relation to true and false, right and wrong, moral and immoral: it must put up with the constraints of intervening just as any journalist does in the editorial or op-ed pages of the *New York Times.* There are no privileges, now that the conflict of faculties is incorrigible. Said may claim, in a desperate attempt to give weight to weightlessness, that "all these hybrid counter-energies, at work in many fields, individuals, and moments provide a community or culture made up of numerous anti-systemic hints and practices for collective human experiences . . . that is not based on coercion or domination."[18] But Hunter's reply to Said is decisive: "Were we to hold this appeal to a self-governing community accountable to any particular governmental problem, such as that faced by the United Nations in dealing with the 'anti-systemic hints and practices' of the warring communities in Bosnia, we would find it connected to the actual political situation by only the slenderest of threads: the theorist's moral prestige. For this appeal too is neither more nor less than a counter-political projection of the theorist's own spiritual comportment."[19] To Bosnia in that sentence one might add, with similar cogency, any political forces that ignore their translation into a hermeneutic occasion. I am not an Irishman for nothing.

But a question remains to be asked: What, or rather whom, does Derrida have in mind as the most immobile forces of the university? Does he really believe that Deconstruction is the only evidence of mobility, or that anyone who does not practice Deconstruction is by definition a tranquil, irresponsible adept of moralism? Let me quote, as an instance of one professor's activity within a university, Empson's brief commentary on a stanza from Thomas Gray's "Elegy Written in a Country Churchyard":

> Full many a gem of purest ray serene
> The dark, unfathomed caves of ocean bear;
> Full many a flower is born to blush unseen
> And waste its sweetness on the desert air.

What this means, Empson says, is that eighteenth-century England had no scholarship system or *carrière ouverte aux talents:*

> This is stated as pathetic, but the reader is put into a mood in which one would not try to alter it. (It is true that Gray's society, unlike a possible machine society, was necessarily based on manual labour, but it might have used a man of special ability wherever he was born.) By comparing the social arrangement to Nature he makes it seem inevitable, which it was not, and gives it a dignity which was undeserved. Furthermore, a gem does not mind being in a cave and a flower prefers not to be picked; we feel that the man is like the flower, as short-lived, natural, and valuable, and this tricks us into feeling that he is better off without opportunities. The sexual suggestion of *blush* brings in the Christian idea that virginity is good in itself, and so that any renunciation is good; this may trick us into feeling it is lucky for the poor man that society keeps him unspotted from the World. The tone of melancholy claims that the poet understands the considerations opposed to aristocracy, though he judges against them; the truism of the reflections in the churchyard, the universality and impersonality this gives to the style, claim as if by

comparison that we ought to accept the injustice of society as we do the inevitability of death. Many people, without being communists, have been irri-
tated by the complacence in the massive calm of the poem, and this seems
partly because there is a cheat in the implied politics; the "bourgeois" themselves do not like literature to have too much "bourgeois ideology."[20]

Christopher Ricks has quoted that passage from Empson to maintain that in
criticism we want principles, not theories; or rather, in my terms, that we want
principles rather than the institution of Theory. He has a point, though not
one as decisive as he thinks. The principles he celebrates are moral principles,
applied in a piece of literary reading and criticism. If they are moral principles, how has Empson come by them? It won't do to point to Samuel Johnson
and say that he is the supreme English critic because he brought his moral
sense to bear on every literary consideration. Aren't we back in the argumentative world in which John Rawls wrote *A Theory of Morals* and a thousand
readers of that book questioned the theory? If by Empson's principles Ricks
merely means his good old-fashioned English decency, I would remind him of
the many occasions on which that virtue failed Empson or he failed it, when
Christianity was the object of attention and Empson vented his hatred on it
and his disgust for its adherents. I admire Empson's commentary on Gray's
stanza just as much as Ricks does, and for similar reasons: it is morally
impressive to have a critic being as just to a piece of writing as Empson is even
as he disapproves of the political attitude on which the poem proceeds. Edifying, too, to find Empson taking such care to decide what he feels about the
poem and its attitudes, and how much he feels, and why. In that chapter of
Some Versions of Pastoral Empson starts from Pope's feeling that the *Aeneid*
was a puff for Augustus: its "dreamy, impersonal, universal melancholy" made
the puff a success. So with Gray's "Elegy." What makes Empson's commentary
great criticism is that he recognizes Gray's trickery and knows that it is not
mere trickery: it would be easy to show that Gray is sincere in holding the
mixture of sentiments in a decent degree of order. Feelings about destiny, as in
the flower's being "born" to a particular one, are mixed with the recognition
that this destiny involves what any decent person is bound to see as "waste."
The sweetness of the flower is also that of a woman who would in better
circumstances have allowed a man to enjoy her sweetness and respond to it in
kind. And so on. There is more to be said along Empson's lines.

I am aware that Empson, despite Paul de Man's essay on the alleged "dead end of formalist criticism," is sometimes thought of as a Deconstructionist before the letter of Grammatology. If that view has any merit—though it seems to me not to have much—it might suggest that Empson's commentary on Gray's "Elegy" is just the sort of post-Kantian faculty work that Derrida has in mind for Deconstruction; pronouncing on the truth and falsehood, right and wrong, moral and immoral quality of a piece of writing. But Empson's books show that, to pronounce in this spirit, there is no need to set up a special faculty and make an outlandish claim for it as a matter of principle. Empson did a lot of such work without making a fuss about it and certainly without claiming that he should have institutional privilege over his rivals. He was prepared to argue with anyone. He didn't ask for special consideration from Helen Gardner, F. A. C. Wilson, John Dover Wilson, or any of his opponents. That strikes me as a principle contiguous to the principles Ricks has in view, and good enough to be going on with.

The moral of the story is perhaps a simple one. There is no need to outlaw a theory or a principle or even to discourage the institution of Theory. But it seems important to decide, on each occasion, what is at stake. Is it a matter of belief, on which we may have to change our lives? The language of spiritual adherence allows for several degrees: we speak of belief, but we also speak of credence, which is not the same thing. We apprehend an idea or a belief or a notion, but we may also entertain each of these; again, this marks a different relation to the object in question. It seems desirable, and perhaps more than desirable, to know not just what the words we read and write mean and what their sense is—to use a crucial distinction of Vygotsky's—but to determine their status as forces that enter our minds. Is their entry a matter of life and death or an issue of little account or a notion that may be useful on a later occasion but not now? Or is Hunter right in his implication that the translation of brute facts into hermeneutic occasions is the only practice we're any good at?

But I may remark, to end with, that when I first read Derrida's early books and tried to take account of their complex relations to those of Husserl and Heidegger, I thought they belonged to the history of skepticism and might safely be allowed to find their place in that story. But Derrida's recent books and essays seem to me not to belong to the history of skepticism but to the history of politics. They retain their skepticism, but now as a quality that should justify an appeal not just to other skeptics but to the polity at large. The deconstructive scruple is now offered as if it were the basis of a political program. It appears that Deconstruction is offering itself not as a political party like any other, but as a political party unlike any other; unlike, because of its more radical stance in epistemology. If we vote for this party, we are to give it the power of adjudicating on true and false, right and wrong, precisely the authority that Kant claimed for philosophy against theology, medicine, and law.

Three Ways of Reading

It may be true that the "culture wars" are over. There are reports of a "general lessening of theoretical polemical fervour."[1] Ideological conflicts have shifted from universities to high schools, public and private. Instead of quarreling about the canon of literature, many high-school teachers are preoccupied by the appalling conditions they have to face, problems of discipline, guns, drugs, violence, urban dread. But if the universities are quiet, who won the war, and why are we not celebrating? I am ready to believe that young scholars, weary of the toil of battle, have given up quarreling about theoretical issues and are pursuing their studies on the assumption that whatever theoretical framework they need is adequately in place. If it is widely supposed that all such frameworks are in any case merely "constructed" rather than innate, natural, or otherwise privileged, then any one of them is just as employable as another.[2] Or each of them is good for a particular job and may be replaced by another one for the next assignment.

But it is my impression that the wars are not over. There has been a cease-fire, which may well be permanent, but only in the sense that the disputants have given up fighting

with their opponents and have resorted to another strategy. Each of them—
and they are many—has withdrawn from the arena and set up a local constitu-
ency, a gathering of the faithful. Feminism, as a case in point, has made for
itself a place apart, where it conducts its business for the benefit of its adherents
and doesn't bother strangers. This strategy requires for its success several enabling institutions: journals given over to feminist issues, regular conferences
where feminists address one another and refine their rhetorical skills, courses
in colleges and universities, anthologies to cater to the interests of the group.
The publication of *The Norton Anthology of Literature by Women* was a crucial
strategic event. There is now somewhere for feminists to go to be together for a
while. Students can assemble around the book; the appropriate discourse can
begin. The designation of college courses as separate entities makes these
procedures easier. Many interests that were once in conflict with other interests
are now pursued separately, on the understanding that each of them concerns
the members of its group and no one else. They are organized like sects within
the Christian community. Presbyterians don't trouble Methodists so long as
Methodists don't interfere with Presbyterians. The quarrels that flare up now
are between one adherent and another: the wars are civil wars.

I can't imagine that anyone regards this as an entirely happy outcome, but
it was inevitable. Cultural formations deal with disputes not by resolving them
but by enlarging the field, making a separate space for those who refuse to
accept the official designation of areas and sites. Lines of demarcation are opportunistically drawn so that people can decide where they want to live. They
can choose their neighbors on probable ideological considerations. These
devices make life easier: at last we are enjoying a truce, if not permanent peace.
No issue has been resolved, but the provision of separate spaces has the effect
of making the issues seem not quite as incorrigible as they were in the bad old
years. Each group has room to breathe.

I should be content with these arrangements. It is a blessing that my
professional life proceeds free from the noise of ignorant armies clashing by
night. But I am not entirely content. I wish the war had ended in the victory of
one party, preferably that of my friends. I would like to have seen something
achieved, some issue resolved, if only to make the turbulence and the accusa-
tions of bad faith appear to have been worthwhile. Lacking a resolution of our
quarrels, I am not convinced that it is time to put away the weapons. Even
now, so late in the professional day, I find myself staying awake to be ready for

the next theoretical assault. But often, when morning comes, I conclude that many continuing issues trouble me now only in their practical consequences. I haven't lost my zeal for the disputes of theory: they are—or I thought they were—disputes among rival systems of belief, issues of life if not of death. I still hope to break a theoretical lance occasionally. But I have come to think that disputes of theory are best engaged as disputes about our ways of reading and interpreting. The idea of arguing with Jacques Derrida, Fredric Jameson, Edward Said, Annette Kolodny, J. Hillis Miller, Stephen Greenblatt, and Stanley Fish about their theories of literature has not lost its charm, but it might be more worthwhile to ask adepts of feminism, Marxism, Deconstruction, the New Historicism, and Cultural Studies what they think they're doing when they read literature. I have come to feel that theories matter only when they coerce someone's way of reading a book. Then they matter a lot.

So I would ask what distinguishes one interpretation of a poem, a novel, or a play from another, not to determine good and bad but to clarify the different assumptions that govern the readings. How does a particular interpretation of a book indicate the ideological axioms on which its reader silently proceeds? What does a particular reader assume goes without saying? And shouldn't we tease out those assumptions? For the moment, I propose to consider three ways of reading and to delineate the different assumptions that govern each of them. I don't imply that there are only three, though I find it hard to believe that their number is infinitely large or that each reader has an entirely individual set of them. I call the three Matthew Arnold, Walter Pater, and Oscar Wilde.

I

On December 8, 1860, Matthew Arnold gave a lecture, the second of three under the title "On Translating Homer." Near the end of the lecture he made a comment about the literatures of France and Germany: "Of these two literatures, as of the intellect of Europe in general, the main effort, for now many years, has been a *critical* effort; the endeavour, in all branches of knowledge,— theology, philosophy, history, art, science,—to see the object as in itself it really is."[3] Arnold repeated the claim in virtually the same words in a lecture on October 29, 1864, which he published as "The Function of Criticism at the Present Time." Clearly he thought that English writers had no reason to take satisfaction in their uncritical or anticritical disposition.

The formula—to see the object as in itself it really is—has been famous since Arnold devised it. It's still serviceable. In fact, it indicates the standard aim of criticism. Arnold takes for granted that there is an object to be attended to: a work of literature. He also assumes that the existence of the work is objective; it has as much independence as any other object in the world. A stone, a shell, an epic poem, or a cathedral is what it is, and it stays the same under anyone's scrutiny: it doesn't dissolve into the mind that contemplates it. The job of criticism is to discover the qualities of a work of literature by analogy with the properties of any other object to which one pays attention. A good Arnoldian reader tries to see what is there in a particular work—what Henry James calls "the figure in the carpet." Such a reader doesn't doubt that the figure is already in the carpet. The writer, not the reader, has put it there.

Arnold's phrase "to see the object as in itself it really is" indicates the commonly accepted aim of criticism. Most critics evidently think that this is what they should be about. Acting on the aim, Roman Jakobson read Shakespeare's sonnet "The Expence of Spirit in a Waste of Shame," Donald Davie read Coleridge's "Dejection" ode, Christopher Ricks has read Eliot's poems and Wordsworth's and, more recently, Beckett's fiction. They have tried to see what is there. To take an example: Lionel Trilling's essay on Wordsworth's "Immortality" ode pursues Arnold's aim with characteristic verve. Trilling reads the poem in the context of Wordsworth's poetry as a whole, and he interprets it as a poem about growing up, coming to terms with one's life, developing a sense of reality. The ode, according to Trilling, is not what it has often been thought to be, a dirge sung by Wordsworth over his departing powers: it is the very opposite, "a welcome of new powers and a dedication to a new poetic subject."[4] Trilling is scrupulous in finding that the poem has this quality; he doesn't add himself to the poem or intrude on its objective character.

This could also be said of Helen Vendler's essay on the same poem. Her interpretation of it differs from Trilling's. She thinks that the "final human value affirmed by the ode is that of thought arising from feeling." But thoughts are, as Wordsworth said on another occasion, "the representatives of all our past feelings." They come at a later stage. The spontaneity of feelings has been replaced by a more regulated scheme of relations, but in substance, thoughts are not different from feelings. Vendler emphasizes that "Those obstinate questionings / Of sense and outward things" to which Wordsworth refers in the ode are the very means by which we construct "our later trust in that inward affectional and intellectual reality 'by which we live.'" The ode is a great poem because Wordsworth has devised in it a language "to join the external world of sense-experience with the interior world of moral consciousness."[5] The fact that Vendler feels no misgiving in referring to the external world and the interior world as different entities makes the Arnoldian point.

Trilling and Vendler seem to be reading different poems, or at least attaching special significance to different parts of the same poem. But these critics are Arnoldian in the fundamental sense that they confine themselves to a description of the poem "as in itself it really is." Or they try to do this. In that respect their readings practice a discipline of scruple. We may reject both readings if we think they have not persuasively described the poem, if we think they have been blind to some of its properties. But their essays on the poem respect its apparent objectivity, its status as an independent structure or entity. It follows that Vendler's dispute with Trilling on the question of Wordsworth's ode is a dispute between parties who are as one in their Arnoldian emphasis: neither of them has any doubt about the validity, the applicable force, of such terms as "objective" and "subjective." Both critics believe that the ode is an object waiting to be seen as in itself it really is.

I have remarked that Arnold's sense of literature and the criticism of literature is still in force. Despite every exorbitant position taken up by this critic or that, most critics read poems and novels to discover what is there. Let me be more specific. Here is Wordsworth's sonnet "Surprised by Joy":

Surprised by joy—impatient as the Wind
I turned to share the transport—Oh! With whom
But Thee, deep buried in the silent tomb,
That spot which no vicissitude can find?
Love, faithful love, recalled thee to my mind—
But how could I forget thee? Through what power,
Even for the least division of an hour,
Have I been so beguiled as to be blind
To my most grievous loss!—That thought's return
Was the worst pang that sorrow ever bore,
Save one, one only, when I stood forlorn,
Knowing my heart's best treasure was no more;
That neither present time, nor years unborn
Could to my sight that heavenly face restore.[6]

A biographical scholar would report that the occasion of the poem was the death of Wordsworth's daughter Catherine in June 1812 at the age of three. A critic in Arnold's tradition would be concerned rather with the poem as an act of feeling, made possible by the English language, its modes and conventions, and Wordsworth's sense of those. I'll quote part of F. R. Leavis's commentary, which is based on the assumption that a reader of the sonnet will want to read it aloud and will not find that pleasure as easily attained as it seems:

> The first word of the sonnet . . . is a key word. The explicit exalted surprise of the opening gives way abruptly to the contrasting surprise of that poignant realization, now flooding back, which it had for a moment banished:

> —Oh! With whom
> But Thee, deep buried in the silent tomb . . .

> Then follows a surprise for the reader (the others were for the poet too):

> That spot which no vicissitude can find.

> It is a surprise in the sense that one doesn't at first know how to read it, the turn in feeling and thought being so unexpected. For the line, instead of insisting on the renewed overwhelming sense of loss, appears to offset it with a consideration on the other side of the account, as it were—there would be a suggestion of "at any rate" in the inflection. Then one discovers that the "no vicissitude" is the admonitory hint of a subtler pang and of the self-reproach that becomes explicit in the next line but one. There could be little profit in attempting to describe the resulting complex and delicate inflection that one would finally settle on—it would have to convey a certain tentativeness, and a hint of sub-ironical flatness. Then, in marked contrast, comes the straight-forward statement.

> Love, faithful love, recall'd thee to my mind,

> followed by the outbreak of self-reproach, which is developed with the rhetorical emphasis of passion:

> But how could I forget thee? Through what power
> Even for the least division of an hour,
> Have I been so beguiled as to be blind
> To my most grievous loss?

> The intensity of this is set off by the relapse upon quiet statement in

> That thought's return
>
> Was the worst pang that sorrow ever bore,

—quiet statement that pulls itself up with the renewed intensity (still quiet) of

> Save one, one only,

where the movement is checked as by a sudden scruple, a recall to precision.[7]

Leavis has more to say about the poem, but I have quoted enough to represent the quality of his attention. Of course there is more to be said. Donald Davie noted how the "heart-breaking poignancy" at the beginning of the poem "comes with the syntactical shift over from statement to question," in the lines "I turned to share the transport—Oh! With whom / But Thee, deep buried in the silent tomb."[8] It would also be necessary, in a full Arnoldian commentary on the poem, to consider the effect of personifying "vicissitude" by making it the subject of its clause, going with the verb "can find." The main effect is to change "vicissitude" from a passive condition to a force, appallingly active in its own cause. It would also be worthwhile to attend to the versification of the poem, to register Wordsworth's mastery of the movement of the lines, how he uses the resources of meter and rhyme to control the phrasing. I note the power of the phrasing—the fingering, as a musician would say—achieved by rhyming "return" with "forlorn" and "unborn," that last word referring immediately to "years" but also to the forlornness of feeling that the child was indeed born, only to be unborn three years later.

II

In 1873, Walter Pater adverted to Arnold's phrase without naming its author. He was not inclined to give names. In the preface to *Studies in the History of the Renaissance* he said: " 'To see the object as in itself it really is' has been justly said to be the aim of all true criticism whatever; and in aesthetic criticism the first step towards seeing one's object as it really is, is to know one's own impression as it really is, to discriminate it, to realise it distinctly." In practice, that "first step" was the only one Pater proposed to take. Whereas Arnold spoke of an object, Pater spoke of an impression, and by that he meant something that occurs in the mind of a qualified reader when he or she looks at a painting or a statue, reads a poem or a novel, listens to a piece of music.

The impression is not entirely subjective; it is provoked by one work of art rather than by another. A different work would cause a different impression. But it is not objective, either; it occurs in that singular mind, it is not the same as the impression in someone else's mind. What happens in Kenneth Clark's mind—to speak of it in that way for the moment—is not the same as what happens in John Berger's or Adrian Stokes's, even though these critics are looking at the same painting. One's experience is relative, Pater would say. So an impression can't be thought of as an object; it is not held in the mind as if it fulfilled that way of being there. In fact, it is misleading to speak of it as being contained in the mind. Rather, "impression" is the name we give to what the mind does, under sensory provocation.

The most celebrated or derided record of an impression, as something not entirely subjective but more subjective than objective, is Pater's commentary on *La Gioconda* of Leonardo da Vinci, the Mona Lisa. It is not a commentary, it is a reverie. Pater doesn't examine the painting for its formal qualities. He doesn't lead us through it as Leavis leads us through "Surprised by Joy," helping us to "live" the poem as an experience. Pater's main concern is to divine the particular sensibility, the structure of feelings that he thinks of as Leonardo's, or at least as Leonardesque, and then to respond to that with his own. The painting embodies a distinctive psychological type which Pater identifies as Leonardo's. By looking at his works, or works deemed however inaccurately to be his, Pater gradually senses a type of human being, a particular discovery among the possible ways of being alive. Then, since he is an aesthetic critic, he lets that sense of the Leonardesque exert itself on his mind, inciting it to a new act of sensibility. The particular impression is what Pater's mind does in return. When he contemplates a particular manifestation of the Leonardesque—say, when he looks at the Mona Lisa—he trusts the impression that the painting incites his mind to produce. It is a new act of his own mind, an extension of his creative life. That is what his "reading" of the painting comes to. The critical problem is then to find the right words to convey that impression. So Pater writes of the Lady Lisa:

> She is older than the rocks among which she sits; like the vampire, she has been dead many times, and learned the secrets of the grave; and has been a diver in deep seas, and keeps their fallen day about her; and trafficked for strange webs with Eastern merchants; and, as Leda, was the mother of Helen

of Troy, and, as Saint Anne, the mother of Mary; and all this has been to her but as the sound of lyres and flutes, and lives only in the delicacy with which it has moulded the changing lineaments, and tinged the eyelids and the hands. The fancy of a perpetual life, sweeping together ten thousand experiences, is an old one; and modern philosophy has conceived the idea of humanity as wrought upon by, and summing up in itself, all modes of thought and life. Certainly Lady Lisa might stand as the embodiment of the old fancy, the symbol of the modern idea.[9]

That passage of Pater's may sound bizarre, a gorgeous flourish of nonsense, so much the rhapsody of a hedonist that it could not establish a tradition of criticism. But it has done exactly that. Critics have Pater's authority, if they want it, when they give more credence to their mental acts in the face of a work of art than to any formal, historical, or otherwise objective qualities the work may be shown to have. They have his authority, too, when they assume that the human mind or spirit is so abundant that no sequence of articulations could exhaust it. Critics can express some of that abundance: by divining it in the artist, they proclaim its possibility in themselves. We call that abundance one's sensibility. Pater responds to it in Raphael, Leonardo, and Michelangelo by trusting his own provoked eloquence.

Virginia Woolf's essays on literature issue from similar trust in her sensibility; they never observe the discipline of objectivity that I've ascribed to Trilling and Vendler. Woolf's own experience, reading certain books, is always uppermost in her account of them. Wallace Stevens's essay on the poetry of Marianne Moore is another case in point: it makes me feel not that Stevens's sense of Moore's poems is inconceivable, but that only he could have conceived it. He is appealing to no common understanding of those poems. So his essay is an intimate disclosure of his own mind and only marginally bears on Moore's poems, their way of being in the world. The essay is contiguous to Stevens's "The Idea of Order at Key West" in which we are told of the woman walking along the beach that "she sang beyond the genius of the sea" and that

She was the single artificer of the world
In which she sang. And when she sang, the sea,
Whatever self it had, became the self
That was her song, for she was the maker. Then we,
As we beheld her striding there alone,

Knew that there never was a world for her
Except the one she sang and, singing, made.[10]

The nicety of the phrasing in that last line—the pointed specificity of "singing" before Stevens releases the second verb, "made"—embodies his concern to make the singer's idealism inescapably present.

It follows that Paterian or impressionist criticism tends to lead, after a while, an independent life. We forget what has occasioned it, and remember the sentences for their personal tone, the murmur of word to word. It is hardly surprising that when W. B. Yeats was compiling the *Oxford Book of Modern Verse* he took the first of Pater's sentences from the passage on the Mona Lisa that I've quoted, broke it into disparate lines, and printed it—not quite accurately—as a poem in "free verse," the first poem in the anthology. By 1936, when the *Oxford Book* was published, Pater's sentence had long since floated free of its context in his book on the Renaissance; it had attached itself to the expression of certain moods or tones of feeling which Yeats thought of as those of modernity.

But I should quote a modern instance of Paterian reading. It would be possible to choose virtually any book or essay by the French or Swiss phenomenologists. I choose Georges Poulet because he has a theory of reading and has practiced what he theorizes. In "Phenomenology of Reading" he starts with a book on a table: it is waiting to be read. Until I take it up and begin to read it, it is external and objective. But as soon as I start to read it, it becomes an interior object, part of "my innermost self." Interior objects have given up their materiality for the new destiny of being read, looked at, listened to. As Poulet says:

> The universe of fiction is infinitely more elastic than the world of objective reality. It lends itself to any use; it yields with little resistance to the importunities of the mind. Moreover—and of all its benefits I find this the most appealing—this interior universe constituted by language does not seem radically opposed to the *me* who thinks it. Doubtless what I glimpse through the words are mental forms not divested of an appearance of objectivity. But they do not seem to be of a nature other than my mind which thinks them. They are objects, but subjectified objects. In short, since everything has become part of my mind, thanks to the intervention of language, the opposition between the subject and its objects has been considerably attenuated. And thus the greatest advantage of literature is that I am persuaded by it that

I am freed from my usual sense of incompatibility between my consciousness and its objects.[11]

It is an extreme example of philosophic idealism. Poulet assumes that in the act of reading and by exercising his imagination he can gain complete access to the "world" of the writer. He reads, say, Flaubert's works, and ignores the differences between one book, one genre, and another. Flaubert's letters are just the same as his novels in the force with which they constitute the writer's world. Poulet places himself at the hypothetical center of that world and surveys it from that vantage point. He takes pleasure in the conviction that there is no incompatibility between his consciousness and the constituents of Flaubert's world. In *Etudes sur le temps humain* he describes what he sees as if he were inside Flaubert's mind. What he sees—according to his reports—is a distinctive sense of life according to which the moments of greatest significance are those in which a sensory event impels someone to have a direct intuition of time as duration. "These are the moments," Poulet says, "when sensation is so perfectly yoked with the general life of things that one becomes, so to speak, the metaphorical expression of the other." Then, "to feel oneself live is to feel oneself live life, to feel the pulse of duration beat."

Poulet's vocabulary is Bergsonian. In the *Introduction to Metaphysics* Bergson distinguishes between intuition and analysis:

Il suit de là qu'un absolu ne saurait être donné que dans une *intuition,* tandis que tout le reste relève de l'analyse. Nous appelons ici intuition la *sympathie* par laquelle on se transporte à l'intérieur d'un objet pour coincider avec ce qu'il a d'unique et par conséquent d'inexprimable. Au contraire, l'analyse est l'opération qui ramène l'objet à des éléments déjà connus, c'est-à-dire communs à cet objet et à d'autres.[12]

[It follows from this than an absolute could be given only in an *intuition,* while everything else falls within the province of analysis. Here by intuition we mean the *sympathy* by which one places oneself within an object in order to coincide with what is unique in it and therefore inexpressible. Analysis, on the contrary, is the operation which reduces the object to elements already known, that is, to elements common to it and to other objects.]

What the intuitionist expresses is sympathy, an experience under the auspices of time, not of space. Intuition gives the critic the pleasure of apprehending himself as a creator.

The example that Poulet chooses is the scene, Chapter 7 of *Madame Bovary*, in which Emma and Rodolphe make love in a forest outside Yonville:

> Les ombres du soir descendaient; le soleil horizontal, passant entre les branches, lui éblouissait les yeux. Çà et là, tout autour d'elle, dans les feuilles ou par terre, des taches lumineuses tremblaient, comme si des colibris, en volant, eussent éparpillé leurs plumes. Le silence était partout; quelque chose de doux semblait sortir des arbres; elle sentait son coeur, dont les battements recommençaient, et le sang circuler dans sa chair comme un fleuve de lait. Alors, elle entendit tout au loin, au delà du bois, sur les autres collines, un cri vague et prolongé, une voix qui se traînait, et elle l'écoutait silencieusement, se mêlant comme une musique aux dernières vibrations de ses nerfs émus.[13]

> [Evening shadows were falling, and the level rays of the sun streamed through the branches and dazzled her eyes. Here and there, all about her, among the leaves and on the ground, were shimmering patches of light, as though hummingbirds winging by had scattered their feathers. All was silent; a soft sweetness seemed to be seeping from the trees; she felt her heart beating again, and her blood flowing in her flesh like a river of milk. Then from far off, beyond the woods in distant hills, she heard a vague, long, drawn-out cry—a sound that lingered; and she listened silently as it mingled like a strain of music with the last vibrations of her quivering nerves.][14]

Poulet comments:

> In this passage Flaubert succeeds in giving the moment a spatial and temporal destiny so particular that one could say (and it is undoubtedly the effect Flaubert wished to produce) that this moment belongs to a different duration from that of ordinary days, a duration whose *tempo* of things is made sweeter, slower, and therefore more perceptible; a duration that spreads out. It is as if time, like a passing breeze, could be felt in the renewed beatings of the heart, in the blood that flows like a stream of milk. It is no longer the bitter consciousness of an interval, there is no more interval; there is only a gliding motion which carries away simultaneously the things and the sentient mind with the sense of an absolute homogeneity between the different elements that compose the moment. The mind, the body, nature, and life all participate in the same moment of the same becoming.[15]

To write those sentences, as a commentary on the lovemaking passage in *Madame Bovary*, Poulet has to assume that Emma's feeling and Flaubert's are one and the same. The fact that Emma is an invented character in a novel can't be allowed to make a difference. Nor does it make a difference that the passage is written in "free indirect style," the style in which a novelist uses not the vocabulary he would use if he were describing the event objectively but the vocabulary the character in the case would use if she were managing her own narrative. Poulet must also assume that Flaubert's feeling, Emma's, and his own are one and the same: his projective imagination can inhabit Emma's feeling, which is deemed to be identical with Flaubert's, without any sense of discrepancy. It follows that Poulet has nothing to say about the passage in any objective sense. There is nothing to be analyzed or even pointed to, because he is himself within the language. He does not mention the voice, the cry, that Emma heard. By way of commentary, he can only repeat the words of Emma's rapture, her swoon of unity with the forest, writing sentences which mime those that Flaubert has invented for Emma by first divining them, apparently, in himself. Poulet has to assume that nothing in the given world importunes his mind: everything yields to the prescriptive force of that mind.

It is no wonder, then, that Poulet breaks off the quotation before it reaches the next and last sentence: "Rodolphe, le cigare aux dents, raccommodait avec son canif une des deux brides cassées.[16] [Rodolphe, a cigar between his teeth, was mending a broken bridle with his penknife.][17] That sight must have shaken Emma out of her swoon. Poulet could not have quoted the sentence, because it is clearly incompatible with his thesis, that every detail in Flaubert's writing is predicated on making the very working of duration visible. Cigar, broken bridle, penknife: these do not dissolve into the mind that sees them. Flaubert's irony cannot be accommodated in Poulet's phenomenology of reading. The interest of such a reading consists in its moving toward independence. Typically, Poulet places a grand theme—human time—in the vicinity of Flaubert's work. If the theme is well chosen, its vocabulary will catch rays and reflections from Flaubert's texts and will minister to Poulet's own meditation, his reverie.

But there is a further degree of independence.

III

Oscar Wilde took up Arnold's phrase and Pater's deformation of it and produced from them a typical exorbitance. In July 1890, Wilde published "The

Critic as Artist," an essay in the form of a dialogue between the flamboyant Gilbert and his straight man, Ernest. At one point Gilbert recalls Arnold's formula and Pater's allusion to it—" 'To see the object as in itself is really is,' has been justly said to be . . . ":

> It has been said by one whose gracious memory we all revere . . . that the proper aim of Criticism is to see the object as in itself it really is. But this is a very serious error, and takes no cognizance of Criticism's most perfect form, which is in its essence purely subjective, and seeks to reveal its own secret and not the secret of another. For the highest Criticism deals with art not as expressive but as impressive purely.

For proof, Gilbert refers to Pater's reverie on the Mona Lisa. Who cares, he asks, "whether Mr. Pater has put into the portrait of Mona Lisa something that Leonardo never dreamed of?": "The painter may have been merely the slave of an archaic smile, as some have fancied, but whenever I pass into the cool galleries of the Palace of the Louvre, and stand before that strange figure . . . I murmur to myself, 'She is older than the rocks among which she sits; like the vampire, she has been dead many times; and has been a diver in deep seas.' " Ernest doesn't point out that Gilbert's recitation of Pater's prose is illegitimate. He should be composing his own reverie, not quoting Pater's. Ernest lets him get away with it: "The highest Criticism, then, is more creative than creation, and the primary aim of the critic is to see the object as in itself it really is not." Gilbert answers: "Yes, that is my theory. To the critic the work of art is simply a suggestion for a new work of his own, that need not necessarily bear any obvious resemblance to the thing it criticises."[18] Only the phrasing is original to Wilde: the conceit itself is implicit in many versions of Aestheticism.

But Wilde's formulation of it has had a suggestive history. There is a nuance of it in Paul Bourget's book on Flaubert, in which he speaks of the malady of thought as thought that precedes experience instead of submitting to it.[19] Jules de Gaultier has a more specific study of it in his *Le Bovarysme: La Psychologie dans l'oeuvre de Flaubert* (1892), in which he describes Bovarysm as man's determination to see himself as other than he is.[20] Poor Emma gives her name to it because de Gaultier finds in her, as in many of Flaubert's characters, a certain predisposition, a "pathological and singular exaggeration of the faculty of imagining oneself to be other than one is."[21] He thinks that the predisposition is at one with a hatred of reality: it is a ruling tendency in Emma, by virtue of which any actual condition of existence arouses in her a contrary conception. The difference between Bovarysm and a worthy use of the imagination is that, in the latter, one conceives an alternative or antinomian reality without proposing to put it into practice, one retains it as a fiction: in the former, one takes it as a program and acts on it.

De Gaultier thinks that the determination to see oneself as other than one is accounts for the entire human comedy and drama. Other writers think of it as mostly comic or pathetic. In "Rhetoric and Poetic Drama" (1919), T. S. Eliot acknowledged that the really fine rhetoric of Shakespeare "occurs in situations where a character in the play *sees himself* in a dramatic light," and he quotes as an instance Othello's last speech, "And say besides that in Aleppo once . . ."[22] But in a later essay, "Shakespeare and the Stoicism of Seneca" (1927), Eliot quotes the same speech to make quite a different point. Othello is addressing Lodovico, Montano, and the officers who have come to arrest him:

> Soft you! A word or two before you go.
> I have done the state some service, and they know't—
> No more of that. I pray you, in your letters,
> When you shall these unlucky deeds relate,
> Speak of me as I am. Nothing extenuate,
> Nor set down aught in malice. Then must you speak
> Of one that loved not wisely, but too well;
> Of one not easily jealous, but, being wrought,
> Perplexed in the extreme; of one whose hand
> (Like the base Indian) threw a pearl away
> Richer than all his tribe; of one whose subdued eyes,
> Albeit unused to the melting mood,
> Drop tears as fast as the Arabian trees
> Their med'cinable gum. Set you down this;
> And say besides that in Aleppo once,
> Where a malignant and a turbaned Turk
> Beat a Venetian and traduced the state,
> I took by the throat the circumcised dog
> And smote him—thus.[23]

Eliot comments: "What Othello seems to me to be doing in making this speech is *cheering himself up*. He is endeavouring to escape reality, he has ceased to think about Desdemona, and is thinking about himself. Humility is the most difficult of all virtues to achieve; nothing dies harder than the desire to think well of oneself. Othello succeeds in turning himself into a pathetic figure, by adopting an *aesthetic* rather than a moral attitude, dramatizing himself against his environment. He takes in the spectator, but the human motive is primarily to take in himself. I do not believe that any writer has ever exposed this *bovarysme,* the human will to see things as they are not, more clearly than Shakespeare."[24]

In 1890, Wilde's extravagance—"to see the object as in itself it really is not"—was regarded as a conceit, a vivacity, but it has now become a fairly common practice in literary criticism. Not universal. Arnold's sober formula still holds as orthodoxy. But Wilde's heresy has many adherents, critics who write about works of literature as if their taking the particular form they take were of no account; or as if the critic were free to wish them to be other than they are. Pierre Macherey has insisted that by its very nature, criticism immediately dissents from the empiricist fallacy; it aspires to indicate a possible alternative to the given. Roland Barthes read books as if he mainly wanted to defeat them, or at least to deflect the force of their rhetoric. When Jacques Derrida writes about Rousseau, Nietzsche, Hegel, Celan, Mallarmé, Ponge, or Genet, he is not much interested in saying what is there, in the works under consideration: he is far more concerned to invent a piece of writing by improvising upon the themes they offer. In *Jacques Derrida* by Geoffrey Bennington and Jacques Derrida, Bennington is the straight man, like Wilde's Ernest, the patient explainer telling us about *différance,* Husserl, sign and signified, translation, and Derrida's relation to Levinas; meanwhile, at the bottom of every page, Derrida, like Wilde's Gilbert, plays grim variations on other themes—circumcision, Augustine, God, the death of Derrida's mother. *The Gift of Death* starts out as if Derrida were explicating Jan Patocka's *Heretical Essays on the Philosophy of History,* and broods to much purpose on Christianity and responsibility. But it soon becomes a heretical essay in residual relation to Patocka's heresies: it winds up as a set of improvisations on secrecy, sacrifice, trembling, mystery, with copious reference to Baudelaire, Heidegger, Levinas, and "Bartleby the Scrivener." I am not complaining. *The Gift of Death* is one of my favorite books, and its tropical plenitude is Derrida at his grave best.

Alternatives to the given are now regularly enforced by critics of different persuasions—Marxist, feminist, psychoanalytic, gay and lesbian, deconstructive. These critics do not feel any piety toward the object as in itself it really is, or to the impression the work has made on them, or to the alternative impression they have formed in relation to the work.

Specifically: Marjorie Levinson has written a book on Wordsworth's poems mainly, it appears, for the satisfaction of chastising him. She is not the first to do this. Arnold, I regret to have to concede, much as he admired Wordsworth in other respects, thought that he had turned away from half of human life. Douglas Bush made much the same comment. The complaint has been taken up by several critics to impugn what Jerome McGann calls the "romantic ideology." But Levinson has extended the tradition into a relentless rebuke. In a chapter on "Tintern Abbey" she accuses Wordsworth of suppressing the social, historical, and economic facts of the case. He doesn't look at what is there in front of him, the scene around the Abbey, the squalor, the misery, the beggars, the pollution of the River Wye. "The 'still, sad music of humanity' drowns out the noise produced by real people in real distress. . . . By narrowing and skewing his field of vision," Levinson says, "Wordsworth manages to 'see into the life of things.'" The poem achieves its "fiercely private vision" by that suppression, by expressing Culture as if it were Nature. Finally, the poem presents mind and memory as barricades "to resist the violence of historical change and contradiction."

Levinson deals with the persuasive force of "Tintern Abbey" simply by rejecting it. We are to tell ourselves that the "prolific contraries of Romantic poetry and criticism"—such as creation-and-perception, innocence-and-experience, subject-and-object—"are not our family of conflicts, which is to say, they are not prolific for us. . . . To pretend otherwise is to forget ourselves through a facile sympathy, and to lose our enabling, alienated purchase on the poems we study."[25] But it doesn't occur to Levinson that "to forget ourselves" may be a morally fine thing to do and that the best way of doing it is by imaginatively participating in lives other than our own, while continuing to know that they are not our own. Participating in Wordsworth's life, for instance. Sympathy need not be facile. Levinson refers to "our enabling, alienated purchase on the poems we study," but she refuses to turn that alienating force on herself or to question her own rhetoric and the sources of her resentment. It is almost as if she hated the reality of Wordsworth's poems and determined to conceive how they might be if they were different and morally better.

Wilde's formula would allow us to deflect the blow of Levinson's criticism.

Wilde's Gilbert says that "to the critic the work of art is simply a suggestion for a new work of his own." We might then read such criticism as if it were literature—which it sometimes is. I have no doubt that Derrida is part of the history of French literature, whether or not he is part of the history of literary criticism. It may be that his books belong, with Rousseau's *Confessions*, to the genre of autobiography; even those which are not explicitly autobiographical. If so, their bearing on the works they discuss may be a minor consideration. Perhaps this device is intolerably cynical: by referring Derrida's work to the history of French literature we seem to be challenging it to take its chances there, in the midst of that prolific and abundant library. Perhaps there is no harm in that. If Levinson's book on Wordsworth is not primarily a book on Wordsworth but a "new work of her own," we might read it as a chapter of her autobiography. We might use it to imagine, yet again, what it must be to be different. Which is, in my view, why we continue to have an interest in writing and reading.

IV

It would be difficult to argue the respective merits of these three forms of reading without disclosing a prejudice. The causes that make one person a realist, another an idealist, and a third a pragmatist are not to be found in the reasons each would give to justify his position: one would have to start further back, when the prejudice in favor of a particular stance went without saying and was not felt to need reasons. In literary criticism, a critic does not start from a formulated position: the formulation comes later, after many essays that seemed to need no such thing. Arnold was Arnoldian in many practices before he found it necessary to give reasons. Pater became Paterian at a much earlier point in his career. Wilde had the intuitions of a dramatist before he thought of turning them to comic account in literary criticism. Donald Davie once gave a talk called "Three Analogies for Modern Poetry" in which he argued that Pound's poetry aspired toward the condition of sculpture, Eliot's toward the condition of music, and Yeats's toward the condition of drama. Davie's own poetry is Poundian, for the most part, and seeks the sculpture of rhyme. But it discloses that affiliation only after the event of many variously disposed poems. A label merely notes a tendency, but it is useful to have a label—it makes for clarity—despite the limiting considerations of "merely" and "despite."

Each of the three ways of reading that I've described gratifies certain desires and runs particular risk. "Arnold" gratifies the desire for knowledge and construes knowledge as a relation in which a subject respects an object. "Arnold" is like a Victorian scientist in that consideration: he is content to regard subject and object as separate entities and to take the subjective presence largely for granted. He is also content that the subject should appear to be a servant, a mere scribe. "Arnold" runs the risk of exaggerating the objective character of a work of literature and of counting too much on the common sense of a realistic epistemology. A poem is in some respects a visible thing, but in other respects it's as mobile as one's breath. A play moves in time, and is moving because of that consideration among many other considerations. "Pater" appeals to the privilege of experience rather than of knowledge. He may not feel any disrespect for the object, but he is especially tender toward the subject, his sensibility, and he is mainly concerned to have the sensation of feeling that the world, seemingly opaque, is—or appears to be—suggestible and translucent. It must be an acute pleasure to feel that everything in the given world is incipiently and subjectively intelligible, available to the practice of divination. But "Pater" runs the risk of displacing the work of literature by his own feelings. He solicits the temptation of loving his feelings more than the paintings, the poems, the fictions. "Wilde" might be accused of not reading at all, as Picasso might be thought not to have read the African masks from which he started in several paintings. Presumably the reading is done silently while the artist prepares to produce his own new work. "Wilde" is indifferent to knowledge and dissatisfied with experience: they are too old, they have run to seed without being fruitful. He is avid for production and performance, the production of new writing, new gestures, new masks, new selves. He willingly takes the risk of thinking that he has surpassed the work of literature by the verve of his performances in its vicinity. But I should not, in turn, make too much of these tendencies and temptations. Even to name a way of reading exposes me to the risk of making it seem fixed in that character: it is fixed only when its practitioner reflects on his purposes with the intention of confirming them and loving them alone. It is more likely that we move from one mood to another. Emerson said in "Circles" that our moods do not believe in one another. It is probable that anyone's moods will include from time to time one or another of the three figures I have sketched.

Finally, it is possible to combine the motives of the three ways of reading by seeing them as mutually obliging. I find an instance of this combination in one of Christopher Ricks's essays. He has quoted a passage from Stevens's "Notes Toward a Supreme Fiction":

> Two things of opposite natures seem to depend
> On one another, as a man depends
> On a woman, day on night, the imagined
>
> On the real. This is the origin of change.
> Winter and spring, cold copulars, embrace
> And forth the particulars of rapture come.[26]

Ricks comments: "Does imagination 'embrace' reality, or is there a turn, with reality embracing imagination? Why is not the imagined, like the imagination, as much a part of reality, albeit differently so, as anything else? Independence of mind imagines interdependences."[27] These sentences allow for our three ways of reading. Ricks assumes, by referring to a "part of reality," that there is at any moment a whole, reality itself or the hypothetical sum of its parts. A poem is one of those parts. Poetry, as the sum of particular poems, is part of a much larger whole—the world, reality, everything that is the case. This is an Arnoldian stance. Ricks then implies, in his second question, that "the imagined" is not as starkly opposite in its nature to "the real" as Stevens on this occasion says it is. A Paterian movement on Ricks's part, much as he disapproves of Pater. He well knows that Stevens, in many other poems and other parts of this one, enlarges the range of the imagined to the point at which it appears to usurp the rights of the real. In those poems Stevens calls the imagined by the name of fiction, and imagines a Supreme Fiction, rival to God's creation because, according to "Final Soliloquy of the Interior Paramour," "We say God and the imagination are one."[28] "Why is not the imagined, like the imagination, as much a part of reality, albeit differently so, as anything else?" Why not? But the difference, unspecified, would allow "Wilde" to claim that it makes all the difference in the world and some difference to the world. He intends adding a new thing to the world while seeming to pay attention to an old thing. "Wilde" declares his independence of mind, releases himself of every obligation to the work of literature, by choosing not to imagine interdependences. Or, having imagined them, to challenge them in performing his new self, striking through yet another mask.

FOUR

The Practice of Reading

It may be well to speak to a text. I have chosen *Macbeth* for reasons that hardly need to be explained. I will quote several passages of literary criticism, directed upon a few speeches from the play, to indicate what I regard as close, patient reading. I am not claiming that these passages say all that might usefully be said or that they are adequate to the play as an artistic whole. But they indicate what literary criticism is. There was a time when it was unnecessary to produce such passages or to say "this is literary criticism." But that is not the case now, a point that explains why I have written this book.

I must approach these passages of criticism by a detour, to indicate why I am citing them in a chapter on current practices of reading. I confine myself to *Macbeth* and its attendant commentaries, but I assume that similar problems of reading are encountered in the humanities generally. Reading a painting must be just as arduous—and as pleasurable—as reading a poem, play, or novel.

I

In the fall of 1946, I. A. Richards spoke at a conference in Princeton on "The Humanistic Tradition in the Century Ahead." The occasion, Richards recalled in an essay in the *Journal of General Education* for April 1947, "was felt to be challenging." The conference had been preceded by one on nuclear physics and another on the social sciences: "it was hardly possible throughout the discussion not to wonder where—in the balance of forces that are shaping the future—the humanities did come in." Richards noted some of the conditions in which the question was necessarily raised: the enormous and still increasing population of the world, 700 million in 1840, 2,200 million in 1947; the rise of mass education and the hopes and fears it provoked; and the exposure of minds to a "range and variety and promiscuity of contacts unparalleled in history." Finally he emphasized the juncture of the sciences with the humanities: "What are meeting now head on are two unreconciled ways of conceiving man and his good and how to pursue it. Both wish him well, but they differ radically as to how he can be helped. The physical and social sciences alike—being applications of methods of observation and calculation—conceive men as units subject to forces playing upon them *from without.* . . . Thus a man's desires and opinions and beliefs, the springs of his action and sources of his triumphs or sufferings, are likewise, for science, to be studied from without. . . . In contrast, the humanities pin a faith, which is experimentally still ungrounded, on the ideal autonomy of the individual man."[1]

It will not be supposed that I regard Richards's account of these matters as definitive. It is no longer true that the main opposition to the humanities comes from the sciences: it comes from the humanities themselves and takes the form of "techniques of trouble"—R. P. Blackmur's designation of the ways we make trouble for ourselves, mocking our purposes. As humanists—in the special and limited sense in which we are teachers of the humanities—we are unable or unwilling to say what we are doing, or why our activities should receive support in the form of salaries, grants, and fellowships. Why should the National Endowment for the Humanities exist? Why should taxes be spent on such a cause? We are timid in describing the relation between training in the humanities and the exercise of the moral imagination. We have largely given up the claim that one's reading of, say, *Little Dorrit* has any bearing, however tenuous or oblique, on the exercise of one's informed sympathies at large. Other aspects of Richards's commentary, too, may be questioned. It is astonishing that he spoke with such confidence of the "ideal autonomy of the individual man." It is now widely if not universally believed that, far from being autonomous even ideally, each of us is socially constituted. The view of mankind that Richards ascribed to scientists is now commonly held by humanists; that each of us is a consequence of extraneous and contingent forces. A claim for one's autonomy, however modestly expressed, is rarely allowed.

But Richards's comments are still useful, even if they chiefly provide opportunities for disagreement. When we put his sentences beside other versions of the cultural conditions that obtain in the humanities—I'm thinking of Blackmur's *Anni Mirabiles* and of several more recent interventions, including E. D. Hirsch Jr.'s *Cultural Literacy,* Sven Berkerts's *Gutenberg Elegies,* and many more—we gain a sense, good enough for most purposes, of our hopes and fears. For the moment I would add only this: those hopes and fears turn upon the question of reading. What we fear is that our students are losing the ability to read or are giving it up in favor of an easier one, a flair for being spontaneously righteous, indignant, or otherwise exasperated. We fear, too, that the impatience our students bring to the slow work of reading literature is a symptom of more drastic trouble, the general decline of literacy in the U.S.A. and the increase in the number of those who are technically literate but choose not to read. What we hope is that we may still be able to show our students the pleasure—different and better, we have to think—of reading in a more exacting spirit.

I must be summary at this point. I believe that the purpose of reading literature is to exercise or incite one's imagination; specifically, one's ability to imagine being different. Such an imagining was one of Hopkins's preoccupations in his journals and spiritual exercises: What must it be to be different? I don't think he meant solely: What would it be to like girls rather than boys? He meant: What is it to be oneself and therefore not someone else? Is it possible to project myself into the state of being of another person? Can I imagine being someone else? Is the imagining valid or merely a form of self-deception? Reading a poem or a novel, attending a play, looking at a painting or a building, listening to music—these experiences should provoke me to imagine what it would mean to have a life different from my own. A good reading is in that sense disinterested, as we used to say and some of us still want to say. I know that disinterestedness is commonly denounced as just another interest, flagrantly masked, so I use the word only in a limited sense. But it is possible to distinguish a reading more or less disinterested from one demonstrably opportunistic. I'll try to do that later.

II

I begin with D. W. Harding's commentary—amplified by a paragraph of scholarship from Helen Gardner—on the "Pity, like a naked new-born babe" passage. Macbeth is trying to talk himself out of murdering Duncan:

> Besides, this Duncan
> Hath borne his faculties so meek, hath been
> So clear in his great office, that his virtues
> Will plead like angels, trumpet-tongu'd, against
> The deep damnation of his taking-off;
> And Pity, like a naked new-born babe,
> Striding the blast, or heaven's Cherubins, hors'd
> Upon the sightless couriers of the air,
> Shall blow the horrid deed in every eye,
> That tears shall drown the wind.

(I.vii.16.25)

Harding believes that one of the qualities that distinguish poets from other people who use language is that poets bring language to bear on their thinking at a notably early stage of its development. He has explained this idea in an essay on the poetry of Isaac Rosenberg:

> Usually when we speak of finding words to express a thought we seem to mean that we have the thought rather close to formulation and use it to measure the adequacy of any possible phrasing that occurs to us, treating words as servants of the idea. "Clothing a thought in language," whatever it means psychologically, seems a fair metaphorical description of much speaking and writing. Of Rosenberg's work it would be misleading. He—like many poets in some degree, one supposes—brought language to bear on the incipient thought at an earlier stage of its development. Instead of the emerging idea being racked slightly so as to fit a more familiar approximation of itself, and words found for *that,* Rosenberg let it manipulate words almost from the beginning, often without insisting on the controls of logic and intelligibility.[2]

So, too, with Shakespeare, allowing for differences in the scale of genius between him and Rosenberg. In "The Hinterland of Thought" Harding recurs to the idea and associates it with Langer's distinction, in *Philosophy in a New Key*, between presentational symbolism and discursive thinking, the latter coming later in cognition than the former. Harding writes:

> A half-way house between presentational symbolism and discursive state-
> ment is to be seen in some of the torrential passages of Shakespeare where
> half-activated images succeed one another with great rapidity and gain their
> effect through not being brought to the full definition of an exact metaphor.
> The *Macbeth* passage about Pity like a naked new-born babe is an obvious
> example. The sense of the passage is that in spite of the seeming helplessness
> of any protest against the horrors perpetrated by unscrupulous power, the
> decent human emotion of pity can in the end mobilize enormous strength.
> But Shakespeare stopped long before this stage of discursive statement. He
> had in mind presumably a mass of items and associations related to the cen-
> tral theme: the new-born babe as an example of extreme helplessness, the
> cherubs on maps blowing the winds, the immense power of the wind and
> the fact that it brings tears to the eyes—and they could be tears of pity—
> especially if it blows something into them, the way it rushes all over the
> world like an invisible messenger carrying heaven's protest against the
> crime, in other words carrying pity, which in spite of being a helpless infant
> is now in charge of the tremendous strength of divine as well as human con-
> demnation of the crime.[3]

There is indeed more to be said about the famous speech. Helen Gardner has explicated it further in reply to Cleanth Brooks's analysis of it in *The Well-Wrought Urn*. Brooks didn't know enough about angels, apparently; he thought cherubins must be avengers. Not so: they are "angels of the presence of God," standing above the throne, "contemplating the glory of God." It is not their task to act upon God's will: "The babe, naked and new-born, the most helpless of all things, the cherubins, innocent and beautiful, call out the pity and the love by which Macbeth is judged. It is not terror of heaven's vengeance which makes him pause; but the terror of moral isolation. He ends by seeing himself alone in a sudden silence, where nothing can be heard but weeping, as, when a storm has blown itself out, the wind drops and we hear the steady falling of the rain, which sounds as if it would go on for ever. The naked babe strides the blast because pity is to Shakespeare the strongest and profoundest of human emotions, the distinctively human emotion. It rises above and masters indignation."[4]

III

The next passages are from F. R. Leavis's *Education and the University: A Sketch for an 'English School'* (1943). In the first one, Leavis is making the point that when we say of a particular passage that in it the metaphors are "realized," this term—necessary as it is—does not introduce a simple or easily applied criterion. The example Leavis uses is Lady Macbeth's speech of welcome to Duncan:

> All our service,
> In every point twice done, and then done double,
> Were poor and single business to contend
> Against those honours deep and broad wherewith
> Your majesty loads our house.
>
> (I.vi.14–18)

Leavis comments: "In 'contend,' it will be conceded, we feel an unusual physical force, yet perhaps very few, when challenged, could say offhand how this comes, in what way it is related to the image implicit in 'deep and broad,' or what this is. The image is that, felt rather than seen, of a full-flowing and irresistible river, and Shakespeare clearly arrived at it by, characteristically, seizing on and realizing the conventional metaphor of the king's being the 'fount of honour.' But he has controlled realization to the requisite degree of incipience, so that the image is not felt to quarrel with the following one of 'loads.' And in this marvellously sure and subtle control of realization Shakespeare's genius is manifested as much as in the vividness of his most striking imagery."[5]

In the next passage the lines Leavis is reading are the "temple-haunting martlet" speech of Banquo to Duncan under the battlements at Macbeth's castle:

> DUNCAN: This castle hath a pleasant seat; the air
> Nimbly and sweetly recommends itself
> Unto our gentle senses.
> BANQUO: This guest of summer,
> The temple-haunting martlet, does approve,

> By his loved mansionry, that the heaven's breath
> Smells wooingly here: no jutty, frieze,
> Buttress, nor coign of vantage, but this bird
> Hath made his pendent bed, and procreant cradle
> Where they most breed and haunt, I have observed
> The air is delicate.
>
> $\qquad\qquad\qquad\qquad\qquad\qquad\qquad\qquad$ (I.v.1–10)

Leavis's commentary reads, in part:

> We note the insistence, throughout the passage, of the element represented
> by "pleasant," "sweetly," "gentle"; it is so insistent that it appears even in a
> place so apparently inappropriate (on editorial inspection) as to elicit from
> the *Arden* editor the comment: "probably a proleptic construction." But
>
>> the air
>> *Nimbly* and sweetly recommends itself,
>
> and the set of associations represented by "nimbly" is equally important on
> the whole: we are in hill air, which is not only sweet but fresh and vital—a
> sharp contrast to the smothering sense, already evoked, of the "blanket of
> the dark." But that is not all; every word in the passage contributes. Why, for
> instance, "temple-haunting"? It co-operates with "guest" and "heaven" to
> evoke the associations belonging to the "sanctity of hospitality": for
> "heaven," reinforced by "temple," is not merely the sky where the fresh
> winds blow. Nevertheless the suggestion of altitude is potent:
>
>> no jutty, frieze,
>> Buttress, nor coign of vantage, . . .
>
> —"above the smoke and stir of this dim spot." But why "martlet"? The bird,
> with its swift vitality and exquisite frail delicacy, represents a combination
> analogous to "nimbly and sweetly." But more; its "pendent bed," secure
> above the dizzy drop, is its "procreant cradle"; and "procreant" is enforced
> by "breeds": all these suggestions, uniting again with those of "temple" and
> "heaven," evoke the contrast to "foul murder"—life springing swift, keen
> and vulnerable from the hallowed source.[6]

Leavis's analysis of the passage was meant to support his claim that "attention
directed upon 'character' and 'psychology' is not favourably disposed for
doing justice to the kind of thing Shakespeare does here with words."[7] The

words are spoken by Banquo, indeed, but Leavis doesn't make much of that fact; he discourages the reader from valuing the speech as evidence of Banquo's character rather than for its bearing on the play as a poetic whole and on Shakespeare's particular way of using words. I find no contradiction between these interests. It is important, for the reasons Leavis offers, to have Banquo's words spoken at this point in the play: important, too, to have them spoken by him. There is no discrepancy between Shakespeare's inventive genius among the words and the enabling propriety of his assigning them to Banquo.

IV

I'll give another example of close reading in response to the first part of Macbeth's speech at the beginning of act I, scene vii. William Empson's analysis concentrates on the first four lines, in which he finds a "resounding example" of the ambiguity by which two or more alternative meanings are resolved into one:

> If it were done, when 'tis done, then 'twere well
> It were done quickly:
> (double syntax since you may stop at the end of the line)
> If th' assassination
> Could trammel up the consequence, and catch
> With his surcease success; that but . . .

words hissed in the passage where servants were passing, which must be swaddled with darkness, loaded as it were in themselves with fearful powers, and not made too naked even to his own mind. *Consequence* means causal result, and the things to follow, though not causally connected, and, as in "a person of consequence," the divinity that doth hedge a king. *Trammel* was a technical term used about netting birds, hobbling horses in some particular way, hooking up pots, levering, and running trolleys on rails. *Surcease* means completion, stopping proceedings in the middle of a lawsuit, or the overruling of a judgment; the word reminds you of "surfeit" and "decease," as does *assassination* of hissing and "assess" and, as in "supersession," through *sedere*, of knocking down the mightly from their seat. *His* may apply to Duncan, *assassination* or *consequence*. *Success* means fortunate result, result whether fortunate or not, and succession to the throne. And *catch*, the single little flat word among these monsters, names an action: it is a mark of human inadequacy to deal with these matters of statecraft, a child snatching at the moon as she rides thunder-clouds. The meanings cannot all be remembered at once, however often you read it; it remains the incantation of a murderer, dishevelled and fumbling among the powers of darkness.[8]

When Elder Olson protested against this dealing with "trammel," Empson explained his point further: "I do not think I have ever heard anyone use the word *trammel* in ordinary life; it still seems necessary to go to the dictionary and find what sort of thing it meant to an Elizabethan. . . . These current uses of the word appear to Shakespeare or his audience as a kind of feeling about what you could do with it; and the literary effect here, though simple in its way, is I think very strong. Macbeth is trying to feel that this is only a kind of engineering problem; if only he can get the murder done efficiently, he thinks, all this fog will lift and he will be able to see clearly again. Both the mechanical analogy and its underlying complexity still seem to me very direct parts of the speech."[9]

V

I have been going back to these and other critics—notably to G. Wilson Knight, John Crowe Ransom, and L. C. Knights—to rehearse the purposes to which they turned their readings of *Macbeth* in particular, of Shakespeare more generally, and of other writers in relation to Shakespeare. Up to a point (and despite Ransom's belated appreciation of Eliot's early poems) the critics might be called the School of Eliot: their critical essays were impelled by his early poetry and *The Sacred Wood*. The motive I find in common among these critics is Eliot's, that of gaining, against increasing difficulty, an intelligent readership for literature. Leavis is most explicit on that issue, just as the considerations that led to his explicitness are most clearly indicated by Q. D. Leavis's *Fiction and the Reading Public* (1932). In that book Mrs. Leavis studies the rise and the disintegration of such a readership, the development of journalism, the book market, advertising, economic considerations, and the significance of Best Sellers in relation to serious fiction. The place to start, in the work of cultivation, was clearly the school, college, university: the crucial discipline was a revised "English School." In schools and colleges, F. R. Leavis reiterates, the critical study of literature must involve "a training of intelligence that is at the same time a training of sensibility." Furthermore: "If literature is worth study, then the test of its having been so will be the ability to read literature intelligently, and apart from this ability an accumulation of knowledge is so much lumber."[10]

Again: "By training of reading capacity I mean the training of perception, judgment and analytic skill commonly referred to as practical criticism—or, rather, the training that practical criticism ought to be."[11] That last qualification put a certain distance, however cordially, between Leavis's program and Richards's. Leavis didn't want to be associated with Richards's behaviorism. The differences between them need not concern us here.

The critics I have referred to worried about the fate of intelligent reading in conditions of mass society, universal education, the Yellow Press, the resurgence of logical positivism, and the dominance of science. They argued that a work of literature differs from a scientific treatise in not being a sequence of discursive statements. A poem, as Brooks said in *The Well-Wrought Urn*, does not properly eventuate in a proposition. Hence the "heresy of paraphrase." A poem is an action, not a proposition. What it offers to an energetic reader is an experience, an event, not a semantic entity. Even if the poem is grammatically divisible into sentences, a proper reading of those sentences takes them as actions—symbolic actions, Kenneth Burke called them—performed in a certain hypothetical context. They are to be questioned not for their truth but for their direction and force within the poem. The "To-morrow and to-morrow and to-morrow" speech is not a philosophy of life, Shakespeare's or Macbeth's, but a sequence of statements issuing from Macbeth's sense of himself at that moment.

It is not true, therefore, as John Guillory has claimed, that the method of close reading, practiced by the New Critics, sustained a conservative ideology of the self. The method was used by critics on the Left and on the Right: it is enough to name, indicating the Left, Empson's *Some Versions of Pastoral*, Burke's *The Philosophy of Literary Form* and *Permanence and Change*, and L. C. Knights's *Drama and Society in the Age of Jonson*. Ransom, Tate, and Robert Penn Warren may be called the Right for this local purpose. Nor is it true, as Guillory has maintained, that the practice of the New Critics in purging political considerations from the study of literature has a "tendentially conservative effect, conservative by default."[12] When we read a work of literature as a symbolic action, we purge the political, but we also purge the metaphysical, the religious, the economic, the historical, or any other ideological discourse. We give none of these any privilege, for the simple reason that we pay attention not to propositions that might be extracted from the work and used to some ideological end, but to statements made under the pressure of the context; and we attend to these not as independent truths or falsehoods but as things said in that context.

VI

I have made another detour, but it enables me to say that in recent commentaries on *Macbeth* what is repeatedly ignored is the distinction between a proposition and an action. The homework that I have been doing on these commentaries has led me to think that we are in the presence of a New Thematics, which represents itself as literary criticism or instead of it. Instead of it, if literary criticism is to be repudiated as the work of formalists and aesthetes. Since the early 1980s, a consensus on *Macbeth* has emerged which I'll try to describe: it satisfies the interests of social science, apparently, or of biographical diagnosis rather than those of criticism. By that difference I mean that the commentaries issue not in analyses of the language of the play but in an invidious account of the ideology that the play allegedly sustains: for that purpose, a reading of the play in the detail of its language is thought to be a nuisance.

The critics of *Macbeth* whom I have been reading include Peter Stallybrass, Marilyn French, Dennis Biggins, Terry Eagleton, Jonathan Goldberg, Madelon Gohlke, Marjorie Garber, Lisa Jardine, Catherine Belsey, Malcolm Evans, Janet Adelman, and Garry Wills. Wills's interests don't come into the story or affect the main issue. Why these critics? They reveal what is happening in criticism more clearly than what happens in *Macbeth*. Many of them—not all—embody the consensus by citing one another and by not citing anyone else. There is common cause between them, or most of them.

It is my understanding that the new reading of *Macbeth* was stimulated by the publication of Alan Macfarlane's *Witchcraft in Tudor and Stuart England* (1970), Keith Thomas's *Religion and the Decline of Magic* (1971), and perhaps— I'm not sure about this—Carlo Ginzburg's *The Night Battles: Witchcraft and Agrarian Cults in the Sixteenth and Seventeenth Centuries* (1966). Scholars have continued to read the play in terms of the Gunpowder Plot, the Gowrie Conspiracy, Scottish conventions of monarchy, and Shakespeare's need to gratify James I. But these books by Macfarlane, Thomas, and Ginzburg drew new attention to witchcraft and fears about it in the sixteenth century, and prompted critics to interpret *Macbeth* afresh, making much of the witches and of Lady Macbeth in some strange relation to them. Biggins's "Sexuality, Witchcraft, and Violence in *Macbeth*" (1975)[13] and Stallybrass's "*Macbeth* and Witchcraft" (1982)[14] mark the first phase of the consensus. Terry Eagleton's *William Shakespeare* (1986) gave it a stirring conceit: "To any unprejudiced reader—which would seem to exclude Shakespeare himself, his contemporary audiences and almost all literary critics—it is surely clear that positive value in *Macbeth* lies with the three witches. The witches are the heroines of the piece, however little the play itself recognises the fact, and however much the critics may have set out to defame them. It is they who, by releasing ambitious thoughts in Macbeth, expose a reverence for hierarchical social order for what it is, as the pious self-deception of a society based on routine oppression and incessant warfare. The witches are exiles from that violent order, inhabiting their own sisterly community on its shadowy borderlands, refusing all truck with its tribal bickerings and military honours."[15] But the agreed account of *Macbeth* was in place before Eagleton's book was published.

The gist of the consensus is that *Macbeth* is Shakespeare's fantasy of male self-begetting and immortality, without recourse to women. It is crucial to the new reading to bring Lady Macbeth and the witches together as sisters in subjugation. They are not forces of evil or the uncanny, but victims of male oppression; they testify to every value a society governed by men excludes.

The earliest essay in this vein, so far as I can discover, is Gohlke's " 'I wooed thee with my sword': Shakespeare's Tragic Paradigms" (1980): "The world constructed by Macbeth attempts to deny not only the values of trust and hospitality, perceived as essentially feminine, but to eradicate femininity itself. Macbeth reads power in terms of a masculine mystique that has no room for maternal values, as if the conscious exclusion of these values would eliminate all conditions of dependence, making him in effect invulnerable. To be born of woman, as he reads the witches' prophecy, is to be mortal. Macbeth's program of violence, involving murder and pillage in his kingdom and the repression of anything resembling compassion nor remorse within, is designed, like Coriolanus's desperate militarism, to make him author of himself."[16] Jonathan

Goldberg took up the theme in "Speculations: *Macbeth* and Source": "The hypermasculine world of *Macbeth* is haunted . . . by the power represented in the witches; masculinity in the play is directed as an assaultive attempt to secure power, to maintain success and succession, at the expense of women. . . . Macbeth looks in the mirror and sees his reflection in the line that extends to James; not in the mirror is Mary Queen of Scots, the figure that haunts the patriarchal claims of *Basilikon Doron*, the mother on whom James rested his claims to the throne of England—and whom he sacrificed to assure his sovereignty." But in the end, "all masculine attempts at female deprivation—including Lady Macbeth's desire to unsex herself—are robbed of ultimate success. . . . What escapes control is figured in the witches."[17]

Perhaps the most thoroughgoing version of the consensus is Janet Adelman's " 'Born of Woman': Fantasies of Maternal Power in *Macbeth*" (1987)[18] and *Suffocating Mothers: Fantasies of Maternal Origin in Shakespeare's Plays: "Hamlet" to "The Tempest"* (1992). She writes of the "decisive masculine act as a bloody rebirth, replacing the dangerous maternal origin through the violence of self-creation," and of the play as representing "both the fantasy of a virtually absolute and destructive maternal power and the fantasy of absolute escape from this power."[19]

These versions of the new reading are not of course identical: we would not expect them to be, coming as they do from exponents of feminism, psychoanalytic criticism, and Old and New Historicism. But they are at one in interpreting the play as a fantasy of self-begetting and immortality. They differ in determining whether the fantasy is fulfilled. Some critics see the end of the play as restoring the old masculine values; others think the forces embodied in the witches are still compellingly at large, like the spirits of Cathy and Heathcliff at the end of *Wuthering Heights*, on the margin of the society they at any moment are capable of threatening. But we have a consensus of alleged fantasy and diagnosis, nonetheless.

It would be helpful if I could quote a few passages of close reading of *Macbeth* from adepts of the New Thematics. Not surprisingly, I can't. Close reading is not what they do. Several reasons suggest themselves. The first is that these critics are queering one discipline—literary criticism—with the habits of another—social science or moral interrogation. Their metier is not verbal analysis but the deployment of themes, arguments, and morally charged conclusions: hence the only relation they maintain to the language of

Macbeth is a remote one. A second consideration: these critics evidently think that Shakespeare's language is transparent to reality and that the reality it discloses can be represented without fuss in political, moral, and psychoanalytic terms. This is a strange assumption, after many years of Deconstruction in which we have been admonished that language is constitutionally opaque and its meanings undecidable. The new readers of *Macbeth* are not impeded by these Derridean considerations. They take language for granted as providing direct access to reality and fantasy. Acting on this assumption, they also take for granted what Geoffrey Hill has called, with rebuking intent, the "concurrence of language with one's expectations."[20] These critics have no sense of the recalcitrance of language, specifically of Shakespeare's English: they think that in reading his words they are engaging with forces and properties indistinguishable from their own. In philosophic terms, they practice the most blatant form of Idealism, even though they profess—many of them—to be Materialists.

It follows that when such critics quote, they do so merely to illustrate a theme, a discursive claim, or a diagnosis they have already produced. Eagleton quotes part of the "To-morrow and to-morrow and to-morrow" speech, but only to say that it shows Macbeth "reduced to a ham actor, unable to identify with his role."[21] That is not what the lines do. The reductive nature of Eagleton's comment may be shown by quoting, as an example of responsible interpretation of the lines, L. C. Knights's comment that Macbeth is "groping for meanings, trying to conceive a time when he might have met such a situation [as his wife's death] with something more than indifference."[22] Lisa Jardine, much in Eagleton's style, quotes Lady Macbeth's "Come you spirits / That tend on mortal thoughts, unsex me here" speech, but says of it merely that it represents "this steady misogynistic tradition" in which Lady Macbeth and other women "are represented as 'not-woman' at the peak of dramatic tension before committing 'unwomanly' acts—generally murder." The fact that the speech represents Lady Macbeth as mother, or at least as imaginatively maternal, is not allowed to count. When Jardine quotes Lady Macbeth's challenge to Macbeth, "What beast was't then / That made you break this enterprise to me?" she remarks only that it is yet another instance of "threatening womanhood."[23] In *The Subject of Tragedy* Catherine Belsey quotes the "Pity" speech and makes no literary comment on it, but uses it to reproach Liberal Humanism for finding "its own reflection, its own imaginary fullness everywhere," in this case by constructing the "feeling, self-conscious, 'poetic' Macbeth, a full subject, a character."[24]

VII

I am not claiming that all recent dealings with *Macbeth* have been ideologically opportunistic or that it is impossible to find a disinterested reading of the play. But such readings are pretty rare. I'll quote two instances, the first from Stanley Cavell. It's worth remarking that Cavell is a philosopher, much of whose thinking is incited by his reading of Emerson, Thoreau, Kierkegaard, Wittgenstein, and Austin. He is also interested in American films and the patterns of behavior and aspiration they present. As if that were not enough, he has published many essays on Shakespeare and on Beckett. In one essay he concentrates on the language of *Macbeth* and its bearing on prophecy and mind reading. I'll quote a passage about mind reading in relation to Macbeth and his wife: "The idea of words as mind-reading is a conception of reading as such—or play-watching—reading the text of another as being read by the other. Uttering words as mind-reading is represented in the language of this marriage, in which each of the pair says what the other already knows or has already said; or does not say something the other does not say, either assuming the other knows, or keeping a pledge of silence. They exemplify exchanges of words that are not exchanges, that represent a kind of negation of conversation. For example: Macbeth prays to "let that be, / Which the eye fears, when it is done, to see" (I.iv.52–53), and Lady Macbeth is soon incanting "That my keen knife see not the wound it makes" (I.v.52).[25]

It may be said that this is not close reading in Leavis's sense, but the perception—of Macbeth and his wife reading each other's minds—could not have issued from anything but close reading. You couldn't deduce it from a psychological profile drafted in advance of detailed attention. In fact, Cavell might have gone further by reflecting even more closely on the language. Take the two passages. In act I, scene iv, Macbeth hears the King say that "We will establish our estate upon / Our eldest, Malcolm, whom we name hereafter / The Prince of Cumberland." The monarchy was not hereditary, but the King's naming his son Prince of Cumberland made a problem for Macbeth and thwarted his ambition. In an aside, he brings forward his thought of killing the King:

> Stars, hide your fires;
> Let not light see my black and deep desires:
> The eye wink at the hand; yet let that be,
> Which the eye fears, when it is done, to see.

In the next scene Lady Macbeth, by herself in a room of the castle at Inverness, is working herself up to murder the King:

> Come, you spirits
> That tend on mortal thoughts, unsex me here,
> And fill me from the crown to the toe top-full
> Of direst cruelty! make thick my blood;
> Stop up th'access and passage to remorse,
> That no compunctious visitings of nature
> Shake my fell purpose, nor keep peace between
> Th'effect and it! Come to my woman's breasts,
> And take my milk for gall, you murd'ring ministers,
> Wherever in your sightless substances
> You wait on nature's mischief! Come, thick night,
> And pall thee in the dunnest smoke of hell,
> That my keen knife see not the wound it makes,
> Nor heaven peep through the blanket of the dark,
> To cry 'Hold, hold!'

"Crown" keeps the King in mind while it refers immediately to Lady Macbeth, head to toe. Thick blood cannot flow as it naturally would to incite dread and remorse. The repetition of "thick" brings night and blood into sinister relation. "Thick night" is almost an allusion to Macbeth's "Stars, hide your fires." But the feature of the language that most vividly makes us think of mind reading is that Macbeth and his wife use the same figure of speech, catachresis, the figure of abuse by which incompatibilities are forced together despite their incompatibility. The standard instance is from Milton's "Lycidas": "Blind mouths! That scarce themselves know how to hold / A sheep-hook." Mouths don't know anything. In Macbeth's speech stars don't hide their fires, light can't see, eyes don't fear. In Lady Macbeth's speech evil spirits may corrupt mortal thoughts, thicken one's blood, forestall compunctious visitings of nature, and replace a woman's milk with gall. Night may be fancied to thicken its darkness with the dunnest smoke of hell, and God—the unspoken referent in "heaven," as in Milton's invocation in *Paradise Lost* to "the will and high permission of all-ruling Heaven"—may choose to cry "Hold!" But a knife can't see the wound it makes. The difference between the catachreses in the two speeches is that Lady Macbeth disappears, by anticipation, into her instrumentality—"my keen knife"—and leaves the play by killing herself. Macbeth survives the figure of abuse and steadies himself, for the moment, in his resolution—"let that be." In act I, scene vii, the roles are nearly reversed; Macbeth tries to talk himself out of the deed, and his wife's violence forces him back to it.

Cavell's reading of these speeches is edifyingly disinterested, in the sense that nothing he says about the language of *Macbeth* could be used for any ideological purpose. It is as if the speeches bespoke the form of his attention and he stood ready to have them perform themselves. His reading is close to the spirit of Maurice Blanchot's in *The Gaze of Orpheus:* "Reading is not writing the book again but causing the book to write itself or *be* written—this time without the writer as intermediary, without anyone writing it."[26] Cavell hands himself over to the words, and divines in them the figure of their bearing.

The second example of close reading may be thought not to be a reading at all but a poet's act of *sprezzatura*. Jorie Graham's poem "The Phase After History" is in three parts. The first imagines two juncos that have flown into a house and become trapped there. One of them escapes, the other doesn't. This part of the poem gives someone's meditation on the arbitrariness of action, the bewildered whirl of energy in which objects are materialized meanings and there is no direction. History is over or still to come. The second part of the poem presents a young student who tries to kill himself and eventually succeeds. Seizing the day, the student makes history of a kind by taking it into his own hand and knife. Each of these parts includes allusions to *Macbeth*, direct quotations, sometimes altered, from speeches by Macbeth and his wife. In the third part, the speaker, evidently the woman of the house, sits on the landing, waiting, listening for a sign of the resumption of historical time:

> listening for the one notch
>   on the listening which isn't me
> listening—

The poem ends the woman's reverie on yet another doomed attempt to create or appropriate history—"something new come in but / what?"—Macbeth's and his wife's, leading to the sleepwalking scene (V.i) in which Lady Macbeth tries to wash her guilt away—"What, will these hands ne'er be clean?" The woman's reverie ends, as if addressed to Macbeth, by bringing eye and knife together:

> Sleep, sleep, but on it the dream of reason, eyed,
> pointing forward, tapering for entry,
>   the *look* with its meeting place at
> vanishing point, blade honed for
>   quick entry,
> etcetera, glance, glance again,
>   (make my keen knife see not the
> wound it makes)—
> So that you 1) must kill the King—yes—
> 2) must let her change, change—until you lose her,
>   the creature made of nets,
>
>   whose eyes are closed,
> whose left hand is raised
>
>   (now now now now hisses the voice)
> (her hair made of sentences) and
>   3) something new come in but
> what? listening.
>   Is the house empty?
> Is the emptiness housed?
>   Where is America here from the landing, my face on
>
> my knees, eyes closed to hear
>   further?
> Lady M. is the intermediary phase.
>   God help us.
> Unsexed unmanned.
>   Her open hand like a verb slowly descending onto
>   the free,
> her open hand fluttering all round her face now,
>   trying to still her gaze, to snag it on
>
> those white hands waving and diving
>   in the water that is not there.[27]

Disinterested attention and an archetypal imagination together see juncos and student in the light of the story of Macbeth and his wife. Graham's interpretation begins by seeing these three situations related one to another and all three to the motif of "after history." Macbeth must kill the King and he must see his wife change—the creature made of nets—into a figure in the sleep and dream of reason, the verb becoming a noun and then a pronoun and then a gesture, a shadow of itself, a shape in the air.

VIII

To what desires in contemporary literate society does the New Thematics correspond? A new form of reading, or a relapse into an old form, is interesting only if it exhibits such correspondence.

My sense of the matter comes back to the notion of transparency. I find a suggestive passage, bearing on this motif, in Matei Calinescu's *Rereading,* where he writes about the general move from intensive to extensive reading; from the slow reading of a few texts, sacred or profane, to the skimming of many books, magazines, and newspapers: "With the growth of 'extensive reading,' the growing prestige of science, and the rise of political democracy, modernity has fostered a powerful longing for transparency doubled by a hostility to those forms of secrecy that were traditionally claimed as a prerogative of power, whether supernatural or human. But the modern ideal of transparency does not apply to the personal secrets of individuals, which, again reversing a long-standing tradition, should from now on be protected by the modern 'right to privacy.' "[28] This desire for transparency takes many forms, all reductive. It shows itself in the determination to construe every work of literature—a play about kings, treason, murder, and equivocation, for instance—as a simple parable, invidiously recited, of men and women. More clamorously, it presents itself as a desire to find great literature rotten with fantasy and corruptly in league with men of power. "There is no document of civilization," we hear Walter Benjamin alleging, "that is not at the same time a document of barbarism."[29]

The broad background to these desires is the assumption that all knowledge is socially constructed and that sociologists of knowledge are fully equipped to understand the processes of this construction. The authors of *The Social Construction of Reality* (1966) tell us that "it will be enough, for our purposes, . . . to define 'knowledge' as the certainty that phenomena are real and that they possess specific characteristics."[30] Even with the weasel qualification "for our purposes," this definition is scandalously loose, but it serves the purposes of those who for one reason or another want to suppress metaphysical, religious, or visionary experience. What sociologists offer, to prove the social constitution of knowledge, is a simplified account of particular social practices. Their definitions are useless in trying to explain how the same social conditions produced writers as different as Shakespeare and Webster, or why Blake's art differs so radically from Reynolds's. As Michel Serres has remarked, "You can always proceed from the product to its conditions, but never from the conditions to the product."[31]

These factors, along with more obvious considerations, such as film, TV, and video, explain why there has been a palpable loss or lapse of interest in verbal culture by comparison with the culture of visual images and artifacts. Guillory has argued, with Hirsch's *Cultural Literacy* in mind, that "if Americans are 'culturally illiterate,' this fact is evidence of the educational system's failure to install a motive for reading in a nominally literate population."[32] What would such a motive be? Pleasure, I hope: but pleasure of a distinctive kind. There is no point in offering our students the experience of reading works of literature as if it could compete, for quick diversion, with more mundane felicities. A different experience is entailed, not an immediate gratification. I'll try to say what it involves, by way of an attempted Sketch of an English School.

IX

The pleasure of reading literature arises from the exercise of one's imagination, a going out from one's self toward other lives, other forms of life, past, present, and perhaps future. This denotes its relation to sympathy, fellowship, the spirituality and morality of being human. It is certainly not a substitute for anything else—for one's commitments in religion or politics, for instance. It is what it is. The reading of literature may be taken as exemplary of artistic experience in general, without implying that literature is superior to any other form of art. It may be true, as Walter Pater maintained, that all the arts constantly aspire toward the condition of music. But in literature that aspiration is qualified by the writer's more fundamental desire to explore and extend the resources of a language. It is once again necessary to assert, in the face of much dissent, that literature exists; that it is not just a form of discourse like any other. By saying this, I may be thought to be endorsing some version of essentialism and claiming that every work of literature embodies some essence, universal, that floats entirely free of the conditions of its production. I make no such claim. But I assert, provoked by the opposite claim now more commonly heard, that a work of literature is accompanied by the circumstances and forces of its production, pressed upon by them, but it is not determined by them. Shakespeare's achievement in *Macbeth*, the powers of invention and discovery he put to work in that play, are such as to make me entertain the conceit that the play was written in almost complete freedom. Still, there is no merit in countering one extravagance with another.

If literature exists, it is necessary to say in what respect it exists. I agree with Paul de Man on this matter: "For the statement about language, that sign and meaning can never coincide, is what is precisely taken for granted in the kind of language we call literary. Literature, unlike everyday language, begins on the far side of this knowledge; it is the only form of language free from the fallacy of unmediated expression. All of us know this, although we know it in the misleading way of a wishful assertion of the opposite. Yet the truth emerges in the foreknowledge we possess of the true nature of literature when we refer to it as *fiction*."[33] As we'll see in a later chapter, de Man didn't always hold to this view of literary language, but that is another story. The fallacy of unmediated expression to which he refers is much in evidence in recent commentaries on *Macbeth:* the critics have not considered what mediation entails in Shakespeare's language or how one's reading should engage with that force.

What, then, are we to ask our students to read? Life, being short, is better spent reading great works rather than mediocre ones. If it is alleged that critical adjudication between one work and another has invariably been effected by men, and that masculine values have been enforced in those decisions, we now have the pedagogical conditions—classes, seminars, conferences, journals—in which an alternative canon, or additions to the canon, may be tried out. I would be surprised to see many works of literature, now deemed canonical, dislodged by this process. But I recognize certain troubling signs, such as the inclination of many students to read only modern if not contemporary works, and—among those—to prefer prose fiction to poetry. It is a bad sign. We find in poems more exactingly than in novels the qualities of language that give point to de Man's emphasis on mediation. But it is hardly likely that the question of merit in a particular work will gain much of a hearing, silenced as it is likely to be by questions of topical relevance and diagnostic availability. There are works of literature that answer to local interests and may be quoted to illustrate a theme or a set of cultural forces. That is probably the readiest use to which teachers are inclined to put them. But a great work of literature, like *Macbeth*, is one that answers to a remarkably wide range and pressure of interests. It is also, like the world according to Whitehead's sense of it, "patient of interpretation in terms of whatever happens to interest us."[34]

Nevertheless, it is sometimes maintained that we should not prescribe great works of literature for students who come from a different cultural setting than our own. In "The Function of Literary Theory at the Present Time" (1989), J. Hillis Miller denounced as "repressive" the practice of "forcing a Latino or Thai in Los Angeles, a Puerto Rican in New York, an inner city African-American in either city to read only *King Lear, Great Expectations,* and other works from the old canon."[35] Miller's sentence is bizarre. "Forcing" is an exaggeration, the proportion of required to elective courses in American colleges and universities being as concessive as it is. In many institutions it is easy to major in English without reading any Shakespeare or Dickens. Miller's "only" is also a wild exaggeration: no such prescription ever arises. These are details, but on the substantive issue I see no reason whatever for not asking Latino, Thai, and Puerto Rican students who have chosen to read English for a degree to read *King Lear, Great Expectations,* and other works from the canon. If those students were reading French, German, or Italian for a degree, they would expect to read Racine or Goethe or Dante, authors far removed from their daily experience, and they would regard themselves as cheated if they didn't get good teaching in the mysteries of the foreign language and its literature. Miller is patronizing those students by claiming that they are not to be asked to read great literature or to be taught how best to read it.

Indeed, my disagreement with him on this issue impels me to claim that the best way to read English, especially in present circumstances, would be to read it as a second language and a second literature. Most of the defects of our reading and teaching arise from the fact that we are reading and teaching English as though our students were already in command of the language. We assume that they know the language well enough and are qualified to move to a study of the literature. We would not make this assumption if we were teaching a foreign language. If we taught English as a second language and a second literature, we would become more responsive to the mediating character of the literary language, the opacity of language as such: we would not assume that the language is transparent to our interests.

Surely I am forgetting the expository writing programs, which take up so much time and energy in our colleges and universities? No: EWPS exist because many junior-high-school and high-school teachers work in conditions so frightful that they can't teach their students how to read and write. If conditions were propitious, EWPS would happily cease, and their teachers would be employed teaching the literature they entered the profession hoping to teach. Instead, the teachers find themselves helping students to become functionally literate, a process for which the reading of great literature is generally considered unsuitable. No student in an EWP class is obliged to read *King Lear*. As Edward Corbett has written, "Literary texts will more often than not serve as a distraction from, rather than a promoter of, the objectives of a writing course."[36] No wonder the students are encouraged to write more than they read, and to write even if they don't read.

A latecomer to the U.S.A., I have never taught a class in expository writing, so I must quote what other teachers report of the experience. In *The Culture of Literacy*, Wlad Godzich gives convincing evidence that only a restricted notion of literacy obtains in EWPS: they "provide for competence in a specific code, with little, if any but the most rudimentary, awareness of the general problematics of codes and codification in language." I don't warm to Godzich's talk of codes; it doesn't answer to my sense of the reading of literature, the activity in which we have seen Harding, Leavis, Empson, and other critics engaged. But Godzich's general argument is persuasive: "It is not an exaggeration to state that the effect of the new writing programs, given their orientation, is not to solve a 'crisis of literacy' but to promote a new differentiated culture in which the student is trained to use language for the reception and conveyance of information in only one sphere of human activity: that of his or her future field of employment."[37] Guillory's reflections on the EWP are even more pointed: they bear on the civic aim of such a program. He refers to

> a new kind of "oral performance" on the basis of the new kind of writing
> practice inculcated in the compositional syllabus. We will have no difficulty

in recognizing what this speech sounds like: it is the speech of the professional-managerial classes, the administrators and bureaucrats; and it is employed *in its place,* the "office." It is not "everyday" language. The point of greatest historical interest about this speech is that its production by-passes the older literary syllabus altogether. Students need no longer im-merse themselves in that body of writing called "literature" in order to acquire "literary" language. In taking over the social function of producing a distinction between a basic and a more elite language, composition takes on as well the ideological identity of that sociolect, its pretension to univer-sality, its status as the medium of political discourse.[38]

Leavis's aim was to train students to form an intelligent reading public, a minority no doubt because the forces at work in society had conspired to that end: his ideal student might well become a man of letters or, as in the case of Q. D. Leavis, a woman of letters, but he or she would also be able, by virtue of that training, to play an effective part in social and public life. That was as much as could be hoped for. But the aim of EWPs is merely to train students to take part in the decorum of social and public life. The divided forces of a plural society—ideologies of race, class, gender, creed—are meant to be recon-ciled in offices of management and the corporations. Meanwhile, the study of literature is confined to a relatively small part of the English School, and its aims are regularly alleged to be elitist.

Not that literature needs to be defended, it merely needs to be read, inten-sively. I can't regard recent readings of *Macbeth* as intensive; they exhibit that premature recourse to the political and the psychoanalytic which is one of the banes of contemporary practice. But I should emphasize, even in a mere sketch of an English School, that a theory of communication is not adequate to the reading of literature. No matter how elaborately such a theory is pro-posed, as by Richards or by Roman Jakobson, it does not answer the require-ments of reading literature. Pierre Bourdieu has argued that "utterances are not only (save in exceptional circumstances) signs to be understood and deciphered; they are also *signs of wealth,* intended to be evaluated and appreci-ated, and *signs of authority,* intended to be believed and obeyed."[39] I would add: some words and sentences are also tokens of largesse, acts of grace and flair, to be appreciated as such. So a theory of performance, not of communi-cation, is required. Performance is the larger motive, within which the sec-ondary motive, communication, can be housed comfortably enough. What we find in *Macbeth* is Shakespeare's performance in the modes of language and theater, copiousness of expression far beyond the requirements of communication though still compatible with those. The speeches analyzed by Leavis, Empson, Harding, and Knights would be largely redundant, their inventive eloquence quite exorbitant, if local requirements of communication were primary.

Performance, and therefore form: bringing words, gestures, and actions to the condition of form. This is the most complex issue in literary criticism, how to divine the form of a work as distinct from the object of reference when we recite the plot of a novel or paraphrase a sonnet. It is a serious limitation in the "close reading" practiced by Leavis's colleagues that it had little or no purchase on the form of a work of literature. Except in their readings of short poems, the New Critics could indicate the form of a work only by delineating its structure of images, as in *The Well-Wrought Urn* or Mark Schorer's essays on English fiction. Form is achieved content, Schorer said: true, and his phrase recognizes the work of performance, but it does not say enough to be useful beyond that. In *The Aesthetic Dimension*, Herbert Marcuse argues that Marxist critics have been misguided in attacking Formalism in criticism: of many works of literature it may be shown that it is by virtue of its form that a work of art is genuinely revolutionary. The form of *Macbeth* is not its five-act structure, though it is related to that. Form is the embodiment, first word to last, of a principle, source of energy, or—in Aristotle's sense—a human action which is the animating motive of the play.

The first requirement, if we are to read literature in the spirit indicated by my approved instances, is a recovered disinterestedness. If we can't or won't sequester our immediately pressing interests, put them in parentheses for the time being, we have no hope of reading literature. If we read merely to have our political or other values endorsed, or to find them abused, by the work of literature, the situation is vain. Received wisdom would have it that disinterestedness is a cloak at once to conceal and to reveal economic capital; to conceal it by making its signs a matter of tone and gesture; to reveal it by showing it in a sublime transformation. The only person who can be disinterested, we are told, is someone who has enough money, leisure, and freedom to enjoy the experience. That is not true, or not entirely true. The few years that Miller's Thai, Latino, and Puerto Rican students spend taking a degree are designed to provide them with conditions of relative freedom in which they can study. During those years, unless the system of higher education has already broken down, these students have the opportunity of standing apart, at least to some extent, from the primary interests that beset them—jobs, money, responsibilities. Lionel Trilling speaks to this theme in *Beyond Culture*. Such students ought to be helped to take pleasure in reading great literature, by having them read it a little apart from the culture that otherwise governs them. They might also be helped to enjoy for a while a quality Blackmur found in Marianne Moore's poems, the perfection of standing aside. If that is not possible, then the system has already failed.

The word I have not used that seems to trouble many critics and teachers is "aesthetics." It is thought to connote moral lassitude, political irresponsibility, decadence. The troubling is unnecessary. If we take the word as it is used by Louise Rosenblatt to indicate the comprehensive, lived experience of reading, there is nothing to be troubled about. Or ashamed of. Perhaps the word can still be used with honor. I have been heartened recently, reading certain critics who might be thought to be entirely "political" and finding them coming round, belatedly perhaps, to the recognition of aesthetics as a necessary discipline of attention. Edward Said in *Culture and Imperialism*, Peter R. Brooks in "Aesthetics and Ideology: What Happened to Poetics"? and George Levine in *Aesthetics and Ideology* are willing to recognize "the aesthetic" as providing what Levine calls a "space where the immediate pressures of ethical and political decisions are deferred."[40] Levine also recognizes "how difficult it is to resist or qualify in any way the primacy of the ideological project of criticism."[41] That recognition is enough for my purpose. But some critics remain invincibly hostile to aesthetics. I can note only that aesthetics means perception, the practice of paying attention to objects that ask only to be perceived. If the word offends, I would be pleased to replace it by "poetics," which I take to mean the inductive study of works of literature with a view to understanding—but only late in the day—the principles of their working. That is what an English School should do, even if the conditions of its work are unpropitious.

FIVE

What Is Interpretation?

Whatever the work of interpretation is, it is something that most literary critics do. Interpretation begins when someone decides to pay attention to a text. In *Truth and Method,* Gadamer refers to the claim of the text to dominate our minds.[1] Interpretation begins when we have acknowledged that claim and set about fulfilling it. We try to understand the text as if its character were hidden and must be brought to light. We move along the interpretive process when we try to make our preliminary understanding of the text explicit to ourselves, thereby turning the occasion into an experience. If we offer to make the experience—or something like it—available to other readers, we have in mind to put the text into the public domain. We may assume that there is an obstacle or some degree of opacity, otherwise the text would move into that domain without any intervention on our part. In common practice, there are obstacles. The domain is already choked with signs and signals. Reading at a certain level of seriousness is no longer what most people do. Or we find that a text is so difficult, such slow work, that many readers give it up. Or we discover that a section of the text, a word or a phrase, makes for difficulty and must be elucidated. We then have another reader in view. To begin with, we interpret the poem, say, for ourselves: we go as far as we can to read it from our own resources. When we can go no further, we go for help to readers we have cause to think are better informed on this particular poem. But in either case interpretation becomes a social act: we do it at first for ourselves and later for other people. If we have encountered a problem, the chances are that some other readers have come upon it, too. More specifically, we assume that there is a public domain which consists mostly of signs and the talk about signs. The signs are visible, audible, or tangible; the talk is casual or formal, ignorant or well-informed. We interpret a text because we want it to exert a force of presence in ourselves, to begin with, and then a similar force among the public signs and the current forms of talk. But interpretation is merely the first stage of reading. It comes to an end when we are satisfied that we have made the text at least provisionally available. Teacher and pupils, critic and readers are agreed that they have a certain text between them and that their minds are not—or not yet—at cross-purposes. Interpretation has established the poem as common ground between the parties engaged. Now the reading can proceed.

In the little I have said, I am taking it for granted that the text is in some measure difficult. We want to know what the Delphic oracle said. We want to read the Bible. It has been argued that the discipline of literary criticism "originates in medieval efforts to interpret what is in many ways the most challenging of sacred Hebrew poetic texts, the Song of Songs."[2] The Bible consists of several books of stories, laments, exclamations, many of them hard to understand and therefore hard to live with or live by. We need help from commentators, rabbinic scholars, interpreters from different religious traditions, adepts of hermeneutics skilled in the ways of biblical writing. The Bible, interpreted in one spirit or another, then becomes part of the public domain: it may eventually appear in an unlikely place, as *Genesis* did, on television. Without those interpretations, many parts of the Bible would be darkness visible. It would still be available to the clerisy of scholars, but not to the laity. Every homily preached in a church is an attempt to add the force of spiritual or moral presence to the public domain of speech, belief, and practice.

Sometimes the work of interpretation begins with the removal of local obstacles. I recall that when I first read Stevens's "The River of Rivers in Connecticut"—

> There is a great river this side of Stygia,
> Before one comes to the first black cataracts
> And trees that lack the intelligence of trees . . .[3]

—I had no idea what the third line meant. Some time later I found that Stevens had explained it to Renato Poggioli: it meant trees living in a place unfavorable to their growth. If I had read Stevens's complete poetry and prose at the time, I might have found that he sometimes used the word "intelligence" to mean not only the cognitive or imaginative capacity of people but also the vital force in anything—a tree, for instance. An interpreter would try to make sense of it; not necessarily Stevens's sense. His explanation of the line to Poggioli still leaves the conceit in place, the tension between the intelligence of trees and the conditions in which it is absent. "Lack" has to mean something like: "suffer the absence of . . ." Reading Stevens's "Credences of Summer," I come to the tenth section, which begins—

> The personae of summer play the characters
> Of an inhuman author, who meditates
> With the gold bugs, in blue meadows, late at night.
> He does not hear his characters talk. He sees
> Them mottled, in the moodiest costumes,
>
> Of blue and yellow, sky and sun, belted
> And knotted, sashed and seamed, half pales of red,
> Half pales of green, . . .[4]

Why half pales of red, half pales of green? Poggioli put the question to Stevens and got this reply:

> In the expression—half pales of red, etc.—the word pales is used in its heraldic sense and I suppose that unconsciously I used the plural in the same way that the plural gules has been used. I should hate to say that I remember anything as long ago as the time when the poem was written. But it seems to me that when using the word pales I validated the use by thinking of the use that had been made of gules. I have forgotten where it is in Keats, but there is a line describing moonlight falling through a stained glass window upon a floor. Keats used words something like this:
>
> "and cast warm gules of red."[5]

Stevens recalled the line in Keats's "The Eve of St. Agnes" (XXV, line 2): "And threw warm gules on Madeline's fair breast."

One more example of interpretation as the removal of obstacles. When you come to Yeats's "The Statues," you are pulled up short by the first sentence: "Pythagoras planned it." You may know who Pythagoras was, but not what he is said to have planned. All you can do is hold the sentence in suspension till the plan begins to come clear:

> Pythagoras planned it. Why did the people stare?
> His numbers, though they moved or seemed to move
> In marble or in bronze, lacked character.
> But boys and girls, pale from the imagined love
> Of solitary beds, knew what they were,
> That passion could bring character enough,
> And pressed at midnight in some public place
> Live lips upon a plummet-measured face.[6]

The plan was evidently embodied in Pythagoras's theory of numbers, the basis of ancient Greek conceptions of harmony. Yeats seems to have believed that Pythagoras devised his theory not only for intrinsic reasons but also because it would bring forward a new type of person, an athletic image of beauty, and suppress the vague, formless beauty of Persian culture. In "On the Boiler" he says: "There are moments when I am certain that art must once again accept those Greek proportions which carry into plastic art the Pythagorean numbers, those faces which are divine because all there is empty and measured. Europe was not born when Greek galleys defeated the Persian hordes at Salamis; but when the Doric studios sent out those broad-backed marble statues against the multiform, vague, expressive Asiatic sea, they gave to the sexual instinct of Europe its goal, its fixed type."[7] The people stared, I presume, because they were not accustomed to this new type of body and couldn't believe their eyes. Perhaps they found it intolerably abstract. Only lovers knew that their passion would adopt the new form and animate it, changing character into personality without refuting the plummet-measured face. The poem is not, of course, the same as the passage in "On the Boiler." It remains to be read as a poem, in its own formal terms. But local obstacles have to be removed.

It is fairly generally accepted that the interpreter of a text can't appeal for authority to the author's intention—at least beyond a certain point—not only because we rarely know what that intention was but also because the author may not have realized his intention in the text; the text may in the event have exceeded the intention or diverged from it. As Gadamer says, "Texts do not ask to be understood as a living expression of the subjectivity of their writers."[8] Nor can the interpreter appeal to a writer's first readers to verify his interpretation—but this is a raw issue, as we'll see. Appeal to the first readers has mainly negative force: we may know what those readers couldn't have known— Milton's first readers couldn't have read Einstein on relativity—but we can't be sure what their relation to their knowledge was. Stanley Fish has proposed to avoid this difficulty by arguing that the meaning of a text is established by the "interpretive community" that receives it and that it changes when a differently configured community emerges. But this is a doubtful claim. Who are those who constitute a community, and how can we assume that their being a community depends on the way they read texts? It may depend on consanguinities of social class, family income, race, religious observance, and many other considerations. If Fish means a community of scholars, his case is still weak. When we consult the critics and scholars who are supposedly members of the same interpretive community, we find mostly disagreement on the interpretation of particular texts. We are impelled to conclude that no reading of a text is universally accepted unless a particular critic happens to speak of it—as T. S. Eliot did for many years—with special authority.

But it is time to describe a particular issue rather than continue generalizing. I choose an occasion on which most of the contentious issues of interpretation were raised. In January 1953, the English scholar-critic F. W. Bateson, editor of *Essays in Criticism,* published a manifesto in that journal: it was called "The Function of Criticism at the Present Time," and it explicitly invoked Matthew Arnold's authority. Bateson's main argument was that contemporary critics, resourceful and ingenious as they were, were irresponsible in many of their interpretations. I. A. Richards, C. S. Lewis, William Empson, John Crowe Ransom, and F. R. Leavis were irresponsible in letting their interpretations—or some of them—float free of scholarly constraint. Richards's commentary on Eliot's "A Cooking Egg," Empson's reading of Shakespeare's "That Time of Year Thou Mayst in Me Behold," Lewis's account of Spenser in *The Allegory of Love,* Ransom's essay on Milton's "Lycidas": these, according to Bateson, did not take into consideration the context of the literary work they offered to interpret. By "context" he meant "the framework of reference within which the work achieves meaning."[9]

Bateson's main attack was turned on Leavis. In *Revaluation*, Leavis juxtaposed a short passage from Marvell's "A Dialogue Between the Soul and Body" and another from Pope's *The Dunciad*. I'll quote the two passages, giving a few more lines of each to indicate the immediate context. Here is the first stanza of Marvell's poem; the speaker is the Soul:

> O, who shall from this dungeon raise
> A soul, enslaved so many ways,
> With bolts of bones, that fettered stands
> In feet, and manacled in hands.
> Here blinded with an eye; and there
> Deaf with the drumming of an ear,
> A soul hung up, as 'twere, in chains
> Of nerves, and arteries, and veins,
> Tortured, besides each other part,
> In a vain head, and double heart?[10]

"Double heart," the only obvious obstacle, is usually glossed as "characterized by duplicity, but it also suggests the physical aspect of double ventricles."[11] And here is the passage from the fourth book of *The Dunciad*, lines 499–504. The speaker is Silenus (Thomas Gordon), a drunken Epicurean philosopher, addressing the "Goddess Dame":

> Then thus: From priestcraft happily set free,
> Lo! Every finished son returns to thee:
> First slave to words, then vassal to a name,
> Then dupe to party; child and man the same;
> Bounded by nature, narrowed still by art,
> A trifling head, and a contracted heart.[12]

Bateson held that Leavis quoted these passages in *Revaluation* in order to claim, mainly on the strength of the last line of each, that they disclose striking affinities between the style of Pope and that of Marvell; that Pope's "wit" represents a continuation of the Metaphysical tradition. Bateson denies that the two passages are evidence of any such continuation. He says:

In terms of literary tradition the meanings of "head" and "heart" are demonstrably quite different in the two passages. In Marvell's lines the vivid
images of the first couplet almost compel the reader to visualize the torture-
chambers of the "vain Head, and double Heart." It is the kind of allegory that
was popularized in the early seventeenth century by the Emblem Books, in
which a more or less conventional concept is dressed up in some striking
new clothes, the new clothes being the real *raison d'être*. In Pope's last line,
however, the abstract or quasi-abstract words which lead up to it make it almost impossible to *see* either the "trifling head" or the "contracted heart."
Obviously Pope's "head" and "heart" belong to the same order of reality as
his "Nature" and "Art." They are simply items in his psychological terminology, one the antithetical opposite of the other, and their modern equivalents
would, I suppose, be the intellect and the emotions. Nothing could be further removed than these grey abstractions from Marvell's picture-language.[13]

Bateson goes on to claim that the vividness of Marvell's imagery has caused
him to blur the argument by forcing the reader to equate the immoral head
and heart with the relatively innocent nerves, arteries, and veins. Marvell's
imagery, according to Bateson, has forced him to say what he couldn't possibly
have intended.

To sustain this position, Bateson invokes what he calls the intellectual context and the social context. He speaks of four stages in the widening scene of
meaning. The first is the plane of dictionary meanings, the second is the literary plane (the tradition or genre to which the poem belongs), the third is the
large intellectual setting, and the fourth is the social context. At that point in
one's reading, Bateson claims, we have the correct meaning: "It can be called
the correct meaning, the object as in itself it really is, since it is the product of
progressive corrections at each stage of the contextual series. And, as the work
assumes its original historical setting, the human experience embodied in it
begins to be realized and re-enacted by the reader."[14] In the end, Bateson
proposes what he calls a balance of literary and sociological criticism.

Within a few months, Leavis replied to Bateson in his own journal, *Scrutiny*. It is clear that he resented Bateson's claim to possess, as Leavis allegedly
didn't, the scholarship to enable a just reading of Marvell and Pope. Leavis
maintained that the production of this scholarship, on Bateson's own showing, amounted to the intrusion of a vast deal of critical irrelevance on the
poem. With all his show of learning, Bateson was incapable of reading the

poems. We may confine ourselves to Marvell's "Dialogue" for the moment. Quoting the first stanza, Leavis says that "of its very nature it eludes, defies and transcends visualization": "So one is surprised to be told, by a scholar (who should know these things), that it is 'the kind of allegory that was popularized in the early seventeenth century by the Emblem Books.' To call it an allegory at all can only mislead, and to say, as Mr Bateson does, that it 'dresses up' a 'more or less conventional concept' in some 'new clothes' (these being the 'real *raison d'être*') is to convey the opposite of the truth about it. For it is a profoundly critical and inquiring poem, devoted to some subtle exploratory thinking, and to the *questioning* of 'conventional concepts' and current habits of mind."[15] Leavis insists that the poem begins with paradoxes which elude or defy visualization. He asks of the lines—

> With bolts of bones, that fettered stands
> In feet, and manacled in hands

—how do we see the Soul? What visual images correspond to "fettered" and "manacled"?: "We certainly don't see manacles on the Soul's hands and fetters on its feet: the Soul's hands and feet are the Body's, and it is the fact that they *are* the Body's that makes them 'manacles' and 'fetters.' . . . Reading this rightly, we feel, as something more than stated, the Soul's protest (paradoxically in part physical—this is where 'imagery' comes in) against the so intimately and inescapably associated matter: the introductory 'with bolts of bones' makes the antithesis, Soul and Body, seem clear and sharp."[16] It follows that Leavis must regard Bateson's appeal to allegory and Emblem Books as an irrelevance. Marvell's poem does not present a picture or, with any degree of piety, embody a genre; it makes any such picture unavailable, it refuses the consolations of an emblem. In fact, the poem does not quite conform to its title, because the entities—Soul and Body—are not separable. As Leavis says, with the later stanzas in mind: "A body that fears to die, and has to fear to die because it has been made to live by the Soul, is not so readily to be set over against the soul, as something clearly distinguished, as the title of the poem seems to imply. . . . The maladies of the Soul—described as that because they are of the kind that Physick cannot reach—are equally the Body's. The Body is exposed, it says, to suffering them by Knowledge and Memory, which it speaks of as belonging to the Soul, but which are nevertheless sufficiently of the body to involve the Body in maladies."[17]

On the passage from *The Dunciad*, Bateson evidently felt that his reading was irresistible. In Pope's lines, he claims, "the concept has almost killed the imagery, the progress being toward a mathematical purity with the sensuous elements segregated into a separate compartment of their own": "How is it that Pope, a master of language if ever there was one, has used his concrete terms with so little precision? In these lines 'slave,' 'vassal' and 'dupe' are virtually interchangeable. And so are 'Bounded,' 'narrowed' and 'contracted.' These tautologies can't have been *meant* by Pope."[18] In a later "Reply" Bateson apparently thought that he had clinched the matter by quoting the Pope-Warburton note on the passage in question as if it had unquestionable authority. The note reads: "A recapitulation of the whole course of modern education described in this book, which confines youth to the study of *words* only in schools, subjects them to the authority of *systems* in the universities, and deludes them with the names of *party-distinctions* in the world. All equally concurring to narrow the understanding, and establish slavery and error in literature, philosophy, and politics."[19] Bateson thought that the note justified his reading of the passage: "Not to put too fine a point on it, Dr Leavis has misunderstood, more or less completely, all three of Pope's phrases. Slavery to 'Words' refers to the way in which Latin and Greek were taught in eighteenth-century schools; the 'Name' to which the adolescent pays homage is not that of a member of the nobility but the philosophical system taught in the universities; and it is party slogans that dupe the young man and not the politicians' promises of pickings and sinecures. . . . That what Pope really meant by the words was in fact something very like 'a slave or dupe of Aristotelianism' is confirmed by the Pope-Warburton note on *Dunciad* IV, 255–271."[20] But that did not reduce Leavis to silence. He continued to find it scandalous that Bateson wouldn't admit a difference between slave, vassal, and dupe. Leavis commented:

> Words should be servants—the servants of thought and of the thinker; the
> badly educated child is made a "slave to words" (the cliché has point, as
> clichés usually have). Such a child, grown to political years, naturally be
> comes "vassal to a Name." The felicity of this expression takes us beyond
> cliché (the "mastery of language" shown here is characteristic of Pope): the
> relation of personal subservience to a great patrician name (and a "mere
> name," it is suggested)—a relation substituting for service of Principle—is

with special point described contemptuously by the feudal term in an age in which feudalism is Gothick. And such an initiate into politics, expecting his reward for faithful service of Party, finds himself a "dupe." . . . "Vassal" and "dupe" express quite different relations, and a moment's thought will show that they couldn't be interchanged. And neither noun could go with "words": "vassal" expresses a relation between persons, and "dupe" implies an exploiting agent. There is hardly any need to argue that "slave" could not, without loss of point, as these words stand, be substituted for "vassal" or "dupe."[21]

With similar arguments, Leavis shows that "bounded," "narrowed," and "contracted" are not interchangeable: " 'Bounded by nature'—this refers to the limitations imposed by innate constitution. The person thus limited is made 'by art'—i.e. by education—even more limited than he need have been. . . . 'Contracted'—which picks up 'trifling' alliteratively, with a gain of expressive value for both terms—has something like the effect of 'double' in Marvell's 'vain head and double heart': it keeps us in touch with the heart as a physical organ. It suggests the muscular contraction, though *this* contractedness is permanent, and not part of the vital rhythm; and the presence of the muscular effect gives to the evoking of life meanly constricted a force that it wouldn't otherwise have had."[22]

Did Leavis give no credence to the Pope-Warburton note that Bateson quoted? He claimed to have read it, but to have found in it "nothing essential that I hadn't already gathered from the text itself." How much, or how little, such a note helps toward a right reading, he argued, "must be determined finally by a study of the text." The note doesn't settle any dispute. Pope's shift from "slave" to "vassal" "has an effect on 'name' that no note could undo even if it tried": "And it shows an odd unfamiliarity with Pope's habit in developing an attack, or a line of argument, to assume that, when he offers to exhibit the ill consequences of a defective education, he must be confining himself to the narrow—and pointless—kind of consistency preferred by Mr Bateson. Pope here exhibits his characteristic strength; his 'vassal' and 'dupe,' far from being disguised repetitions of 'slave,' are both creative words. . . . Pope there, so far from submitting the development of his case against the 'whole Course of Modern Education' to the canons of the 'contextual' interpreter, has turned his art to imputing, with whatever lack of strict logical cogency, a sinister responsibility for the social and political scene in general."[23]

Leavis's case against Bateson, now that I have nearly stopped rehearsing it and intend offering some general commentary, is that he cannot read a poem. He is disabled from doing so by his confidence in what he calls contextual criticism, as if that relieved him from the labor of reading the words on the page. What *is* this "complex of religious, political and economic factors that can be called the social context," Leavis asks; a complex such that it enables us to restore the poem to its original historical setting and find there, with the conviction of certainty, the right interpretation? It is an illusion, Leavis insists: it is nothing more than "the arbitrary odds and ends of fact, assumption, and more or less historical summary" that Bateson produces as if it had some evident authority other than the force of his own assertiveness. In truth, it merely gives Bateson license for not, in any serious sense, reading the poem.[24] Leavis is not making a case for ignorance. Knowledge, he says, "is needed for the critic's work, but the most essential kind of knowledge can come only from an intelligent frequentation of the poetry—the poetry of the age in question, and the poetry of other ages." In the measure in which you commit yourself "to ideas and theories like Mr Bateson's you debar yourself from that."[25] Leavis brushes aside Bateson's accusation that he read every work of literature as if it were written yesterday: "One judges a poem by Marvell not by persuading a hypothetical seventeenth-century 'context,' or any 'social context,' to take the responsibility, but, as one alone can, out of one's personal living (which inevitably is in the twentieth century)."[26]

I have no doubt that Leavis had the better part of this dispute. He won on points, if not by a technical knockout. He convicted Bateson of being thoughtless in the presence of Marvell's poem and of Pope's. Thoughtless, too, in taking for granted the applicable force, for the purpose of interpretation, of contexts that were largely of Bateson's own devising. So much is clear enough. But the parts of the dispute that seem to me not to have been decisive are those in which Leavis appeals to "one's personal living," as if that force should always be enough. I remain unconvinced, too, by his claim that the poem is determinately *there,* as if it were an object like any other. One's personal living would not be enough in reading the passages from Stevens and Yeats that I have quoted. Information is required. Leavis would probably retort: so much the worse for poems if they need, for an adequate interpretation, extraneous or private lore. As for the poem's being *there,* Leavis maintains that it is there in a sense in which it is impossible for any produced context to be there.

"There is nothing," he contends, "to correspond—nothing answering to Mr Bateson's 'social context' that can be set over against the poem, or induced to establish itself round it as a kind of framework." But Bateson was right to challenge Leavis to show in what sense the poem is present. It is there as certain words in a particular order on a printed page, but, as Bateson insists, "the meanings of the words, and therefore *a fortiori* the meaning of the whole poem, are emphatically not *there*."[27] Where are they? Predictably, Bateson maintains that they are where they started out as being: "To discover their meaning we have to ask what they meant to their author and his original readers, and if we are to recover their full meaning, the connotations as well as the denotations, we shall often find ourselves committed to precisely those stylistic, intellectual and social explorations that Dr Leavis now deplores. There is no alternative—*except to invent the meanings ourselves.* Dr Leavis is in fact opening the door to sheer subjectivism."[28]

Leavis didn't reply to that charge. Presumably he regarded it as absurd. Indeed, I can't think of any passage of his practical criticism that is subjective, in the nefarious sense intended by Bateson, though there are passages in which he gives way to prejudice, as in some parts of his commentary on Eliot's "Four Quartets" in *The Living Principle*.[29] Besides, while we normally think of subjectivism as emotional self-indulgence, it could just as reasonably be referred to Bateson's confidence, excessive as it is, in the critical force of his "contexts."

The dispute between Bateson and Leavis was severe, and not only on Leavis's part. It began with a clear challenge from Bateson to Leavis. As editor of *Essays in Criticism*, Bateson claimed, in effect, that his journal could compete with Leavis's *Scrutiny* in point of literary criticism and could improve on that criticism by calling on a greater power of scholarship. Leavis could not have allowed the claim to pass. But one of the consequences of the tone of the dispute was that it concealed the issues on which Leavis and Bateson were in agreement. They agreed on the primacy of interpretation and on the necessity of getting it right. They differed on the means of getting it right. Bateson appealed to historical scholarship as he conceived of it. Leavis thought the appeal vain. Both of them evidently thought that by getting the interpretation of, say, Marvell's poem right, one could put a stop to the vagaries of interpreting it. Neither of them mentions a possible change in the values to which he might appeal and over which he might have little or no control. Each of them assumed that if he interpreted Marvell's poem or Pope's correctly, the poem would stay in that interpretation: it would continue to be there, as Leavis liked to claim.

This accounts for the priestly tone of both Leavis and Bateson: they write as if they were engaged in a theological conflict and as if the real issues were doctrinal. It is significant, too, that the normal forum of teaching, for each of them, was not the large heterogeneous class of a modern university but the tutorial—teacher and two undergraduates—of an Oxford (Bateson) or Cambridge (Leavis) college. Each of them insists, to the last letter, on his own interpretation. The passions they express are those attached to a canon. Leavis regularly claimed that his tutorials were models of collaboration between teacher and pupils, their minds meeting as equal partners across a poem or a novel, but the intensity with which he replied to Bateson has the marks of an ecclesiastical commission of inquiry. There is to be no latitude in the hermeneutic act, no talk of plural interpretation. So I will quote, to illustrate the opposite attitude, a passage from Michel de Certeau's *Practice of Everyday Life,* in which de Certeau—though himself a Roman Catholic priest—takes evident pleasure in the ruses by which people circumvent the authority of institutions:

> Formerly, the Church, which instituted a social division between its intellectual clerks and the "faithful," ensured the Scriptures the status of a "Letter" that was supposed to be independent of its readers and, in fact, possessed by its exegetes: the autonomy of the text was the reproduction of sociocultural relationships within the institution whose officials determined what parts of it should be read. When the institution began to weaken, the reciprocity between the text and its readers (which the institution hid) appeared, as if by withdrawing, the Church had opened to view the indefinite plurality of the "writings" produced by readings. The creativity of the reader grows as the institution that controlled it declines. This process, visible from the Reformation onward, already disturbed the pastors of the seventeenth century. Today, it is the sociopolitical mechanisms of the schools, the press, or television that isolate the text controlled by the teacher or the producer from its readers. But behind the theatrical decor of this new orthodoxy is hidden (as in earlier ages) the silent, transgressive, ironic or poetic activity of readers (or television viewers) who maintain their reserve in private and without the knowledge of the "masters."[30]

Leavis, a more powerful polemicist than Bateson, detested the public institutions that governed the expression of convictions and values, but he did not trust the silent, transgressive ironies of ordinary readers to undermine their authority. Only an educated minority could have the slightest mitigating effect on the corrupting forces of Lord This and Sir That. Leavis gave his professional life to the education of that minority. But he had no hesitation in trying to substitute his own authority, limited as it was bound to be, for the unholy writ of the BBC and the Fleet Street press.

It follows that neither Leavis nor Bateson allowed for what I may call open interpretation, according to which plural readings may live side by side without troubling one another. In *The Sense of an Ending* Frank Kermode quotes Whitehead as saying that what distinguishes a classic from other works is that the classic is "patient of interpretation." It doesn't really matter, taking the long view appropriate in such a case, how differently *King Lear* is performed or read, though I hold myself free to prefer one performance, one reading, to another. Walter Benjamin touches on the theme of patience in an essay on storytelling. He recites a story from the fourteenth chapter of the third Book of Herodotus's *Histories:*

> When the Egyptian king Psammenitus had been beaten and captured by the Persian king Cambyses, Cambyses was bent on humbling his prisoner. He gave orders to place Psammenitus on the road along which the Persian triumphal procession was to pass. And he further arranged that the prisoner should see his daughter pass by as a maid going to the well with her pitcher. While all the Egyptians were lamenting and bewailing this spectacle, Psammenitus stood alone, mute and motionless, his eyes fixed on the ground; and when presently he saw his son, who was being taken along in the procession to be executed, he likewise remained unmoved. But when afterwards he recognised one of his servants, an old, impoverished man, in the ranks of the prisoners, he beat his fists against his head and gave all the signs of deepest mourning.[31]

Benjamin comments:

> From this story it may be seen what the nature of true story-telling is. The value of information does not survive the moment in which it was new. It lives only at that moment; it has to surrender to it completely and explain itself to it without losing any time. A story is different. It does not expend itself. It preserves and concentrates its strength and is capable of releasing it even after a long time. Thus Montaigne referred to this Egyptian king and

asked himself why he mourned only when he caught sight of his servant. Montaigne answers: "Since he was already over-full of grief, it took only the smallest increase for it to burst through its dams." Thus Montaigne. But one could also say: The king is not moved by the fate of those of royal blood, for it is his own fate. Or: We are moved by much on the stage that does not move us in real life; to the king, this servant is only an actor. Or: Great grief is pent up and breaks forth only with relaxation. Seeing this servant was the relaxation. Herodotus offers no explanations. His report is the driest. That is why this story from ancient Egypt is still capable after thousands of years of arousing astonishment and thoughtfulness.[32]

Benjamin's commentary suggests a number of possibilities. One is that interpretation, so far as it involves discursive paraphrase, is perhaps what we should not be doing. Susan Sontag's *Against Interpretation* means what its title says, subject to the consideration that the book itself contains interpretation. What it mainly expresses is Sontag's desire that interpretation should be translucent, that it should let the being of the work of art appear with as little critical or discursive commentary as possible. The work should be allowed to shine with its own light. But the inconvenience attached to this ideal is the fact that someone has to direct an opera or a play, someone has to conduct the orchestra through the score, someone has to read the poem or novel. Among the arts, only a film, a painting, a sculpture, or a TV program is immune to interference; and that immunity lapses when those who look at it start talking about it.

There are also works of literature that disable interpretation in advance. In "The Music of Poetry" T. S. Eliot argues that there can't be poetry of great musical beauty that makes no sense; but there are poems in which we are moved by the music and take the sense for granted, "just as there are poems in which we attend to the sense and are moved by the music without noticing it." Eliot has in mind the nonsense verse of Edward Lear: "His non-sense is not vacuity of sense: it is a parody of sense, and that is the sense of it. 'The Jumblies' is a poem of adventure, and of nostalgia for the romance of foreign voyage and exploration; 'The Yongy-Bongy Bo' and 'The Dong with a Luminous Nose' are poems of unrequited passion—'blues' in fact. We enjoy the music, which is of a high order, and we enjoy the feeling of irresponsibility towards the sense."[33] Eliot also refers to William Morris's poem "The Blue Closet," a delightful poem, as he says, though "I cannot explain what it means and I doubt whether the author could have explained it." Eliot thinks the poem "has an effect somewhat like that of a rune or charm." Its clear intention, he claims, is "to produce the effect of a dream."[34] We don't need to know what the dream means, though we probably think it means something. In fact, an interpreter could go a certain distance into Morris's poem, far enough to think that Lord Arthur, Lady Louise's lost lover, comes back one Christmas Eve and takes the four ladies, Lady Louise, Lady Alice, and the two damozels, with him to the "happy golden land." It is a dream of eternal love or of happiness glimpsed at last, as if through a blue veil or gauze. In the end the dream fails:

> And ever the great bell overhead,
> And the tumbling seas mourn'd for the dead;
> For their song ceased, and they were dead.[35]

The rhyming of the same word—"dead"—draws attention to the semantic difference between the rhyming words: the first is a plural noun of indefinite extent, the second an adjective qualifying the two ladies. The effect of the difference is to direct attention to the verb, which couldn't be more decisive, "they were dead." The dream is broken. But Eliot is right when he implies that we may be reading this enchanting poem badly if we try to turn it into an ascertainable story by interpreting it.

The best attempt to give a theory of such literature, so far as my reading goes, is Elizabeth Sewell's *Field of Nonsense*. She emphasizes that in the literature of Nonsense "all the world is paper and all the seas are ink." Nonsense is the form of words that renders language a "closed and consistent system on its own," like a game. Such forms can't be interpreted, because interpretation has a bias in favor of breaking the rules of the game and opening the work to the light of common day. Sewell argues that the Alice books and the poems of Lear and of Carroll have an interest in creating the conditions of order but can only "engage the force of disorder in continual play." That is why "Nonsense can admit of no emotion"; the system must remain closed, the mind of the reader must be isolated "from all possible contact with real life and real people."[36] Eliot's statement—"we enjoy the feeling of irresponsibility towards the sense"—is what we keep coming back to. In a particular poem or passage of a poem there may be local sense or a semblance of sense or an echo of some irrelevant sense, but we don't feel under any obligation to register it. The experience of reading the literature of Nonsense is that of dealing with words as if their acoustic value came first—as if we could engage with words as such—and the question of their having an external or public meaning were kept genially in parenthesis. Interpretation is unhappy with that license.

Those who think that interpretation is not, finally, what critics should be doing have another activity in view that they wish to recommend. Helen Vendler presents herself as an aesthetic critic and proposes to distinguish aesthetic criticism from interpretation. Adverting to W. J. T. Mitchell's statement that the present tendency in criticism—he was writing in 1986—is a "shift in emphasis from *meaning* to *value*," and that meaning-centered critics are interested in interpretation while value-centered critics are interested in the "problems of belief, interest, power, and ideology," Vendler said that meaning and value are, to her, marginal terms: "Paraphrase, interpretation (in the usual sense), and ideological polemic are legitimate preliminary activities putting the art work back into the general stream of statements uttered by a culture. All of these statements (from advertising to sermons) can be examined for their rhetorics of persuasion and their ideological self-contradiction or coherence, but such examinations bracket the question of aesthetic success. It is impossible, of course, to name a single set of defining characteristics that will discriminate an aesthetic object from one that does not exert aesthetic power, but that is no reason to deny the existence of aesthetic power and aesthetic response."[37] It is hard to quarrel with those claims, or with their continuation in this passage:

> The aim of a properly aesthetic criticism, then, is not primarily to reveal the *meaning* of an art work or disclose (or argue for or against) the ideological *values* of an art work. The aim of an aesthetic criticism is to *describe* the art work in such a way that it cannot be confused with any other art work (not an easy task), and to *infer* from its elements the aesthetic that might generate this unique configuration. (Ideological criticism is not interested in the uniqueness of the work of art, wishing always to conflate it with other works sharing its values.) Aesthetic criticism begins with the effort to understand the individual work (aided by whatever historical, philosophical, or psychological competence is necessary for that understanding); it is deeply inductive, and goes from the single work to the decade of work, from the decade of work to the lifetime of work, from the lifetime of work to the interrelation with the work of other artists.[38]

I am so far in agreement with this emphasis on aesthetic criticism that I wish it could be taken for granted as an indication of the work we do in criticism. It follows that interpretation is not the whole story but only the first part of it, a necessary labor of explication. Without such labor we could hardly think ourselves engaged with the poem at all. It is as important to make a beginning as to make an end. Of course Vendler's statements of intent do not indicate what form an aesthetic criticism should take in a given case or whether aesthetic criticism and formalism are one and the same, as I take them to be. That is why I applaud a sentence by Guy Davenport: "A work of art is a form that articulates forces, making them intelligible."[39] The title of the book in which that sentence appears is also to be commended: *Every Force Evolves a Form.*

SIX

Doing Things with Words

On December 10, 1982, the *Times Literary Supplement* published an essay by Paul de Man on the polemical scene of literary theory. "The Return to Philology" was partly a response to Walter Jackson Bate's attack on modern literary theory as subversive and nihilistic.[1] In his reply, de Man separated himself from those who allegedly "think of the teaching of literature as a substitute for the teaching of theology, ethics, psychology, or intellectual history." He approved of Theory so far as it entailed a return to philology, "to an examination of the structure of language prior to the meaning it produced."[2] Evidently he intended a strict analysis that would be concentrated on the properties of language in a particular work. The merit of philology, he claimed, was precisely that it upset the assumptions on which the teaching of literature as a humane discipline proceeded:

> As a result, the attribution of a reliable, or even exemplary, cognitive and, by extension, ethical function to literature indeed becomes much more difficult. But this is a recurrent philosophical quandary that has never been resolved. The latest version of the question, which still de-

termines our present-day convictions about the aims of literature, goes back to the rise of aesthetics as an independent discipline in the latter half of the eighteenth century. The link between literature (as art), epistemology, and ethics is the burden of aesthetic theory at least since Kant. It is because we teach literature as an aesthetic function that we can move so easily from literature to its apparent prolongations in the spheres of self-knowledge, of religion, and of politics.

Finally, de Man urged that "literature, instead of being taught only as a historical and humanistic subject, should be taught as a rhetoric and a poetics prior to being taught as a hermeneutics and a history." By "prior to" I think he meant "instead of."

It is questionable whether de Man's essay was a fair description of the scene of Theory in 1982, or even of his own pedagogy. His practical criticism often worked toward a rhetoric and a poetics. In *The Resistance to Theory* his essay on Michael Riffaterre includes a remarkably close analysis of Victor Hugo's "Ecrit sur la vitre d'une fenêtre flamande."[3] But de Man's account of the teaching of literature seems to me inaccurate. I wish I could find some evidence that literature is mainly taught as an aesthetic function or that teachers concentrate on linguistic analysis, rhetoric, and poetics. In my experience it has become extremely difficult to persuade students even to imagine what an aesthetic reading of a novel or a poem might be. For the most part, literature is taught not as rhetoric and poetics but as spilt politics. Teachers do not start with literature and move to considerations of self-knowledge, religion, ethics, and so forth. In common practice, the teaching of literature is a substitute for the teaching of politics: it is what David Bromwich has called the conduct of politics by other means.

I assume that a theory of art or literature is a systematic reflection on the principles embodied in a wide range of artistic or literary productions. We call such a theory Poetics, a consideration of the linguistic possibility that is realized in the form of a poem or a novel. The theory is ancillary to the works it addresses: if it declares itself independent of those works, it becomes something else, an essay in ideology. It is my understanding that Theory, in the philological sense described by de Man, is now rare. Perhaps the self-discipline it requires is too hard to maintain. In the years since de Man's essay was published, we have had more ideologies than theories. These have

asserted their independence first by making a problem of their own procedures and then by using works of literature chiefly as illustrations of social,
political, and economic forces at large. This activity is the heterogeneity that
we call Cultural Studies. More than a decade ago Fredric Jameson described
Theory as a "new discursive and conceptual space . . . distinct from traditional
criticism or philosophy."[4] This space is now occupied by various ideologies.
An ideology, in my sense of it, is a system of ideas, vocabularies, and practices
that has become second nature to its adherents and is deployed as an instrument of power. It is the structure of attitudes that is taken for granted in a
particular group. In the classroom, an ideologue tries to transform students as
social subjects and, by so doing, to further the interests of the social group that
the ideologue represents. Women's Studies, Feminism, Gender Studies, Gay
and Lesbian Studies, African American Studies, Marxist Criticism, Psychoanalytic Criticism, Deconstruction, New Historicism, Cultural Studies, Postcolonial Studies: the list is incomplete, if only because it omits the Bourgeois
Liberalism that many societies still take for granted. Each of these is taught as
an independent set of interests: the motto for such studies might be Caliban's,
"This island's mine."

So far as I can see, there is little communication among the several interests. Inevitably, disputes arise within a particular ideology, but they are comparable to the quarrels on policy and strategy in a political party. A quarrel
breaks out when an adept of, say, Feminism feels that a colleague has veered
from the path of righteousness or has otherwise undermined the principles of
the guild. There is some borrowing of method among the studies, but mostly
each develops a self-propelling vocabulary or code. Contradictions between
one interest and another are quietly ignored. Deconstruction, for instance,
contradicts Marxist criticism on the grounds that the concept of history, as
Jacques Derrida says, "has always been in complicity with a teleological and
eschatological metaphysics . . . with that philosophy of presence to which it
was believed history could be opposed."[5] In Marxist theory, the epistemological privilege of history is taken for granted. Deconstructive and other qualms
on that question are ignored. The New Historicism doesn't trouble itself about
the issues of language and reference that Deconstruction "puts in question." If
you follow Foucault or Gramsci, you exempt yourself from de Man's epistemological scruples. In each of these ideologies, teachers see themselves as
"organic intellectuals" (in Gramsci's phrase) articulating the desires of simple

folk who apparently can't speak for themselves. It may be difficult for professors to act on Gramsci's program, "to remain in contact with the 'simple people' and, moreover, find in this contact the source of its problems to be studied and solved."[6] But they do the best they can. In the classroom these ideologies satisfy an otherwise frustrated desire in teachers and students to intervene directly in political life on behalf of women, gays, blacks, minorities, and the wretched of the earth. Such studies appease one's will-to-power, even if the political object is achieved only notionally or not at all. It is doubtful that they have much provenance outside the seminar room.

I am not claiming that teachers who do not declare an ideological position are free of ideology. The desire for a common culture or for shared interests so self-evident that they may be deemed to be one's second nature is indeed ideological: it involves a partisan system of representations, enforced by repetition and, if necessary, the suppression of rival values. There is no truth in anyone's claim to be beyond ideology. Kant's appeal, in *The Critique of Judgment,* to the faculty of taste as a "sense common to all mankind" was unwise, and regrettably it has been used by those who want to sustain the notion that each of us is spiritually the same, at a level of being far deeper than that of our differences. It would be more reasonable to claim that equality, universality, and disinterestedness are sentiments to be imagined, not actual states of being or gifts of God to be enjoyed. Literature could then be presented as one of the means by which we are enabled to imagine being other than we are. There would be no good reason to denounce aesthetics as an instrument of "bourgeois hegemony" even if it could be shown that those who hold office have an interest in sedating their citizens, making people feel that they are already spiritually equal, fully human, regardless of the economic distinctions that press on them. Instead, we would study aesthetics as a set of principles operative in literature, and read works of literature as practices of experience to be imagined. These practices are related to other activities—religious, social, political, economic—but they are not to be confused with them. Meanwhile, Theory, in de Man's understanding of it, has dispersed into sundry ideologies and become the conduct of politics by ostensibly literary means.

The political definition of reality is not new. Many years ago Thomas Mann wrote that "in our time the destiny of man presents its meanings in political terms." W. B. Yeats countered Mann's claim by writing a poem, "Politics," in which he says, in effect, that it would be just as cogent to replace "political" in

AMERICAN RIVER COLLEGE

Mann's sentence with "sexual" or "erotic." Every strong word embodies an ambition to take over the world. But the political vocabulary has been dominant in higher education for many years. The first result is that all values deemed to reside in individuals rather than in groups, classes, or societies are discredited. These values are clearly enough indicated by such words as self, person, subject, identity, consciousness, intention, imagination, author, voice, and genius. For more occult reasons the same discredit is supposed to fall on metaphor, symbol, myth, and analogy. If there is a single motive common to the ideologies, it is to deride any presumption of subject or self.

As a case in point: in an essay on Wyndham Lewis, Jameson compares a passage from *The Childermass* with one from Joyce's *Ulysses*. The comparison is not turned toward considerations of style, force, or inventiveness. For ideological reasons it is worked in Lewis's favor. Jameson finds it disgraceful that Leopold Bloom's reveries are characterized by the "stylistic *tone* in which all contradictions are ironically resolved as well as by the overall unity of Mr. Bloom's personality" (emphasis in original). He praises Lewis for achieving "not the unification but rather the dispersal of subjectivity."[7] Presumably unity of tone is a mark of petit-bourgeois illusions. In the same invidious mode, Jameson insists on taking the word "aesthetic" to mean "impressionist." He speaks of Conrad's "impressionism" as the "vocation to arrest the living raw material of life, and by wrenching it from the historical situation in which alone its change is meaningful, to preserve it, beyond time, in the imaginary."[8] The aim of the "impressionistic strategy of modernism" is to "derealize the content and make it available for consumption on some purely aesthetic level."[9] The force of "purely" and "consumption" in that sentence, and the tactical appeal to the "historical situation" and the "living raw material of life" in the preceding one—crowding four prejudicial words into a phrase—call for rhetorical analysis. The sentences sound aggressive to me, and the target is the subject.

Criticism is still a practice of doing things with words on the page. We continue to read. We interpret. For many years we thought we understood what interpretation was and worried only about its difficulty in a particular case. Now we're not so sure. The conflict of ideologies has made us question what interpretation means and doubt that we should be doing it. I have tried to clarify the matter in the preceding chapter, but a further note may be useful.

In April 1933, I. A. Richards published in the *Criterion* an essay called

"Fifteen Lines from Landor." The fifteen lines were the opening passage of book 3 of *Gebir*, a poem in seven books published in 1798. When Richards gave the lines to his students at Cambridge, Harvard, and Radcliffe, he excised the first three lines "to heighten the difficulty." He didn't tell the students anything about the poem, the author, the speaker, or the context. Richards's essay, an extension of his *Practical Criticism* (1929), considered the various interpretations of the lines as his students offered them. Mostly, the students tried to paraphrase the lines or otherwise expound them. The question Richards asked was: What do the lines mean? Or: What is the passage, as a system of meanings? These may not have been the best questions. It would have been difficult for the students to ask Richards what he meant by "meaning." At the end, he attempted his own paraphrase. Not to everyone's satisfaction, by the way. In the July 1933 *Criterion*, Charles Mauron disagreed with him and gave his own version of Landor's lines. But Mauron did not question Richards's understanding of interpretation. They agreed, evidently, to take "the reader" for granted. They didn't ask how such an abstract entity could be invoked. Concentrating on the words on the page, they assumed that printed words stand for spoken words. Spoken words stand for mental acts. The speaker is an implied person. Mental acts are forms of the speaker's imagination, tokens of a mind exercising its freedom, subject to the jurisdiction of the language spoken. It was sufficient, for the purposes of the reading, to start with an assumed capacity of the speaker's mind and to work from there. Richards did not distinguish between Landor, biographically ascertained, and the unnamed narrator who supposedly speaks the lines in *Gebir*. He assumed that interpretation is the cognitive act by which someone receives the meaning of a speech, preferably intact. The value of this giving and receiving is the personal and civil good of communication. How do we know when an interpretation is correct? Richards says: "When an interpretation hangs together (without conflicting with anything else: history, literary tradition, etc.) we call it correct—when it takes into account all the items given for interpretation and orders the other items, by which it interprets them, in the most acceptable manner."[10] Acceptable to whom? We may let that pass. A good paraphrase shows that the message has been received. When the New Critics warned against the heresy of paraphrase, they meant merely: go ahead and paraphrase, so that we'll know we're talking about the same poem, but don't mistake your paraphrase for the poem.

I refer to Richards's concept of interpretation without implying that he invented it. For many years his concept was generally accepted and practiced. The main difference between Richards's early books and, say, Empson's *Seven Types of Ambiguity* is that Empson was preoccupied with the conflicting elements in mental acts, and he labored over bits of speech to disclose those conflicts. He valued literature as the site of various tensions or ambiguities in peoples' minds, and of occasional resolutions. Richards's idea of interpretation as the reception of a more-or-less complex message wasn't put under much pressure till Susan Sontag published *Against Interpretation* in 1964. In that essay Sontag argued that we should attend to the presence and force of a work of art rather than to a putative meaning that might be abstracted from it. The argument was more persuasive when the work of art was a painting, a sculpture, or a film rather than a poem or a novel, but many readers found it salutary. Communication did not necessarily entail a message sent and received; certainly not a discursive message. The main force of Sontag's essay was to question whether the axiom of giving and receiving, in the experience of art, entailed further discourse and commentary as proof that the experience had been accomplished.

The common understanding of interpretation was challenged again in October 1966 when Derrida said, in a lecture at Johns Hopkins University:

> There are two interpretations of interpretation, of structure, of sign, of play. The one seeks to decipher, dreams of deciphering a truth or an origin which escapes play and the order of the sign, and which lives the necessity of interpretation as an exile. The other, which is no longer turned toward the origin, affirms play and tries to pass beyond man and humanism, the name of man being the name of that being who, throughout the history of metaphysics or of ontotheology—in other words throughout his entire history— has dreamed of full presence, the reassuring foundation, the origin and the end of play. The second interpretation of interpretation, to which Nietzsche pointed the way, does not seek in ethnography, as Lévi-Strauss does, the "inspiration of a new humanism."[11]

Nietzsche pointed the way in *Beyond Good and Evil* and in his notes on will-to-power. Derrida maintained, replying to a question from Serge Doubrovsky, that he wasn't proposing to get rid of a subject or a center, but that the center is a "function, not a being, . . . I don't destroy the subject, I situate it."[12] Situate it,

I think he meant, in free linguistic play. Derrida's recent work shows that he has no interest in the first interpretation of interpretation and that he practices the second as will-to-power exercised on a text. The object of the exercise is the production of new writing, no longer in any sense auxiliary to the text that provoked it. Roland Barthes takes a similar stance in *S/Z* when he says that "to interpret a text is not to give it a (more or less justified, more or less free) meaning, but on the contrary to appreciate what *plural* constitutes it."[13] Readers are free to engage with that plural as they wish. Barthes's reading, in his later books, is under the sign of pleasure: the plural consists of the promiscuous relations offered by the book one is reading. We have come a long way from Richards's students who tried to figure out what the speaker of the words meant. Or from Reuben Brower's students at Harvard, according to de Man's account of *Humanities 6:* "Students, as they began to write on the writings of others, were not to say anything that was not derived from the text they were considering. They were not to make any statements that they could not support by a specific use of language that actually occurred in the text. They were asked, in other words, to begin by reading texts closely as texts and not to move at once into the general context of human experience or history."[14] I doubt that such ascetic discipline is widely practiced. It is more probable that teachers move quickly to discuss the specious contiguities—political, ethical, moral—that the philologist de Man wanted to keep apart.

If I am right in thinking that the motive common to many ideologies in the classroom is the mortification of the subject, this may explain why so many current interpretations are essays in rebuke. Many critics consider themselves superior to the work of literature, especially when the work expresses a personal or subjective experience. They know so much more than the poem and they forget that the poem is what they know. If there is a palpable subject, it must be scolded, made to feel ashamed of itself. Marjorie Levinson has argued that "the literatures of the past, if left to themselves, confront us as despotic structures." We should disable those literatures by reading them "tendentiously—for ourselves."[15] Reading Wordsworth's sonnet "The World Is Too Much With Us," Levinson claims that it took 150 years to hear the poem "with a certain ring." But she doesn't consider the possibility that her own reading may ring false—especially when it claims the authority of "we" and "ourselves"—or that it conveys mainly the whine of resentment.

So where are we? It seems to me that a feasible plan of criticism might start with this passage from Bakhtin's "Discourse in the Novel": "The study of verbal art can and must overcome the divorce between an abstract 'formal' approach and an equally abstract 'ideological' approach. Form and content in discourse are one, once we understand that verbal discourse is a social phenomenon—social throughout its entire range and in all its factors, from the sound image to the furthest reaches of abstract meaning."[16] But I don't see why a formal approach must be abstract. It isn't abstract when it construes form as—in Marcuse's phrase—achieved content. But Bakhtin's social emphasis is justified, provided he doesn't mean the reduction of the individuality of the work of art to an ideological lesson. Further justification may be found in books by Emmanuel Levinas, Michel de Certeau, and Gilles Deleuze and Félix Guattari.

I don't see any problem in acknowledging the priority of discourse as a social phenomenon. But there is no merit in giving the idea of society a sentimental aura, as if a *sensus communis* happily and gratuitously followed from the fact that certain people share a country and speak more or less the same language. We are social animals, but in practice that doesn't commit us to solidarity. Merely to talk about society rather than about particular people isn't enough: people live in groups, classes, villages, and ghettos rather than in humankind. But the social emphasis in any determination should also take into account the habit of mind that Levinas describes: "One begins with the idea that duality must be transformed into unity, and that social relations must culminate in communion. This is the last vestige of a conception that identifies being with knowledge, that is, with the event through which the multiplicity of reality ends up referring to a single being and where, through the miracle of clarity, everything that encounters me exists as coming from me. It is the last vestige of idealism."[17] With this major qualification, the social emphasis is just. Nothing is to be gained by positing a categorical discrepancy between individuals and society. Or by exaggerating the creative or inaugural character of the subject; even though it would be wicked to deride one's possession of an inner life and the soliloquies in which it may be expressed. It is also self-evident that social discourse remains silent until someone chooses to speak or write. At that moment the subject, formed of conscious and unconscious forces, acts upon the language, simultaneously brings itself and the language to the pitch of performance. We need a theory of such performance. Speech Act theory is good enough, provided it does not give an exaggerated account of the autonomy of the speaker. De Man, J. Hillis Miller, and other rhetoricians have expounded prosopopoeia as a nuance of Speech Act theory: it is the figure that gives a face to the faceless or conjures into a semblance of existence that which otherwise is merely notional. It is the figure of address, notably in Hardy's poems of love and loss. As the act of summoning or conjuring, it can also be deployed as the figure of reading. We come back to de Man's program of rhetoric and poetics, though what that requires has still to be worked out.

What difference would this program make to one's reading of the lines that Richards chose from *Gebir?*

> When on the pausing theatre of earth
> Eve's shadowy curtain falls, can any man
> Bring back the far off intercepted hills,
> Grasp the round rock-built turret, or arrest
> The glittering spires that pierce the brow of Heav'n?
> Rather can any with outstripping voice
> The parting Sun's gigantic strides recall?

The speaker mainly feels, in the few lines before these, that although he is inspired by Shakespeare, he lacks the orphic power of former poets. Perhaps every modern poet suffers the same lack, the speaker says. Richards's commentary is brief—he doesn't do any close work, doesn't say anything about "the pausing theatre" or "intercepted" or "outstripping voice," details that a full commentary would deal with. I wonder whether my reading of Landor's lines would improve if I kept reminding myself that the implied speaker comes into notional existence with the performance of the words and disappears thereafter; that no one lives autonomously, and that—as Deleuze and Guattari maintain in *Kafka: Toward a Minor Literature*—"the most individual enunciation is a particular case of collective enunciation." Interpretation of the passage from Landor may proceed as appreciation of the plural that constitutes it. Maybe it would improve my reading in these respects: I would attend to the negotiations of the language without hoping to see them coming to rest in an empirical speaker deemed to have existed before the poem. I would think of the speech as issuing from a grammatical or rhetorical rather than an existential source. In *The Pleasure of the Text*, Barthes, quoting Nietzsche on interpretation as will-to-power, says: "Then perhaps the subject returns, not as illusion, but as *fiction*. A certain pleasure is derived from a way of imagining oneself as *individual*, of inventing a final, rarest fiction: the fictive identity. This fiction is no longer the illusion of a unity; on the contrary, it is the theatre of society in which we stage our plural: our pleasure is *individual*—but not personal."[18] I wouldn't mind inventing myself in this way, creating a fiction and calling it for the moment me. It may be that we lose very little by thinking of a self in literature as a grammatical subject, textual rather than ontological; though it would seem odd to refer to Leopold Bloom or Falstaff or Isabel Archer as grammatical subjects. It would impede conversation if that were the only way we were permitted to speak of them. Besides, as a reader of Levinas, I would feel squeamish about thinking of other people—even imagined people—as fictive or notional: it's a habit I wouldn't like to take up.

SEVEN

Orality, Literacy, and Their Discontents

Let us suppose that we are reading the *Collected Poems* of
W. B. Yeats and we come to "A Deep-Sworn Vow":

Others because you did not keep
That deep-sworn vow have been friends of mine;
Yet always when I look death in the face,
When I clamber to the heights of sleep,
Or when I grow excited with wine,
Suddenly I meet your face.[1]

If I were to describe the poem, I would say something like
this. It is an encomium, a poem of tribute. Technically, it has
six lines, each line varying in the number of syllables from
seven to ten. The lines have masculine end-rhymes in the
pattern abc/abc, the "c" rhyme being the sole repeated word
face. The first "face" is metaphorical—the face of death—the
second is literal. There are internal rhymes of which the
most forceful is the one that connects the strong accusation
of "keep"—"you did not keep / That deep-sworn vow"—
with "deep" and "sleep" and the near-rhyme of "meet." It is
an unusual feature of the poem that the first word of the
first and the last line—"Others" and "Suddenly"—diverge

from the generally iambic meter: they are, respectively, a trochee and a dactyl. In syntax, the poem consists of two unequal sentences, the first occupying two lines, the second the remaining four: the sentences are strongly linked by the conjunction "yet." The implied speaker may be man or woman and is of a certain age, since the experiences alluded to are those of mature or declining life. I would also note a surprising feature of the poem, that although in the end it becomes intensely personal, it starts out with a distancing word—"Others"—and goes on immediately to a remarkably truculent piece of syntax, the intrusion of the phrase "because you did not keep / That deep-sworn vow" before the subject reaches its verb. "Because" commits the speaker at once to a tone of recrimination that has to be transcended before the poem can become what it generically is, an encomium. The tone of resentment is extended in the demonstrative "that"—"That deep-sworn vow"—a phrase of such severity that the ending of the line with the casual "have been friends of mine" is astonishing. It is not "were friends of mine" but "have been," as if the speaker's casualness had entered a dismissive syntax. The poem goes from the syntactical clottedness of "Others because" to the comparative intimacy of "you" and "mine" before reaching the speaker "I"—"Yet always when I look death in the face...." The second part of the poem reverses this direction, goes from the "I"—spoken four times, as if compulsively—to the you of "your face," and says nothing more of "others." It is as if the face had taken possession of the whole scene of life, now that the speaker is alluding only to experiences extreme or fundamental—death, sleep, the excitement of wine—in that unusual order.

But the four uses of "I" are not the same. The first one—"when I look death in the face"—is metaphysical or melodramatic, as if the speaker were a match for the allegorical force or image of death. The second "I" is psychological. The clambering to the heights of sleep is odd: we usually think of sleep as deep rather than high, something to sink into rather than climb to. And the next "I" is biological, the excitement being erotic and again strange in a context usually found to be narcotic or depressant. With a certain bravado the speaker has looked death in the face, but there is no bravado in the last line when looking turns to meeting: "Suddenly I meet your face." Not "Suddenly I see your face." The other people are relegated to gone times. The unity of the poem, if we choose to interest ourselves in that, is of the temporal kind, a phase of the speaker's implied life: it is enforced by the connectives "because," "yet," "when," and "suddenly."

So much about the poem, but it is not clear enough. My reference to the implied speaker is a weasel phrase. I don't mean W. B. Yeats, biographically ascertained, although biographers have quoted the poem as if it documented his life. Literary critics are instructed to think of the speaker of a poem as a hypothetical person; in this case someone speaking from a situation only barely and discreetly denoted. There are no details, no names, no references to Maud Gonne or another. We may speculate about the vow, who gave it to whom, why it was so deep-sworn, why it was not kept. But we know that these speculations are vain, they won't enhance our sense of the poem. All we have in the end is a voice, carried by the diction, the syntax, the rhythm, the trajectory of the sentences; and sustaining in its turn a declared burden of experience. A situation is implied from which the voice issues and to which it returns. It is not much to have, but it is enough.

I have referred to voice, but it is not self-evident that I am justified in doing so. What we indisputably have are black marks on a white page, marks that by convention we take as signs of words. It could be argued that voice is an abstraction from the poem, and perhaps a mystification. But I'm not sure that I can either avoid using the word in this way or justify the use by appeal to its worthwhile consequences. I construe the voice as a sign of personal presence, hypothetical no doubt, the presence of a textual self, not necessarily ontological, but sufficiently stable to last for the brief spell of the poem. I put the matter in these terms to avoid claiming for the voice existence as if outside the poem, or before and after the reading of it. There are voices in literature that give the impression of coming from characters who have existed before a word was spoken: Stephen Dedalus, Isabel Archer, Elizabeth Bennet. But Yeats's poem doesn't make such a claim. The speaker is anonymous, and present merely for the occasion. However, it is still true that the poem marks an act of will, or the semblance of such an act, not the speaker's will-to-power or will-to-knowledge but the will-to-acknowledge a presence more compelling than its own, the presence, the face of the other person. If the poem has a center of gravity and attraction, it is the aura of that person, the force-of-presence acknowledged by the speaker's voice. The conventions of reading allow us to imagine that someone said these words, and that they are delivered to us after the fact by the printing press. We may read them in such a manner as to restore the words to a voice and to turn these transactions into an experience worth having.

It hardly matters whether my description of the poem is adequate; because the question I want to ask is nearly independent of that consideration. Why, in reading the poem, am I so concerned to divine the voice of the implied speaker, as if this were the first consideration, even to the extent of regarding the content of the poem as of moment chiefly in distinguishing that voice from another one I might imagine? It seems to follow that I am less interested in the objective meaning of the words or the sentences than in the subjective meaning, the intention, of the speaker. Even if I were to describe the poem more elaborately, I would still be preoccupied with the speaker and the tone of voice that implies recognition of the conditions of the speech, the occasion, the audience, the sense of decorum which the recognition observes. Am I listening for the particular voice because I am yearning for the authority of an origin, paternal no doubt? Or for an acoustic presence corresponding to the grammatical subject "I"? Do I want to find the speaker's voice an instance of authority, the self-fashioning force with which every constituent of the case is brought together, perhaps brought to heel? Or—to make the charge a little easier—am I listening for a particular voice in the poem as if I were searching for an immigrant, vulnerable in the opaque world of print? The philosopher J. L. Austin has remarked that "written utterances are not tethered to their origin in the way spoken ones are."[2] Am I wishing that they were, and determined to find the origin even without the tether?

In everything I have said about Yeats's poem, I have treated the words on the page as if they were a transcript of someone's speech, real or imagined. Except for my reference to lines and sentences, I have attended mainly to acoustic or phonetic properties: syllables and rhymes. This practice on my part is nostalgic, no doubt; it marks my desire to retain the orality of expression even through the mediation of print. But such nostalgia is not merely personal to me, it is part of the history of writing and reading. For many centuries after the invention of script—about 3500 B.C. in Egypt and Mesopotamia, about 700 B.C. in Greece—manuscripts were mainly prepared as transcripts of sounds, like scores for modern music, or as imitative allusions to physical objects. The fact that many such manuscripts were also elaborately decorated works of art does not refute their first use. But that use was a contentious matter. Near the end of Plato's *Phaedrus* Socrates raises the question of writing as distinct from speaking, and he quotes the Egyptian god Thamus as saying that the invention of script damages the power of memory in those who write. Socrates goes on to attack script on the grounds that, like a painting, it has nothing to say for itself, it can't take part in a dialogue: a crucial disability. Writing may be useful to remind oneself of something, he concedes, but it shouldn't be taken seriously otherwise: the only true writing is what is written in one's soul.

But the *Phaedrus* had little or no impact. Brian Stock has noted that "most of Plato's writings disappeared at the end of antiquity; they were not known again in the West until the Renaissance."[3] During those centuries, script established itself as a worthy sign of speech and was used accordingly. Therefore the reading of a manuscript was for long a slow and noisy affair as the reader tried to convert written words into sounds. The skill of silent reading was a late achievement. I speculate that one of the reasons why, in reading Yeats's poem, I try to divine the speaker's voice is that for many centuries reading entailed the conversion of script to audible sounds; the reader's voice tried to be in unison with the original voice designated, however inadequately, by marks on clay, bone, parchment, vellum, or cloth.

Historians of orality are in apparent agreement that orality is the sign of lives social and convivial rather than individual. In an oral society people are members of a "collective assemblage"—to use a phrase explicated by Deleuze and Guattari in *A Thousand Plateaus*—before they are isolated individuals (if they are ever such). The dialect of the tribe is not only the context in which people engage in social life: it provides the means by which an individual may speak. It follows that reality in an oral society is construed as mainly temporal: hence its appropriate paradigm is the in-and-out of one's breathing. Temporal, dependent on memory: reality is interpreted as historical, it assumes a narrative form of understanding, as in the epic. Memory is the enabling capacity, repetition is its convention, formulaic narration a practice of its genre. The speech of the place is not soliloquy but conversation.

It follows, too, that politics has been directly associated with conversation and oratory. Hannah Arendt, thinking of the involvement of scientists in the development and use of the atomic bomb, said that the "reason why it may be wise to distrust the political judgment of scientists *qua* scientists is not primarily their lack of 'character'—that they did not refuse to develop atomic weapons—or their naivete—that they did not understand that once these weapons were developed they would be the last to be consulted about their use—but precisely the fact that they move in a world where speech has lost its power."[4]

These conditions of orality were radically, though only gradually, changed by literacy and especially by the development of alphabetic movable type in Europe in the middle of the fifteenth century. Writing and reading are for the most part solitary activities conducted in a world of mainly spatial relations. Historians of orality and literacy—I'm thinking mainly of Albert Lord, Milman Parry, Marshall McLuhan, Eric Havelock, Elizabeth Eisenstein, Walter J. Ong, Jack Goody, Michel de Certeau, and of other scholars who are building on their work—generally agree that after the achievement of silent reading, the act of seeing words on a page entered into the constitution of knowledge. The separation of the eye from what it saw became a constitutive element, not merely an instrument, of knowledge: it sustained the conviction that knowledge entails what Havelock calls the "recognition of the known as object."[5] Orality suffered a severe blow when people started believing that our primary relation to the world is one of knowing, and that knowledge should be substituted for other ways of being active in the world.[6] It follows from that change of mind that reality was assumed to be fully described by knowledge, the distinction between subject and object was used as the chief device of knowing, and knowledge was supposed to be fully achieved by science. We reach the stage, which Brian Stock has described in relation to the early Middle Ages, in which objectivity was identified with a text.[7] Those beliefs were consequences of writing. Further consequences included the move from custom and tradition to law, from an oral promise to a written contract, and the designation of a noble family by genealogy rather than by the scale of its local affiliations. Reality was now deemed to be separate from the mind that engaged it: its qualities were supposedly those of script—relative stability, objectivity, an enduring existence out there, waiting to be observed and interpreted. Observation was the official form of attention. Method became the habit of observation amounting to a conviction. God was believed to have given mankind two books—the Bible and the book of Nature—gifts that could be appreciated only by people who lived in a world of readable script and plane geometry. If a conviction of chaos and opacity were to befall such people, it would have to be internalized and construed as a disability in the subject, the mind. Otherwise it would count as a textual or geometrical flaw, appalling in its consequence. After the Copernican revolution in astronomy, many people indeed felt that a flaw had been discovered in the divine text, the assumed perfection of the circle was broken and, as Donne wrote in such a mood, " 'Tis all in pieces, all coherence gone."

But orality and literacy are never mutually exclusive. It is possible to make the opposition between them appear more severe than it is. Stock has noted that many societies have practiced orality and literacy together. Orality is never merely displaced by writing; if in a particular society it is, it is changed by the pathos of that displacement. De Certeau has pointed out that "orality becomes something else from the moment when writing is no longer a symbol but rather . . . the instrument of a 'production of history' in the hands of a particular social category." He mentions the confidence that intellectuals of the Enlightenment and the French Revolution felt about the power of the printed word: "writing was to refashion society in the same way that it had indicated the power that the enlightened bourgeois was ascribing to itself." To the degree that writing becomes the communication of works through which a society constructs its progress, orality is changed, displaced, as if excluded from the official record. "It is isolated," according to de Certeau, "lost, and found again in a 'voice' which is that of nature, of the woman, of childhood, of the people." It becomes pronunciation, apart from the technical logic of print and its ideology. It becomes music, song, opera, a "space where the organizing power of reason is effaced" and the singing voice stretches or leaps toward a sublime beyond reason. What orality speaks of is whatever reason designates as superstition, passion, stirrings of an indeterminate self, the sublime: "it is voice separated from contents."[8]

But the transition from one technology of expression to another is never abrupt. De Certeau has noted that "epistemological configurations are never replaced by the appearance of new orders; they compose strata that form the bedrock of a present."[9] The relation between an old medium and a new one is archaeological rather than historical or linear. This describes the possibility, which may not be available to everyone, of choosing to live a life mostly archaic or nostalgic, by not capitulating to the zeitgeist. Even if people think in linear terms, there is always an overlap between one technology and its apparent successor. Havelock has pointed out that Greece remained an oral culture for centuries after the invention of script. There were continuities as well as changes between scribal and print cultures. Walter Ong has argued, notably in his *Orality and Literacy* and *Interfaces of the Word,* that a new medium of verbal expression not only does not wipe out the old one but, for a time, appears to reinforce it. However, in doing so, the new medium transforms the old, so that it is no longer what it was: and in the end the values of the new medium enforce themselves.

This sequence is confirmed by thinking of the impingement of print technology on English literature. Elizabethan styles in prose and verse were far more elaborate, more copious, more oral than the common speech of the places from which they arose. The oral character of Shakespeare's sonnets, Thomas Nashe's *The Unfortunate Traveller,* and John Lyly's *Euphues* is emphasized rather than suppressed by print: every word seems to be italicized. The printing of Donne's sermons, or of Lancelot Andrewes's, did not curb their oral and oratorical flights. It was only later in the seventeenth century that the particular values of print imposed themselves and established a new decorum. This entailed a revised *sermo humilis,* a plain style supposedly correlated to the quiet act of observation and the morality of speaking truths deemed most convincing when they were plainly delivered. Stability was enforced by grammars and dictionaries. Meaning was declared to issue, as in the rhetoric of the Royal Society, from the correspondence of word to thing rather than from an intentional relation between words and their speaker. Indeed, the ease with which words in a culture of print could be separated from their speaker and from a natural world accounts for the development of new forms of writing and new styles, especially in the seventeenth and eighteenth centuries.

These arose from the first consequence of writing, that words can reach people to whom they are not directly addressed. In conversation, what I say to you and you to me and what we make of the exchanged words are nearly simultaneous, active in the shared context. But if I write the same words, they may be read by people I have never met. What I say and the decorum of my speech are governed by the local situation as I construe it. But what I write must observe a different decorum, since I can't know who may read my words. My sense of readership is not the same as my sense of a particular audience. These equivocal conditions, especially in the seventeenth and eighteenth centuries, made possible the proliferation of anonymous pamphlets and pseudonymous squibs, a vital facility in years of religious and political vehemence. Anonymous publication was crucial to Jesuits in the sixteenth century, to the purveyors of the Marprelate Tracts, and to those high-toned writers who wanted to avoid the stigma of being professional authors, scribblers, ink-stained and low class. The separation of print from an identifiable voice was a necessary device, too, for writers who had to disguise themselves at a time of Licensing Acts and the paper wars between political disputants, some of them Whig and Tory. The printing press also made it possible, for writers so disposed, to thwart the common desire to hear particular voices even through the mediation of print. Think of Jonathan Swift's breakages in the text of *A Tale of a Tub*, Laurence Sterne's blank page and the squiggle of print in *Tristram Shandy*, or—moving forward a century—think of Mallarmé's refusal of acoustic eloquence in *Un Coup de Dés*. In our own time Concrete Poetry deploys words as objects from which every trace of a singular authoritative voice has been removed. Print also makes possible omniscient narration, the indirect free style, various forms of impersonation, and styles of willed neutrality, as if the story were being told, but told by no one. It may also incite writers to devise rhetorical stratagems precisely to recover the flourishes of speech and gesture that a culture of print supposedly suppresses. Thomas Sheridan's *Lectures on Elocution* (1762) and *Lectures on the Art of Reading* (1775) were evidently designed for that purpose. Yeats's "A Deep-Sworn Vow" was composed to be printed and published, but it labors to intuit a voice, an entity that the technology of print is especially skilled in suppressing.

One of the most remarkable instances of the subterfuge enabled by the printing press is the first two pages of the "Sirens" chapter in Joyce's *Ulysses* (Chapter 11). Every chapter of *Ulysses* is predicated not only on the story of Leopold Bloom, Stephen Dedalus, Molly Bloom, and the other characters but on a particular art or practice. In this chapter the art is music, notably the fugue, but the pages may also be read as the overture to the opera that follows. The first edition of *Ulysses* made that clear by having a blank page between those first pages and the rest of the chapter, a gesture that John Kidd's edition will reproduce. Not surprisingly, the chapter has many references to nineteenth-century operas and ballads. The first sixty-three lines contain sixty fragments or motifs, each opaque in itself but giving promise of development later in the chapter. I'll comment on a few of these, but only to show that their mode of existence depends on the values of print and would be impossible in speech.

The first line is a regular sentence, but it is not otherwise informative:

"Bronze by gold heard the hoofirons, steelyringing." We have to hold the sentence in suspension and postpone our interpretation of it till the references are clarified, much later, in lines 64 and 65: "Bronze by gold, miss Douce's head by miss Kennedy's head, over the crossblind of the Ormond bar heard the viceregal hoofs go by, ringing steel." Bronze and gold were the principal metals in Homer's world, but here they denote Bronze Lydia Douce and Gold Mina Kennedy, barmaids in the Ormond Hotel. It is four in the afternoon of June 16, 1904, the time agreed between Molly Bloom and Blazes Boylan for a sexual conjunction at 7 Eccles Street. To proceed: the second line can be seen but not heard or spoken—"Imperthnthn thnthnthn." Light breaks upon those letters only in lines 99–100, where we find Miss Douce threatening to report the boots to Mrs. de Massey if she hears any more of his "impertinent inso-lence," and the boots goes off mimicking her threat. What we see on the page is impossible to speak with any accuracy: "Imperthnthn thnthnthn, bootssnout sniffed rudely, as he retreated as she threatened as he had come." Impertinent insolence, entirely plausible as speech, becomes on the page a shadow of itself, five letters followed by six unspeakable typings of the same three letters, thn. Reading further: line 22 has "Lost. Throstle fluted. All is lost now." The refer-ence is fulfilled six hundred lines later when Richie Goulding whistles the tenor aria "Tutto è sciolto"—"All is lost"—from Bellini's *La Sonnambula*: "Most beautiful tenor air ever written, Richie said: *Sonnambula*." For Bloom, as for Bellini's Elvino, it seems, all is indeed lost.

Ulysses, on the whole, is enamored of voice, speech and song. In many chapters the contents of print, newspapers, broadsheets, advertisements, and cheap fiction end up as gossip and lore. But there are many passages in the book that, like the boots's mimicry of Miss Douce, can be read but not spo-ken. I wonder whether the mixture of voice and print doesn't account for recent attacks on the book. Leo Bersani and some other critics have claimed that it is not as avant-garde as its first readers thought it. In *The Culture of Redemption* Bersani argues that it is at bottom a realistic novel much like any other, devoted to character and personality; devoted, I would say, to the continuities of voice. Voice is the form of character and personality. But *Ulysses* entertains two ideologies of utterance. It is basically a book of voices. But it also contains passages of pure print that can't be restored to voice. What is disturbing in the opening pages of the "Sirens" chapter is the impression, conveyed by the printing press, that much can appear to be going on without a human presence to propel it. Beckett's later fiction is disturbing for the same reason: voices are set adrift on the page, but no impression of a self, body and soul in unity, attends their unstoppable eloquence. Deliverances of print seem to parody human action by showing that for certain events on the page a responsible human presence is not necessary. This explains why Joyce at once endorses the axioms of voice and character and yet in many passages, as Derek Attridge has said, "challenges momentarily our untroubled belief in the human subject as unitary, unconstrained, and capable of originating action from a single center of consciousness."[10] One of Attridge's examples is a sentence from the "Sirens" chapter we have been reading:

> —In the second carriage, miss Douce's wet lips said, laughing in the sun.
> He's looking. Mind till I see.

This is one of many occasions in *Ulysses* on which organs of the body are set free to act independently of the person in any unitary sense. In the first chapter Stephen Dedalus expresses his bitterness about Mulligan by reducing him to one of his attributes: "Across the threadbare cuffedge he saw the sea hailed as a great sweet mother by the wellfed voice beside him" (I.106). In that sentence Joyce appears to be conceding, according to the rhetoric of print, that unity of being can be dispersed just as easily as a dissociated life may be ascribed to Miss Douce's lips. The unity of being that we fondly think of as predicated on unity of body and as constituting a self may be dismembered. But I'm not sure that this amounts to a discrepancy on Joyce's part between the values of voice and of script. It may be that the structure of his feeling includes nostalgia and a refusal on principle to indulge it: nostalgia, I mean, for a world of voice and of the particular striving of print to recover it.

There is another possibility, that Joyce is at once acknowledging Yeats's oral values and showing how easily the printing press can thwart them. Shortly after the opening of the Abbey Theatre, Yeats wrote an essay called "Literature and the Living Voice" in which he made an invidious contrast between Irish and English culture: "Irish poetry and Irish stories were made to be spoken or sung, while English literature, alone of great literatures, because the newest of them all, has all but completely shaped itself in the printing-press. In Ireland to-day the old world that sang and listened is, it may be for the last time in Europe, face to face with the world that reads and writes, and their antagonism is always present under some name or other in Irish imagination and intellect. . . . When literature belonged to a whole people, its three great forms, narrative, lyrical, and dramatic, found their way to men's minds without the mediation of print and paper."[11] Yeats chose the theater—and founded the Abbey Theatre—as symbol of the Ireland he hoped to summon into existence. The consanguinity of theater, oratory, and conversation made the Abbey, at least for a few years, the emblem of a culture he saw as oral and acoustic. He also thought that in an age of print the orality of "the People" might still be found, far from systems of power. It might be recovered by Lady Gregory in rural Galway, by Synge in the Aran Islands, and by Yeats himself in Sligo. Joyce had no interest in that program. In "The Day of the Rabblement" and "The Holy Office" he ridiculed the Abbey and the Irish literary revival it represented. Even though he wrote a play, *Exiles,* he was on principle a man of the book; but it was a book in which he listened to the voices of his recalled and imagined Dublin and used the printing press to declare, on occasion, his independence of a city he never forgot. He gave it the blessing of ear and a nearly blind eye.

But there is a question: was Yeats right in saying that there must always be antagonism between an oral culture and a culture of script and print? We know that in his poems and plays he liked to come upon conflict and to maintain it, if only for the energy produced by the conflicting forces. Like Bakhtin in his work on dialogism, Yeats longed to set voices astir, expressing different values, even in the world of print; though in the end, it may be that one voice emerges more authoritatively than any other. He was not by inclination a peacemaker. But there are other writers who prefer to reach agreeable conclusions. Paul Ricoeur is one of them. He proposes, in effect, that we read the text twice; once for print, one for the voice. He would let the ideology of writing have its day first and then give the reader the freedom of another destiny by recourse to voice: "We can, as readers, remain in the suspense of the text, treating it as a worldless and authorless object; in this case, we explain the text in terms of its internal relations, its structure. On the other hand, we can lift the suspense and fulfil the text in speech, restoring it to living communication; in this case, we interpret the text. These two possibilities both belong to reading, and reading is the dialectic of these two attitudes."[12] Ricoeur seems to say: let Structuralism do its best with the text, and then let Hermeneutics take the harm out of the structuralist abstractions and restore the text to voice and time. I don't see any problem in this.

But there is no need to be especially tender toward the culture of literacy: it has given us some of the greatest works of literature we know, but it has also been turned to sinister purpose. Lévi-Strauss has claimed that "the only phenomenon with which writing has always been concomitant is the creation of cities and empires, that is the integration of large numbers of individuals into a political system, and their grading into castes or classes." The primary function of written communication, he argues, is "to facilitate slavery."[13] That claim may be exorbitant. Derrida has questioned, in the *Grammatology*, Lévi-Strauss's version of the distinction between orality and literacy. One may also be inclined to discount Lévi-Strauss's argument by recalling that he was sentimentally disposed toward the Nambikwara tribe and the other oral societies he studied. But Ricoeur's sentences prompt me to say that while we admire the new styles made possible by print and by the untethering of printed words from their origin in voice, the works of literature we most admire in the age of script and print are those which acknowledge the orality they may appear to have transcended. Dante, Chaucer, Shakespeare, Milton, Blake, Jane Austen, Emily Dickinson, Henry James, Yeats, Eliot, Joyce, Toni Morrison, Cormac McCarthy: none of these abandoned the ways of orality. Milton had his Muse. Blake was an engraver, a painter, a man of print, but his words and designs were responsive to a prophetic voice. Benjamin Franklin was a printer, but the sentences he wrote have their origin and point in a rhetorical tradition still predicated on the oral persuasion of person to person, preacher to congregation.[14]

But what about the electronic media, computers and information technology? If the technology of print enforced its values but still allowed voices to be heard, surely the electronic media will be even more hospitable to voices? Isn't TV almost entirely voice and body? Aren't e-mail and the internet a constant exchange of implied voices? Surely orality must come into its own again?

The prudent answer is: not necessarily. What orality had to fear from script and print was the fate of being silenced, its values displaced. What it has to fear from the electronic media is the abjection of being teased and mocked. Walter Ong is helpful on this question. He calls the present age, so far as it is governed by electronic developments, an age of "secondary orality." He means that the conditions provided by electronic technology are similar to those of primary orality—the orality of an oral society—in superficial respects, but different in profound respects. They are similar, in that the events we witness are oral and are suffused by oral elucidation; but they are different in that TV merely mimes orality, displays simulations of spontaneity, and pretends to show social formations as open and permeable. According to the pattern of consequence he has already indicated, Ong expects to see the institutions of this secondary orality causing the production, at least in the short term, of more books than ever; but these books will more and more clearly submit to the values of the new media. I suppose he means that most of the books on the best-seller list will be parasitic upon TV programs. That is already and dismally the case. Perhaps Ong means that increasingly writers will write as if for TV, or to reach a readership of people accustomed to the situations and the dialogue we see and hear on TV. And presumably readers will gradually come to insist on the styles and the conventions they see on TV.

This seems probable to me. Every new technique, from the printing press to photography, film, audiotape, video, and computer games, has had some impact on the common understanding of the world. Those of us who grew up into a literature still open to voices are likely to be bewildered, perhaps dismayed, by further developments. But all is not lost. I have been much encouraged by one of the arguments in de Certeau's *The Practice of Everyday Life*. He acknowledges that at any given moment a particular system of power is in place, a syntax of social and political practice. But he claims that people nevertheless engage in local ruses and tactics "that are neither determined nor captured by the systems in which they develop."[15] That is to say: local and individual practices do not fully yield to the system of power that for the most part controls them. Instead, they feature constant sleights of hand, bouts of opportunism, inventive trickery. De Certeau speaks of these tactics as constituting an art of powerless people, those who live under an alien god whom, in small ways, they can disable or circumvent.

I end with these few speculations. In the electronic age we are all powerless: power is in other hands. But we can still practice what de Certeau calls tactics, diversionary exercises, ruses. Perhaps these are what we should be teaching our students: tactics of evasion, the skill of detecting simulacra presented to us as real. We might teach our students the art of irony and train them to note discrepancies between one image and another, or between an image and its official discourse. In such an undertaking we might practice what Stanley Cavell calls "aversive thinking," following Emerson, who in "Self-Reliance" says, "The virtue in most request is conformity. Self-reliance is its aversion."[16]

Aversive thinking about the age of the TV screen proposes a critical relation to the world we live in and the instruments by which power is exerted. If we want a motto for this, apart from Emerson's phrase, I offer Kenneth Burke's account, in *Counter-Statement* and other books, of the aim of literature and criticism alike, aesthetically considered: to prevent a society from becoming too completely, too hopelessly, itself.

Murray Krieger Versus Paul de Man

The yellow moon of words about the nightingale
In measureless measures, not a bird for me
But the name of a bird and the name of a nameless air
I have never—shall never hear . . .

—Wallace Stevens, "Autumn Refrain"

In the spring of 1981, at a conference to mark the transfer of
the School of Criticism and Theory from the University of
California at Irvine to Northwestern University, Murray
Krieger gave a lecture at Northwestern under the title " 'A
Waking Dream': The Symbolic Alternative to Allegory."
M. H. Abrams and Paul de Man were the official respondents
to the lecture. Abrams's response has not been published, so
far as I know. De Man's appears in *Romanticism and Contemporary Criticism,* a posthumous collection of his papers.[1] A
revised version of Krieger's lecture was published in Morton W. Bloomfield's *Allegory, Myth, and Symbol* (1981) and in
Krieger's *Words About Words About Words* (1988).[2] I'll rehearse the exchange between Krieger and de Man not to adjudicate their differences but to extend the discussion a little
further. It turns, as it must, on the question How to read?

I

Krieger's aim was to salvage as much as possible of the heritage of symbolism from the damage he thought de Man and other writers had inflicted on it. "A Waking Dream" was part of Krieger's larger project, to recuperate certain literary values by showing that they have taken due account of the considerations ranged against them. Properly interpreted, these values are worth retaining because they have acknowledged and subsumed the grounds of the attack. Organicism, for instance. In another book Krieger offered to show that, "built into the mystical dialectic of organicism, with its magical imposition of unity, is a negative thrust that would explode it." Would explode it, he means, if given complete freedom. The call for unity that is clear in the rhetoric of organic form, he says, "occurs only in the company of its opposite, the call for a *variety* that gives to any attempted unity a dynamics that threatens its stability."[3] The values of organicism deserve to be retained if they are willing to question themselves, experimentally, impelled by a scruple: it is as if they doubted the merit of their totalizing impulse, short of rejecting it. In this spirit, Krieger would speak up for metaphor, if it were cooled a long age by reflecting on metonymy; for epic, if it acknowledged the force of the mock-heroic tradition; for sacred writing, if it recognized the rights of a profane motive; and for aesthetic unity, if it held itself susceptible to acts of play, as in Schiller, to the Sublime, as in Edmund Burke, and to the daemonic, as in Goethe.

In "The Waking Dream" Krieger's point of departure was the traditional distinction between symbol and allegory as it appeared, however diversely, in Goethe, Schelling, and Coleridge and as it persisted, with a radical shift of emphasis, in Mallarmé, Symons, and Yeats. Appropriately, Krieger quoted the well-known passage in *The Statesman's Manual* in which Coleridge makes the distinction as sharp as it was ever to be in his ruminations: "A symbol . . . is characterized by a translucence of the Special in the Individual or of the General in the Especial or of the Universal in the General. Above all by the translucence of the Eternal through and in the Temporal. It always partakes of the Reality which it renders intelligible; and while it enunciates the whole, abides itself as a living part in that Unity, of which it is the representative . . . . Now an Allegory is but a translation of abstract notions into a picture-language which is itself nothing but an abstraction from objects of the senses; the principal being more worthless even than its phantom proxy, both alike unsubstantial, and the former shapeless to boot."[4] The context of Coleridge's sentences is an attack on Hume's atheism. Coleridge acclaims the "great PRIN-CIPLES of our religion, the sublime IDEAS spoken out everywhere in the Old and New Testament" (24). He contrasts scriptural history "with the histories of highest note in the present age"—he means Hume and Gibbon—"in its freedom from the hollowness of abstractions" (28). Coleridge then refers to a "system of symbols, harmonious in themselves, and consubstantial with the truths, of which they are the *conductors*" (20). It is among the miseries of the present age, he claims, "that it recognises no medium between *Literal* and *Metaphorical*. . . . Faith is either to be buried in the dead letter, or its name and honors usurped by a counterfeit product of the mechanical understanding, which in the blindness of self-complacency confounds SYMBOLS with ALLEGO-RIES" (30). Then he makes the distinction I have quoted.

I remark the religious context of the distinction in the hope of making sense of it. It is clear from "consubstantial with the truths, of which they are the *conductors*" that the crucial instance of a symbol is the birth of Christ, the force of the Incarnation, that union of the divine and the human, eternity and time, spirit and body. A symbol is what it is because it denotes the natural world—God's Book of Nature—and partakes of the Word of God. "The power delegated to nature is all in every part," Coleridge says, "and by a symbol I mean, not a metaphor or allegory or any other figure of speech or form of fancy, but an actual and essential part of that, the whole of which it repre-sents" (79).

Krieger alludes to Coleridge's context by referring to the "monistic concep-tion of metaphor" as a "romantic reversion to the sacramental union put forth in Christian theology,"[5] and again by quoting, from the *Biographia Literaria*, Coleridge's definition of the primary imagination as a "repetition in the finite mind of the eternal act of creation in the infinite I AM" (277). But Krieger confuses the issue, I think, when he says that "through the typological *figura*, the unredeemed sequence of chronological time can be redeemed after all into the divine pattern, that eternal, spatial order which exchanges history for eschatology" (277). "Pattern" and "spatial" in that sentence are neither necessary nor desirable. The redemption of historical time does not entail recourse to a spatial figure. Eternity is not a supernatural mode of space.

This error—as I am bound to regard it—has serious consequences. It forces

Krieger to define in static, spatial terms forces that, being temporal, call for temporal description. He interprets each of these by transposing it into a spatial category, as if only there could it be significant. He defines form as the "imposition of spatial elements on a temporal ground without denying the figurative character of the word *spatial* and the merely illusionary escape from a temporal awareness that is never overcome" (280–281). Myth is the "shape that the imagination imposes on the flow of experience to make it conform to itself" (272). I don't see why a shape is especially conformable to the imagination, or why Krieger continues with this talk of spatial elements. Why not deem a myth to be a story, offered to its recipients as true and giving them reasons to live according to its import? It is a narrative, or a group of narratives, issuing from the life of a community and returning to that life. It is not construed as a shape. I recognize that we have a richer vocabulary to describe an entity in space than a force in time, but we gain nothing by confounding them. There is no merit in transposing into the spatial category such terms as myth, form, sacrament, *figura*, and metaphor.

Krieger finds the modern attack on symbol and the correspondingly high valuation of allegory most comprehensively deployed in de Man's "Rhetoric of Temporality," and he quotes from that essay part of the following:

> Whether it occurs in the form of an ethical conflict, as in *La Nouvelle Héloïse*, or as an allegorization of the geographical site, as in Wordsworth, the prevalence of allegory always corresponds to the unveiling of an authentically temporal destiny. This unveiling takes place in a subject that has sought refuge against the impact of time in a natural world to which, in truth, it bears no resemblance. . . . Whereas the symbol postulates the possibility of an identity or identification, allegory designates primarily a distance in relation to its own origin, and, renouncing the nostalgia and the desire to coincide, it establishes its language in the void of this temporal difference. In so doing, it prevents the self from an illusory identification with the non-self, which is now fully, though painfully, recognized as a non-self.[6]

It follows that de Man, to avoid convicting Romantic poets of bad faith and mystification, must argue that the crucial relation in their poetry is not between mind and the natural world but between mind and time. They must be shown to be allegorists, not symbolists, so far as they know themselves and their genuine life in time. This is de Man's aim in several essays.

Krieger deals with this critical situation by claiming, in effect, that Romantic poets and their readers may honorably deal with symbols, provided they
know the risk they run; chiefly, the risk of self-delusion: "I want us to earn a
chance to retain some of the symbolist's ambitious hopes for what man, as
fiction-making creature, can accomplish in language, without falling prey to
the ontologizing impulse that symbolist theory has previously encouraged. To
do so we must balance a wariness about projecting our myths onto reality
with an acknowledgement that we can entertain the dream of symbolic union,
provided it does not come trailing clouds of metaphysical glory. Within the
aesthetic frame of a fictional verbal play, the poem can present us with a form
that creates the illusion of simultaneity, though even as we attend it we remain
aware of its illusionary nature."[7] "Dream" and "illusion" keep the stakes pretty
low, unless Krieger has in mind only the sense in which everything in language
is fictive. But there is a difference between a fiction and an illusion; we are in
thrall to our illusions, but not to the fictions we make. I don't think that
Krieger has given up the ontologizing impulse.

He takes, as an example of such innocent knowledge—innocent because
"we remain aware of its illusionary nature"—the last stanzas of Keats's "Ode to
a Nightingale":

> Thou wast not born for death, immortal Bird!
>   No hungry generations tread thee down;
> The voice I hear this passing night was heard
>   In ancient days by emperor and clown:
> Perhaps the self-same song that found a path
>   Through the sad heart of Ruth, when, sick for home,
> She stood in tears amid the alien corn;
>   The same that oft-times hath
> Charm'd magic casements, opening on the foam
>   Of perilous seas, in faery lands forlorn.
> Forlorn! the very word is like a bell
>   To toll me back from thee to my sole self!
> Adieu! the fancy cannot cheat so well
>   As she is fam'd to do, deceiving elf.
> Adieu! adieu! thy plaintive anthem fades
>   Past the near meadows, over the still stream,
> Up the hill-side; and now 'tis buried deep

> In the next valley-glades:
> Was it a vision, or a waking dream?
>   Fled is that music:—Do I wake or sleep?

Keats's speaker, as Krieger says, wakes up from the momentary trance, "his all-unifying fancy," to return to his sole self:

> Yet the final words of his poem ("Do I wake or sleep?") suggest that the final
> moment of demystification is not necessarily privileged as the only authen-
> tic reality. . . . The perspective that sees the fancy as cheating is itself not a fi-
> nal reality, and the magic of the fancy is not altogether dispelled. Even more,
> the experience itself is still cherished, even in the aftermath of loss. The
> struggle in the speaker between the poet's willed visionary blindness that has
> permitted the fancy and the mortal's dull, perplexed brain that has resisted
> it has not relaxed: once again—or rather still—the struggle between myth
> and history. The music has fled, we learn in the opening of the final line,
> though its continuing effects lead to the uncertainty about the present re-
> flected in the question that concludes the poem.[8]

Krieger implies that the poet who exercises his "fancy" is not in bad faith, provided he wakes up from the trance and acknowledges that he has been dreaming. The redemptive force is—it is my word, not Krieger's—irony. Irony as a higher degree of knowledge recovers the lower degree by exceeding it. When the poet brings irony to bear on his dream, he retains the dream as a valid experience, not a naivete. What de Man calls the "fallen world of our facticity"[9] is not the whole world or the whole story.

II

De Man's response to Krieger is strange. He begins by praising the New Critics—including Krieger—for letting the efficacy of their technical pro-cedures, "as they developed in close contact with the points of resistance they encountered in the understanding of texts, reach beyond and even turn against the limits of their own ideologies."[10] But then he scolds Krieger for preferring one trope to another—symbol to allegory—as if de Man himself had not spent much of his energy overturning that preference. In Krieger's terms, according to de Man's reading of them, "allegory is equated with a thematic assertion of finitude, defeat, and mortality of which symbol is the

aesthetic sublimation and redemption." Krieger "thus recovers the fragmenta-
tion of time and of the self in the beautiful song of the severed head, reconciles
the clear-eyed scepticism of knowledge with the fervor of vision, the language
of fusion with that of separation, the gesture of conceding with that of asserting or countering" (183). The test case, according to de Man, is Krieger's
reading of the last two lines of the poem:

> Was it a vision, or a waking dream?
> Fled is that music:—Do I wake or sleep?

De Man comments, "Guided by the apparent symmetry of the two *or* con-
structions (a vision or a waking dream; wake *or* sleep), Krieger can suspend
the uncertainty of the wake/sleep opposition and make it into a stable cognition by stressing the symbolic complementarity of 'a vision' with 'a waking
dream'—in which the 'second alternative' is not 'wholly a denial of the first'; it
is a cliché, but not an unreasonable one, to call a waking dream a vision (184)."
The past of recollection ("Was it . . . ") and the present of writing or thinking
("Do I . . . ") can be brought together, de Man concedes, "because sleeping
relates to waking as vision relates to waking dream, that is to say, in the mode
of the symbol" (184). De Man doesn't offer to refute Krieger's general argument or to deny him the pleasure of his synthesis. He has already engaged
some of these issues in an essay on Michael Riffaterre.[11] He doesn't want to go
over that ground again, so he leaves Krieger's hoped-for synthesis without
further comment. But he remarks that Descartes points out, in the first two
Meditations, that when we dream, we always dream that we are awake. De
Man says, "Unlike reverie or day-dream, dream and wake (or sleep) are mutually exclusive, not symbolically complementary."[12] But de Man's main question is not whether Krieger's synthesis is valid but whether Keats's ode can be
invoked in support of it. He concentrates on the word "Forlorn!" which leads
to the last two lines of the poem:

> This moment in the text, and this moment alone, occurs as an actual present
> in the only material present of the ode, the actual moment of its inscription
> when Keats writes the word "forlorn" and interrupts himself to reflect on its
> arbitrary sound. At that precise moment, is it possible to say whether Keats,
> in the present of that moment, is awake or asleep? Thematically speaking, it
> is the very moment at which the subject in the text states that it awakens; tex-

tually speaking, however, it is also the moment at which this same subject starts to dream—for as we also all know since Freud, such plays of the letter are also the work of the dream, accessible to us only within a system in which the difference between waking and dreaming cannot be decided and can, henceforth, not be assimilated to a symbolic reconciliation of opposites. The actual inclusion, in the texture of the lyric, of an alien piece of metalanguage makes the "Ode to a Nightingale" one of the very poems, the very allegory, of the non-symbolic, nonaesthetic character of poetic language.[13]

Very odd. So far as I understand it, it comes to this. Krieger, allegedly, takes the apparent symmetry of the questions—Was it A or B? Do I wake or sleep?—as proof of Keats's eventually standing aside from the rhetoric of his symbolism to the extent of questioning its status. By doing so, he earns the right to use the song of the nightingale as a symbol. De Man answers, in effect: No, because the symmetry of the questions is specious, there is no ascertainable difference between each of the states in the pairings; vision or waking dream, dream or waking. There is no place, not a crevice, into which Keats's ostensibly later knowledge can insert itself. "Forlorn" breaks the unity of tone it claims.

But surely the moment at which Keats steps outside the rhetoric of his meditation and withdraws the word "forlorn" from it is not dream work but the work of wide-awake self-scrutiny. Plays of the letter may take place in dreams, but they also occur—are acted on—in waking consciousness. In the ode the difference between waking and dreaming can be decided: dream work may play with the word "forlorn," but it does not run to a comparison of that word to a bell tolling Keats back from the nightingale to his sole self. That is an act of syntax which the dream can't perform. Dreams have images, but no syntax. Hazlitt says, in his essay "On Dreams," that the difference between sleeping and waking "seems to be that in the latter we have a greater range of conscious recollections, a larger discourse of reason, and associate ideas in longer trains and more as they are connected with one another in the order of nature; whereas in the former, any two impressions, that meet or are alike, join company, and then are parted again, without notice, like the froth from the wave."[14] There is enough difference, then, to justify the symmetry of the questions. David Bromwich says, with good reason, that it doesn't matter whether Keats wakes or sleeps, "because he is free to renew his journey, and to return again," but this doesn't support de Man's claim that the question is specious because its terms can't be distinguished.[15] They can be distinguished well enough.

The symbolic reconciliation of opposites that Krieger proposes to show seems to be intact. "Forlorn" is not an alien piece of metalanguage but the moment in which Keats separates himself from the rhetoric of his trance. In the essay on Riffaterre, de Man claims that the question "Was it a vision or a waking dream?" is "destined to remain unanswered."[16] Not necessarily. Any reader is free to think that, on balance, Keats's experience was more a waking dream than a vision; or vice versa. But the question is not opaque, whether it is answered or not. Translated into prose, it might be phrased: was it a vision, "something apparently seen otherwise than by ordinary sight," as the OED has it, though with concentrated attention; or was it a casual, disordered reverie, a loose association of images from which I have now returned to my sober senses?

I think Krieger is right, therefore, to maintain that Keats has found a place for irony, the later knowledge. Several places, I would say: the one surrounding "Forlorn!"; the one between the past tense of "Was" and the interrogative present of "Do I . . . ?"; and the places on each side of the interpellated sentence "Fled is that music." The oddity of that sentence makes a further space; music, not bird; and "Fled," with its implication of flying away from danger. These are acts of alert discrimination, not words of trance. As in Keats's "Sleep and Poetry,"

> The visions all are fled—the car is fled
>   Into the light of heaven

(lines 155–156)

—because they can't face the "sense of real things" come "doubly strong."

III

De Man's last words in reply to Krieger are memorably gruff, when he refers to the "Ode to a Nightingale" as "one of the very poems, the very allegory, of the non-symbolic, nonaesthetic character of poetic language."[17] In his early writings, de Man hovered between describing poetic language in this way and in virtually the opposite way. In "Criticism and Crisis"—a lecture he gave at the University of Texas in spring 1967—he spoke with dismay of Husserl's claim for European supremacy and of the pathos of such a claim "at a moment when Europe was about to destroy itself as center in the name of its unwarranted claim to be the center." Then he talked about literary criticism: "Similarly, demystifying critics are in fact asserting the privileged status of literature as an authentic language, but withdrawing from the implications by cutting themselves off from the source from which they receive their insight. For the statement about language, that sign and meaning can never coincide, is what is precisely taken for granted in the kind of language we call literary. Literature, unlike everyday language, begins on the far side of this knowledge; it is the only form of language free from the fallacy of unmediated expression."[18] But in the Gauss Seminar at Princeton, still in the spring of 1967, and while repeating that "unmediated expression is a philosophical impossibility," de Man denied the privilege he had accorded, at Texas, to literature:

> Literature, presumably, is a form of language, and one can argue that all other art forms, including music, are in fact protoliterary languages. This was, in fact, Mallarmé's thesis in his Oxford lecture, as it is Lévi-Strauss's when he states that the language of music, as a language without speaker, comes closest to being the kind of metalanguage of which the linguists are dreaming. If the radical position suggested by Lévi-Strauss is to stand, if the question of structure can only be asked from a point of view that is not that of a subject using a privileged language, then it becomes imperative to show that literature constitutes no exception, that its language is nowise privileged in terms of unity and truth over everyday forms of language. The task of structuralist literary critics then becomes quite clear: in order to eliminate the constitutive subject, they have to show that the discrepancy between sign and meaning (*signifiant* and *signifié*) prevails in literature in the same manner as in everyday language.[19]

I can't explain how literature, merely by moving from Austin, Texas, to Princeton, New Jersey, lost the privilege of being free from the fallacy of unmediated expression.

But it is clear that de Man, en route in 1967 from Structuralism to Deconstruction, was determined to go far to seek disquietude. By the time he had written "The Rhetoric of Temporality" he had read or reread Benjamin's *Ursprung des deutschen Trauerspiels.* The repudiation of symbol in favor of allegory, in "The Rhetoric of Temporality," is taken directly from Benjamin's book. Benjamin, who had his own reasons for hating time and history, resented the attempt of certain modern writers to "redeem the time"—the later Eliot, I imagine, though Benjamin doesn't mention him—or to show daily life under a possible blessing of miracle, Incarnation, or some other transfiguring value. If you want to transform the lives people have to live, he implied, you must do so by direct political action or by exemplary action, as in Brecht's theater. Hence his hatred of the enhancing tropes, especially of symbol and myth. (Fredric Jameson hates them for the same reason.) Benjamin's method was to deride any literary or dramatic form that appeared to alleviate the malady of the quotidian. Tragedy was the main culprit. The dialogue between Lear and Cordelia near the end of the play is apparently designed to make the audience feel that the gouging of Gloucester's eyes is not the whole story; that suffering, as in the crucifixion of Christ, may be suffused with a redemptive aura of value and meaning. Benjamin rejected the consolation prize and countered Tragedy with the *Trauerspiel,* which—as in the plays of John Webster, Cyril Tourneur, and Thomas Middleton—left the fragments of time entirely unredeemed. Benjamin writes: "Whereas in the symbol destruction is idealized and the transfigured face of nature is fleetingly revealed in the light of redemption, in allegory the observer is confronted with the *facies hippocratica* of history as a petrified, primordial landscape. Allegories are, in the realm of thoughts, what ruins are in the realm of things."[20] That is the gist of de Man's attack, too: allegories are honest because they don't pretend to offer any hope of unity of being, they don't give even a fleeting intimation of redemption, they show time for what it is, mere facticity, one damned thing after another and then nothing. Symbolism is a fraud. It is not surprising that de Man was gruff with Krieger's attempt to retain its glow.

When he responded to Krieger's lecture, de Man was already moving away from the trope of metaphor as the essential poetic figure, since it entailed sundry mystifications of likeness, reference, creativity, constitutive power, ontology, and epistemology. I think this accounts for the impression, in his reply to Krieger, that the whole discourse had ceased to interest him. He was already abandoning Aristotle's theory of the primacy of metaphor and endorsing Vico's claim that language begins in the trope that "gives sense and passion to insensate things."[21] This is the Speech Act of positing or summoning, apostrophe, prosopopoeia, the act by which I call someone or something into existence as a subject. Keats heard a nightingale and was charmed by its song,

but in the poem he doesn't describe what he heard, he summons a nightingale—type of all nightingales from all ages—to appear. In the essay on Riffaterre, de Man writes, agreeably enough, of the "delicate and ever-suspended
balance between reference and play that is the condition for aesthetic pleasure." But the reference to reference soon drops away, and he writes of the
"epistemological tension that produces prosopopoeia, the master trope of
poetic discourse." Indeed, "prosopopoeia, as the trope of address, is the very
figure of the reader and of reading."[22] The particular force of prosopopoeia is
that it achieves the uncanny effect of making the invisible appear to be visible;
it produces a hallucination, or rather a hallucinatory effect. Repeating a few
sentences from his reply to Krieger, de Man produces a quandary dismal
enough for any devotee of Benjamin:

> How then is one to decide on the distinction between hallucination and per-
> ception since, in hallucination, the difference between *I see* and *I think that I*
> *see* has been one-sidedly resolved in the direction of apperception? Con-
> sciousness has become consciousness only of itself. In that sense, any con-
> sciousness, including perception, is hallucinatory: one never "has" a
> hallucination the way one has a sore foot from kicking the proverbial stone.
> Just as the hypothesis of dreaming undoes the certainty of sleep, the hypoth-
> esis, or the figure, of hallucination undoes sense certainty. This means, in
> linguistic terms, that it is impossible to say whether prosopopoeia is plausi-
> ble because of the empirical existence of dreams and hallucinations or
> whether one believes that such a thing as dreams and hallucinations exist
> because language permits the figure of prosopopoeia. The question "Was it a
> vision or a waking dream?" is destined to remain unanswered. Prosopopoeia
> undoes the distinction between reference and signification on which all se-
> miotic systems, including Riffaterre's, depend.[23]

But on second reading this may not be as dismal as it seemed. When Hardy, in
a series of love poems, belatedly calls on his dead wife to come forth, of course
she doesn't obey, as Lazarus obeyed Christ. But in a fictive sense she appears to
appear. If we think of this appearance as a semblance rather than a hallucination, we take the harm out of de Man's conclusion. Semblances are all that
works of art and literature offer to give. The "Ode to a Nightingale" doesn't
produce a nightingale or sing a song. We see nothing, hear nothing. But we
have semblances of things seen and heard.

IV

My disagreement with Krieger's "A Waking Dream" begins with his first paragraph: "The war between the poets and the philosophers, out of which Western literary theory began, is with us still. Though it has taken many forms, it is there now, stimulating yet new varieties of dispute. As a war, it continues to partake of the oppositional force of the Platonic dialectic, forcing us to choose which of the two ways we will accept as a path of knowledge, or which of the two we shall reject for having no valid claim to lead us there."[24] I don't think that is the best way of reading. Suppose it were not a question of knowledge but of—as I hold—action and experience, as in Kenneth Burke's *Grammar of Motives:* "To consider language as a means of *information* or *knowledge* is to consider it epistemologically, semantically, in terms of 'science.' To consider it as a mode of *action* is to consider it in terms of 'poetry.' For a poem is an act, the symbolic act of the poet who made it—an act of such a nature that, in surviving as a structure or object, it enables us as readers to re-enact it."[25] The written or printed poem is like a musical score; it permits us to act it out, follow its action. If we read a poem as symbolic action, we retain its qualities in temporal form. Form itself becomes a temporal sequence involving, in Burke's terms, the "creation of an appetite in the mind of the auditor, and the adequate satisfying of that appetite."[26] One of his examples is the formal perfection of Shakespeare's presentation of the Ghost to Hamlet, a choice instance of the auditor's desires excited, thwarted, sidestepped, but in good time richly satisfied.

The first merit of this approach to reading is that it does not start a war between poets and philosophers about knowledge. Or between poets and scientists on the same issue. If the realm of literature is action and its content is experience real or imagined, such wars are unnecessary. Novelists may use the work of physicists, as Pynchon does in *Gravity's Rainbow,* but they do not compete with physicists. To each his own labor. A dispute would break out only if novelist or physicist claimed to run the whole show. It is not likely to happen. Meanwhile, current disputes about the allegedly social constitution of knowledge are matters in which a poet may take a lay interest. They are not a poet's problem in any consideration of craft or profession. Even when a statement is made in a poem or a novel, it does not come up for judgment in respect to truth or falsity but only in relation to the feelings in the case at that point. I. A. Richards's old theory, according to which statements in a work of literature are not statements but pseudo-statements, is not much valued nowadays, but it should be taken seriously, provided we agree that a pseudo-statement is a statement the truth or falsity of which is not, on the particular consideration, an issue. If I were to say, in conversation or print, that " 'tis better to be vile than vile esteemed," I should be hooted for committing a falsehood and for the further sins of vanity and self-pity. But the sentence is appropriate as the first line of a sonnet by Shakespeare, since the implied context there makes it a feasible thing for the speaker to say. The statement is not true, according to reputable ethics and moral doctrine, but it is true to the life of the implied speaker. Or take Sidney's sonnet:

> With how sad steps, Oh Moon, thou climb'st the skies!
> How silently, and with how wan a face!
> What, may it be that even in heavenly place
> That busy archer his sharp arrows tries?
> Sure, if that long-with-love-acquainted eyes
> Can judge of love, thou feel'st a lover's case,
> I read it in thy looks; thy languished grace,
> To me, that feel the like, thy state descries.
> Then, even of fellowship, Oh Moon, tell me,
> Is constant love deemed there but want of wit?
> Are beauties there as proud as here they be?
> Do they above love to be loved, and yet
> Those lovers scorn whom that love doth possess?
> Do they call virtue there ungratefulness?

The first line is untrue; the moon does not climb the skies with sad steps. But the speaker, a bruised sad lover, might well call upon the moon, in fellowship, to respond to his complaint. The poem is a symbolic act in the mode of apostrophe or prosopopoeia; it summons the moon as a subject, gives it a face, and speaks to it. The moon is, as we say, a symbol of the transience of love, of the conviction that new love, as in the "Ode to a Nightingale," cannot pine at beauty's lustrous eyes "beyond to-morrow." As a symbol, is it vulnerable to an analysis such as de Man's? I don't think so. I can't speak for Krieger, but in his terms I would find the symbol justified by the fact that after the first quatrain, in which Sidney's speaker addresses the moon as victim of love and Cupid's arrows, he gives the moon—with the steadying words "acquainted" and "judge"—a different role. The moon is no longer a mere victim but an adjudicator, a witness qualified to report on lunar conventions and dispositions. The question of knowledge, true or false, does not arise in reading Sidney's sonnet or Shakespeare's: what arises is a question of feeling, action, experience, and the values they adumbrate. Nor does the question of knowledge arise in "Ode to a Nightingale." I agree with Helen Vendler that art, in this ode—by which she means the song of the nightingale—"has no conceptual or moral content." I assume she is referring to the song and not to the poem when she says that "ravishingly beautiful and entirely natural, it is a stream of invention, pure sound, in no way mimetic, on which we as listeners project our own feelings of ecstasy or grief."[27] The song is pure expression, expression in itself nothing but sensation. But Keats's speaker, too, projects his feelings on it. Krieger says:

> Indeed, the bird seems to function for the enraptured speaker as a metonymic metaphor. The magic of the speaker's momentary indulgence leads him to identify the single, mortal bird with its voice and song and to make the voice and song identical with those of the distant past. All nightingales become one bird because the songs are one song, heard but unseen. On the strength of this transfer Keats treats the bird itself as immortal, in contrast to his own mortality and that of the historical or mythological personages who earlier heard the same bird (voice, song). Humanity's individual lives are tied together by the bird once it has been turned into the all-unifying metonymic metaphor, so that history across the ages has been turned into the instantaneous vision of myth. Thanks to a repetition so complete that it achieves the identity of eternal recurrence (de Man's objections notwithstanding), time is redeemed.[28]

Metonymic metaphor is evidently Krieger's name for the metaphor that knows it's a metaphor, or rather for the use of metaphor that accommodates this knowledge. I don't find any problem in reconciling the nightingale's song as pure expression with the song as that into which Keats's speaker projects his feelings and desires. But I don't see how Krieger is justified in collapsing the differences between the "identity of eternal recurrence" and the "instantaneous vision of myth." Again he is thinking of myth as the spatial culmination of history, as if the redemption of time were necessarily to be achieved out of time or beyond it.

My main disagreement with Krieger is, I hope, clear. He makes the question of symbol and allegory an epistemological issue; I want to make it—or keep it—a question of action, suffering, and experience. I concede that he has Coleridge's authority on his side. Coleridge, too, made the symbol an epistemological issue, such that the crucial question was the relation between knowledge and faith. But I argue that a symbol is not an object as if seen in space; it denotes an action or a multitude of cognate actions. The force of Keats's nightingale is not semantic, it is a symbol by virtue of the feelings we (you, I, anyone) project on it. It is not a constituent of knowledge but of desire. It is worth mentioning that when Arthur Symons formulated the theory of Symbolism, in light of the diverse practices of Nerval, Villiers de L'Isle Adam, Rimbaud, Verlaine, Mallarmé, and Laforgue, he placed it in a world beyond knowledge. Or at least beyond any mode that passed for knowledge. "The forces which mould the thought of men change," he said, "or men's resistance to them slackens; with the change of men's thought comes a change of literature, alike in its inmost essence and in its outward form: after the world has starved its soul long enough in the contemplation and the rearrangement of material things, comes the turn of the soul; and with it comes the literature of which I write in this volume, a literature in which the visible world is no longer a reality, and the unseen world no longer a dream."[29] Only in such a world could poems of *symbolisme* have been elicited from words. To achieve such poems, Coleridge's epistemological doctrine of the symbol had to be abandoned. Symbolisme is a poetry that has released itself from the Incarnation by giving each word its autonomy as a word, independent of its old duty in the mundane world. In such a world as Symons intuits, words are not burdened with the duty of reference; there is no longer an empirical world to claim such priority. As a result, words are set free to act not as signs pointing beyond themselves and beyond the poem, but as presences in relation to other presences. They are like sounds in music or pieces in a board game: nothing in themselves but everything in their relation to their fellows. Ontology and epistemology do not arise. The relation between one word and another in a symbolist poem is an event of kinship or difference, marked by internal affiliations—acoustic, promiscuous, self-delighting.

I see more clearly now where I differ from Krieger. He wants to keep symbols close to knowledge, I want to keep them close to desire. I agree with

David Lloyd that a symbol "functions as a means to a narrative organization of desire rather than a mode of mimetic representation."[30] Lloyd has in view the relation between Yeats's symbols and the political state they summon into existence: "Both nationalist poetry and nationalist violence have the same end: to organize the incoherent desires of the population towards the goal of popular unity, which is the essential prerequisite of an effective political struggle for national liberation. The narrative of symbolism is one which progressively leads its subjects on by way of symbols which are consubstantial with the nation which they represent."[31] If a symbol is predicated on desire rather than on knowledge, it is invulnerable: if it ceases to organize the desires in question, it ceases to be a symbol and must be replaced by a more effective one. But, so long as it does its work, I don't see how it could be refuted by allegory or by any other figure.

Part II

What Happens in *Othello*

I begin with a poem by John Peale Bishop called "Speaking of Poetry." It ponders the situation of *Othello* in one loose interpretation of it, and it goes beyond the text to imagine details we are not shown. But mainly it introduces and repeats the word "ceremony" as if to say that the play does not consist merely of its palpable events, the intrigue, the movements of plot leading to catastrophe. The poem designates as ceremony the play in its aspect of form, style, and decorum, and says that the acts and events must become a ceremony in the end. Short of that, I suppose they would be merely a rigmarole and sordid in that character:

The ceremony must be found
that will wed Desdemona to the huge Moor.

It is not enough—
to win the approval of the Senator
or to outwit his disapproval; honest Iago
can manage that: it is not enough. For then,
though she may pant again in his black arms
(his weight resilient as a Barbary stallion's)
she will be found

when the ambassadors of the Venetian state arrive
again smothered. These things have not changed,
not in three hundred years.
(Tupping is still tupping
though that particular word is obsolete.
Naturally, the ritual would not be in Latin.)

For though Othello had his blood from kings
his ancestry was barbarous, his ways African,
his speech uncouth. It must be remembered
that though he valued an embroidery—
three mulberries proper on a silk like silver—
it was not for the subtlety of the stitches,
but for the magic in it. Whereas, Desdemona
once contrived to imitate in needlework
her father's shield, and plucked it out
three times, to begin again, each time
with diminished colors. This is a small point
but indicative.

Desdemona was small and fair,
delicate as a grasshopper
at the tag-end of summer: a Venetian
to her noble finger-tips.

O, it is not enough
that they should meet, naked, at dead of night
in a small inn on a dark canal. Procurers
less expert than Iago can arrange as much.
The ceremony must be found

Traditional, with all its symbols
ancient as the metaphors in dreams;
strange, with never before heard music; continuous
until the torches deaden at the bedroom door.[1]

So much for the poem's admonition. The play is not *Othello* till Shakespeare has found the appropriate ceremony for its events, converting them to sense and presence.

Now I recite another admonition, more familiar than Bishop's, a passage from T. S. Eliot's essay "Shakespeare and the Stoicism of Seneca." Eliot maintains that there is some relation between Seneca's tragedies and Shakespeare's, but that it is nothing as emphatic as an influence. Seneca's tragedies are present in Shakespeare's as a new attitude. Stoicism is a posture or manner rather than a creed. The most that can be said is that in Shakespeare's tragedies at certain high moments there is a distinctive tone, derived in some respect and however circuitously from Seneca. It is also to be found in Marston and Chapman. It arises, Eliot says—with Othello in view—from the "attitude of self-dramatization assumed by some of Shakespeare's heroes at moments of tragic intensity."[2] Seneca's Stoicism is the "refuge for the individual in an indifferent or hostile world."[3] Eliot has in view a gesture or a style rather than a morality. Othello in the last scene of the play is speaking in a well-established style that mediates his self-regard. Without waiting for Shakespeare to find a ceremony for the play, he is finding a Senecan one for his sole self. In another essay, "Seneca in Elizabethan Translation," Eliot supports a distinction—which I find invidious—between the aesthetic and the moral attitudes by contrasting the dialogue of Greek tragedy with that of Senecan tragedy: "Behind the dialogue of Greek drama we are always conscious of a concrete visual actuality, and behind that of a specific emotional actuality. Behind the drama of words is the drama of action, the timbre of voice and voice, the uplifted hand or tense muscle, and the particular emotion. The spoken play, the words which we read, are symbols, a shorthand, and often, as in the best of Shakespeare, a very abbreviated shorthand indeed, for the acted and felt play, which is always the real thing. The phrase, beautiful as it may be, stands for a greater beauty still. . . . In the plays of Seneca, the drama is all in the word, and the word has no further reality behind it."[4] According to that distinction, the moral attitude is Greek and thrives on a Greek sense of reality. The aesthetic attitude is Senecan and takes false pleasure in the autonomy of words: as the early Yeats wrote, "Words alone are certain good."

But I should note, in passing, that Eliot does not always act upon this contrast in his own poems. In "Marina" he takes as epigraph a passage from Seneca's *Hercules Furens* that recalls the entire situation in which Hercules speaks the words. It is not true in that case that the words Seneca has given his tragic hero have no further reality behind them. On the other hand, Eliot's "Gerontion" is a Senecan poem. As desperately as Othello, Gerontion is using a

Senecan style as ceremony to cheer himself up and to enable him to see things as they are not. Still, the contrast Eliot proposes between Greek and Senecan tragedy is illuminating. If we place beside his understanding of Greek tragedy his appreciation of Dante, and place beside his sense of Senecan tragedy his feeling for the poetry of incantation—in Poe, Tennyson, and Swinburne—we make the distinction especially helpful toward our understanding of *Othello.*

The contrast turns upon two styles and therefore two senses of life. In one, the words spoken are translucent, or at least they give that impression. They are signs, instruments, or vehicles in the service of reality construed as not entirely verbal. The words point toward the diversely constituted world they designate. In the other style, the words are self-engendered and therefore seem to be self-regarding; they serve no master other than themselves, their internal possibilities. Such words seem to know that they are words and that they have many qualities in addition to those they give to the task of reference. One word, in that style, leads to the next by virtue not of reference but of zeal in the cause of self-creation. Such words seem to perform themselves, consulting chiefly their own possibilities: they do not observe any duty, least of all that of recognizing an objective world of lives already in their courses. To adapt a passage from Stevens's "Man with the Blue Guitar," these words are like "catching at Goodbye, harvest moon, / Without seeing the harvest or the moon."[5] No wonder the incipiently Christian Eliot felt it an urgent matter in 1927 to rebuke such a Senecan style, just as he rebuked the practice of "art for art's sake" and similar impieties.

In *Othello* we have both of these styles and both of these senses of life. In the end and too late for consolation the play displaces one of them with the other, repudiates Seneca, in effect, and restores a Greek sense of reality, truth, and word. It is Desdemona who does this: to note her achievement, the highest ceremony, is to mark her supreme value for the play. I am not saying that the play is a conflict of words. It is what it appears to be, a tragedy of deception, suspicion, and revenge. But it finds these motives, to begin with, as lethal properties of language waiting to be performed as styles of behavior. If we want a motto for such habits and likelihoods, we have one in Iago's saying of Othello to Roderigo:

> Though I do hate him, as I do hell's pains,
> Yet, for necessity of present life,

I must show out a flag, and sign of love,
Which is indeed but a sign.

(I.i.154–157)[6]

Iago is Othello's ancient, his ensign or standard-bearer. It is his duty to show forth true colors, flags, signs that refer truthfully beyond themselves to meanings at large in the world. A sign that is but a sign is a lie, a signifier that does not truly signify. Or it serves a different value than truth.

But signs have to be interpreted, and the devil can quote Scripture to his purpose. When Iago tells Roderigo that love is "merely a lust of the blood, and a permission of the will" (I.iii.335), there is no merit in claiming that this, too, like nearly everything else Iago says, is a lie. It isn't; it is sound moral doctrine about a certain kind of love. Of course there are many bogus signs in the play. On the value of one's reputation, Iago says one thing to Cassio and the opposite to Othello. Words may be promiscuous, as Brabantio notes when he says, in reply to the Duke's platitudes,

These sentences to sugar, or to gall,
Being strong on both sides, are equivocal:
But words are words; I never yet did hear
That the bruised heart was pierced through the ear:

(I.iii.216–219)

Bruised hearts are often pierced through the ear, and through the eye. Desdemona is a case in point. Brabantio is a better critic of equivocation than of the separation of words from deeds, two linguistic possibilities. He thinks that Othello enchanted Desdemona in chains of magic and practiced foul charms upon her, because he can't imagine that Othello's words or his personal bearing could have done it. He is a prosaic reader of signs.

Unlike Iago, who reads nearly any significance into his texts, or pretends to, but always stays within the range of plausibility. In act 2, scene i, when Iago and Roderigo have watched Cassio greet Desdemona, Iago says to Roderigo, "Didst thou not see her paddle with the palm of his hand?" "Yes, but that was but courtesy," Roderigo reasonably answeres. "Lechery, by this hand," Iago insists, as if his hand were to be vouched for without equivocation, "an index and prologue to the history of lust and foul thoughts: they met so near with their lips, that their breaths embrac'd together" (II.iv.254–256). This little episode is index and prologue to the scene in which Iago, seeing Cassio leave Desdemona's company, says to Othello, "Ha, I like not that."

> OTHELLO: What dost thou say?
> IAGO: Nothing, my lord, or if—I know not what.
> OTHELLO: Was that not Cassio parted from my wife?
> IAGO: Cassio, my lord? . . . no, sure, I cannot think it,
> That he would sneak away so guilty-like,
> Seeing you coming."
>
> (III.iii.35–41)

The Folio has "steal away," a more suggestive wording in relation to theft and Desdemona as Othello's private property. These incidents also prefigure the episode in which Iago stations Othello to eavesdrop on his conversation with Cassio, to see Bianca give Cassio the handkerchief, and to assume that the conversation in its laughter and vulgarity has been about Desdemona rather than Bianca.

"The drama is all in the word," Eliot says, "and the word has no further reality behind it." Perhaps there is no need to make the contrast between Greek and Senecan styles so sharp: it is enough that we recognize in Senecan style a rhetoric of equivocation and think it sinister on the whole. The fact that we are dealing with a particular capacity of language is maintained again in Eliot's essay on Swinburne, in which he ascribes to Swinburne much the same linguistic character as he has ascribed to Seneca. "When you take to pieces any verse of Swinburne," Eliot claims, "you find always that the object was not there—only the word."[7] He then makes the point more general:

> Language in a healthy state presents the object, is so close to the object that the two are identified. They are identified in the verse of Swinburne solely because the object has ceased to exist, because the meaning is merely the hallucination of meaning, because language, uprooted, has adapted itself to an independent life of atmospheric nourishment. In Swinburne, for example, we see the word "weary" flourishing in this way independent of the particular and actual weariness of flesh or spirit. The bad poet dwells partly in a world of objects and partly in a world of words, and he can never get them to fit. Only a man of genius could dwell so exclusively and consistently among words as Swinburne. His language is not, like the language of bad poetry, dead. It is very much alive, with this singular life of its own. But the

language which is more important to us is that which is struggling to digest
and express new objects, new groups of objects, new feelings, new aspects,
as, for instance, the prose of Mr. James Joyce or the earlier Conrad.[8]

This passage is dark but not obscure. Eliot is arguing against himself while
making an effort to be fair to his own genius. His own poems do not "present
the object," are not "so close to the object that the two are identified." Presumably he means that in the works he praises, language and object are identified
under the privileged auspices of the object, as in Dante. But Eliot's own poetic
language is far more akin to Swinburne's, as Eliot describes it in the first few
sentences of this passage, than it is to Dante's. Especially in *Prufrock and Other
Observations*, what is observed is an internal capacity of language, animated
by the "auditory imagination" as Eliot describes it in *The Use of Poetry and the
Use of Criticism*. One word stirs another, issuing from the echoes and recesses
of the English language. It is true that Eliot never uses a word loosely or
interchangeably with other words in its semantic vicinity, as he maintains that
Swinburne does. Eliot's language is more conscientious than Swinburne's,
while being of the same character and disposition. But in the passage I've
quoted from the essay on Swinburne, Eliot extricates himself from mixed
allegiances by reaching—in his reference to digesting and expressing—toward
Shakespeare and Donne, not named because they needn't be. Joyce stands for
Dante and Donne, as Conrad for Shakespeare.

Nonetheless, the contrast persists. In *Othello* there are many occasions on
which a character deliberately produces hallucinations of meaning in someone's mind, as Iago causes Othello to see with his own eyes a state of affairs
between Desdemona and Cassio that is not there. There are other occasions
on which a dramatic irony is introduced, a discrepancy between what a character says and the different meaning the audience is likely to take from it.
Hilda Hulme has argued that the audience construes "Othello's occupation's
gone" in a sense beyond Othello's local intention:

> *Occupation,* as Othello intends it, appears to refer to his victorious general-
> ship, now gone for ever, as his "tranquil mind" is lost. But in this dramatic
> situation, as Iago and the rest of us understand it, the word must also refer to
> his loss of Desdemona; from that place where he has "garnered up" his heart,
> he counts himself discarded (IV.ii.57). It is noteworthy that the verb *occupy,*
> "to cohabit with," was, in Shakespeare's day, in process of being dropped

from decent usage, so that the meaning of "occupation" which Othello himself ignores would be the more vividly present to the Shakespearean audience. Doll Tearsheet, for instance, cries out that Pistol's claim to being a
captain will bring all captains into disrepute; the word "captain" will become

> as odious as the word occupy, which was an excellent good
worde before it was il sorted.
>
> (*2 Henry IV,* II.iv.161, Quarto 1600)

I do not want to make too much of this tiny point, but it seems to me that
there is here another indication of the dangers in Othello's position: he
stands at a certain distance from the world of common men; only rarely
does Shakespeare allow the audience to identify itself with him; at this point
of the play we are listening to his words with ears more sensitive, less noble,
than his own.[9]

I would add only this. Othello's standing at a distance from the world of
common people makes him ready at any moment to withdraw into a static
and purely picturesque world; as in the great speech in which he deploys in a
pageant or tapestry the entities to which he says "Farewell":

> O, now, for ever
> Farewell the tranquil mind! farewell content!
> Farewell the plumed troop, and the big wars,
> That make ambition virtue! O, farewell!
> Farewell the neighing steed, and the shrill trump,
> The spirit-stirring drum, th' ear-piercing fife,
> The royal banner, and all quality,
> Pride, pomp and circumstance of glorious war!
> And, O you mortal engines, whose rude throats
> Th' immortal Jove's dread clamours counterfeit,
> Farewell! Othello's occupation's gone!
>
> (III.iii.347–357)

It is a mark of his high Senecan style that these entities appear slowly, one in
procession after another, and that the character of the language is statuesque.
One phrase incites another of the same quality, and while they are all eventually comprehended by the word "occupation," each is autonomous while
the procession goes on. The instigation of one phrase is the quality of its
predecessor rather than the tragic situation that calls for expression in imme-

diately personal terms. The phrases are certainly far removed from the anguish that impelled Othello to compose the semblance of his loss. His belief that Desdemona has been unfaithful to him has put an end to contentment, but he identifies that contentment with military career, pomp and circumstance, not with his marital and domestic satisfactions. The recital of that career makes a parade in which Desdemona does not appear.

But this speech is merely an extreme instance of the flair of Senecan style: it is a style that delights in setting words free from their standard duty toward objects and referents. Several occasions of this freedom feature stories which may be true or not. Iago is not the only storyteller. There is Othello himself, and as early as act I, scene iii we are allowed to imagine how he won Desdemona. He didn't practice witchcraft, but he told her stories that amounted to witchcraft, or at best a traveler's tall tales. His speech to the senators is a story about his success as a storyteller:

> Her father lov'd me, oft invited me,
> Still question'd me the story of my life,
> From year to year; the battles, sieges, fortunes,
> That I have pass'd:
> I ran it through, even from my boyish days,
> To the very moment that he bade me tell it.
> Wherein I spake of most disastrous chances,
> Of moving accidents by flood and field;
> Of hair-breadth scapes i' th' imminent deadly breach;
> Of being taken by the insolent foe;
> And sold to slavery, and my redemption thence,
> And with it all my travel's history;
> Wherein of antres vast, and deserts idle,
> Rough quarries, rocks and hills, whose heads touch heaven,
> It was my hint to speak, such was the process:
> And of the Cannibals, that each other eat;
> The Anthropophagi, and men whose heads
> Do grow beneath their shoulders: this to hear
> Would Desdemona seriously incline.
>
> (I.iii.128–146)

What are we to make of this? Heads that touch heaven, heads beneath someone's shoulders: likely stories. Desdemona is remarkably susceptible to stories—"She'd come again, and with a greedy ear / Devour up my discourse"—she can't separate her sense of Othello from his yarns or bring irony to bear on them. Such traveler's tales were indeed current, and Shakespeare could have found them at hand in Mandeville, Raleigh, Holland's Pliny, and—the likeliest source—John Pory's translation of Leo Africanus's *Geographical History of Africa,* published in 1600.[10] We are not obliged to agree with Iago that Othello secured Desdemona by bragging and telling her "fantastical lies," but the charge is not self-evidently absurd. Othello's report of his success allows us to think of his rhetoric rather than his truth:

> . . . . my story being done,
> She gave me for my pains a world of sighs;
> She swore i' faith 'twas strange, 'twas passing strange;
> 'Twas pitiful, 'twas wondrous pitiful;
> She wish'd she had not heard it, yet she wish'd
> That heaven had made her such a man: she thank'd me,
> And bade me, if I had a friend that lov'd her,
> I should but teach him how to tell my story,
> And that would woo her. Upon this hint I spake:
> She lov'd me for the dangers I had pass'd,
> And I lov'd her that she did pity them.
> This only is the witchcraft I have us'd.

(I.iii.158–169)

But it was enough, since it was the witchcraft of narrative. Othello's repeated phrases are the formulae of epic narrative, tuned now for domestic interiors; they belong to fable rather than to truth. Desdemona seems to know that she has fallen in love with stories that she identifies with the storyteller, but she doesn't consider extricating herself from the web of words, true or false. Her view of it as an adventure is consistent with its having begun as a sequence of adventure stories:

> That I did love the Moor, to live with him,
> My downright violence, and scorn [storm?] of fortunes,
> May trumpet to the world . . .

(I.iii.248–250)

The trumpet is the right instrument to sound her life now. "I saw Othello's visage in his mind," she says, but she fell in love with his narrative voice and

then with his noble Moorish body; till finally she received his mind as completion of his person, voice, and name. The repetitions of "strange," "passing
strange," "pitiful," "wondrous pitiful," "She wish'd she had not heard it, yet she
wish'd / That heaven had made her such a man" hold her within a strictly
verbal or narrative setting. The conceit of wishing that heaven had made her
such a man, if we take *her* as an accusative, is an entirely verbal extravagance; if
we take it to mean "I wish heaven had made such a man for me," the sentence
refers ambiguously to Othello or, by a later irony, to Cassio, a friend who loved
her. Later, in act III, scene iii, Desdemona reminds Othello that Cassio "came
a-wooing with you," so a motif of tragic possibility is introduced quite early in
the play. Words, words, words.

Some of the stories are out-and-out lies. Iago's story to Othello about
Cassio's dream of Desdemona is a lie, but a plausible one, and extraordinarily
erotic:

> I lay with Cassio lately,
> And being troubled with a raging tooth,
> I could not sleep.
> There are a kind of men so loose of soul,
> That in their sleeps will mutter their affairs,
> One of this kind is Cassio:
> In sleep I heard him say "Sweet Desdemona,
> Let us be wary, let us hide our loves";
> And then, sir, would he gripe and wring my hand,
> Cry out, "Sweet creature!" and then kiss me hard,
> As if he pluck'd up kisses by the roots,
> That grew upon my lips, then laid his leg
> Over my thigh, and sigh'd, and kiss'd, and then
> Cried "Cursed fate, that gave thee to the Moor!"
>
> (III.iii.419–433)

The toothache may be true. The rest is an act of pure and impure imagination,
art for art's sake, narration for the sake of narration. The fact that it has an
immediate purpose does not constrain its self-performative zest. No wonder it
begins with the freedom of a dream. In *The Interpretation of Dreams*, Freud
says that the mind in dreaming "does not think, calculate or judge . . . ; it
restricts itself to giving things a new form."[11] Iago can give things a new form
the more easily because there was never an old form he respected.

Othello's story about the handkerchief, his first gift to Desdemona, presents a different problem. In act III, scene iii Desdemona drops the handkerchief, Emilia picks it up and gives it to Iago, Iago tells Othello that he has
seen Cassio wiping his beard with it. In the next scene, after some talk of
hands, Othello asks Desdemona to produce the handkerchief. Desdemona lies
about it, pretends she still has it. Othello then tells her a long story about its
provenance; how a sibyl made it from silk of hallowed worms and dyed it in
mummy; how an Egyptian gave it to Othello's mother:

> She told her, while she kept it
> 'Twould make her amiable, and subdue my father
> Entirely to her love: but if she lost it,
> Or made a gift of it, my father's eye
> Should hold her loathly, and his spirits should hunt
> After new fancies: she dying, gave it me,
> And bid me, when my fate would have me wive,
> To give it her; I did so, and take heed on't,
> Make it a darling, like your precious eye,
> To lose, or give't away, were such perdition
> As nothing else could match.

(III.iv.56–66)

It is impossible to say whether this is true. Othello may have made it up on the
spot to browbeat Desdemona. There may be magic in the web of the handkerchief, or he may just now have put it there. It is all news to Desdemona,
who is sorry that she has mislaid his first gift but can't really believe it means
the end of the world. Othello storms out, and Desdemona thinks something
else must be the matter, some affair of state; it can't be just the handkerchief.
The scene could be played either way. Othello could be shown telling Desdemona the truth; or mischievously talking himself into attaching erotic significance to the handkerchief, one superstitious word inciting another to the
point of putting magic in the web of the narrative. In the first case Othello
would be justified in feeling cross: a gift from a lover should be treasured. In
the second, he is indulging himself in what Eliot (taking the word from Jules
de Gaultier) called *bovarysme,* a determination to see things as they are not; or
worse still, pretending to do so to make Desdemona distraught. The story
begins with a handkerchief and ends with talk of perdition.

The contrast between Greek tragedy and Senecan tragedy in Eliot's description of them is one we may play fast and loose with, short of abandoning it. The values we think of as Greek, for the moment, are those of observation with a view to telling the truth. Or rather, telling the truth of things established in the world independently of one's volition. Botticelli is Greek in the *Birth of Spring* when he includes in the meadow twenty-one plants distinguishable by a botanist. Vermeer is Greek in painting a street in Delft such that I might think I lived there. But the values we think of as Senecan, for the moment, are counterfactual, they regard events as nuisances and plan to circumvent them. As in Gide's *Counterfeiters,* where Edouard decides that he will not make use of Boris's suicide for his book. There is something "peremptory, irrefutable, brutal, outrageously real" about things that happen, he notes, and he determines to ignore their insistence. "I accept reality coming as a proof in support of my thought, but not as preceding it."[12] That attitude has the authentic Senecan willfulness. In another version it entails what Stephen Greenblatt calls improvisation.

I'll say a little about this concept as Greenblatt uses it in his *Renaissance Self-Fashioning.* The gist of what I have to say is that Greenblatt finds in politics and especially in the practices of colonial power what I see as capacities of language, available to anyone. It is a matter of choice whether one recites these as an allegory of political power.

Greenblatt means by improvisation one's ability to transform someone else's reality into a manipulable fiction. Improvisation is made possible "by the subversive perception of another's truth as an ideological construct."[13] Two of the characteristic acts of improvisation are displacement and absorption. Displacement is the process by which a "prior symbolic structure is compelled to coexist with other centers of attention that do not necessarily conflict with the original structure but are not swept up in its gravitational pull."[14] The effect of this, presumably, is to induce either a feeling of psychic mobility or the Stoic consolation of feeling released from official structures of meaning and definition. The sense of mobility may be enjoyed or feared. Some people want to believe that they may at any moment choose a new mask and live through it for the time being. Others need to feel secure in their sole identity and worry only about losing it. Absorption is the "process by which a symbolic structure is taken into the ego so completely that it ceases to exist as an external phenomenon."[15] As in "The Man with the Blue Guitar," where Stevens speaks of reducing the monster to myself.

The improvisations of power depend on two assumptions. The first is that "one is not forever fixed in a single, divinely sanctioned identity." Iago makes this claim most vigorously when he tells Roderigo that " 'tis in ourselves, that we are thus, or thus: our bodies are gardens, to the which our wills are gardeners, so that if we will plant nettles, or sow lettuce, set hyssop, and weed up thyme; supply it with one gender of herbs, or distract it with many; either to have it sterile with idleness, or manur'd with industry, why, the power, and corrigible authority of this, lies in our wills" (I.iii.319–326). The most thoroughgoing example of improvisation and displacement I can think of is not in *Othello* but in Nabokov's variation on *Othello,* the story "That in Aleppo Once." Here—and the divergence from the play is astonishing—the power of improvisation is appropriated by the Desdemona figure, who inscribes her husband in a monstrous series of stories, some of them plausible, many of them apparently lies. Her husband can defend himself only by conceiving the notion that his wife has never existed; but he confesses that he is dreadfully unhappy and that the whole episode may end, like Othello's first act of punishment, in Aleppo.

The second assumption on which improvisation relies is that a language is just as ready to serve one cause as another: it lives without preference or conviction. Greenblatt, like Joel Altmann in *The Tudor Play of Mind,* makes much of the practice of *argumentum in utramque partem* in Renaissance education, the cultivation of the scholar's power to argue persuasively on either side of a question. But he emphasizes not sophistry but the power of narrative improvisations to replace ostensibly stable structures of feeling. These structures, the narrator silently assumes, have no rights, they are merely ideological. Iago is Greenblatt's chief example of such narrative interventions and improvisations. He rarely argues. But he makes everybody submit to the stories he tells for them. He tells those around him stories that have only one likely conclusion; or he gives them fragments of a story that they can complete with only one end. If the stories they have told themselves are high-flown or idealistic, Iago brings them low by showing that worldly motives can account for the facts just as well.

I have little to say about Greenblatt's main argument. He holds that Othello's conversion to Christianity constitutes his identity, and that, as a convert, he is extreme in his acceptance of Christian doctrine on the subject of marriage and sex. According to this doctrine as enunciated by Jerome, among others, adultery is not only the sin of copulating with another's spouse, it is also the sin of loving to excess one's own spouse. Jerome recalled and endorsed the Stoic epigram that all excess of love is adulterous. Iago's whole strategy, Greenblatt claims, is "to play upon Othello's buried perception of his own sexual relations with Desdemona as adulterous."[16] It must be deeply buried; I can't find any occasion in the play on which Othello confesses this sin. At the end he claims that he loved Desdemona not wisely but too well. It is a confession of imprudence, not of sin.

However, Greenblatt's emphasis on improvisation is useful in linguistic terms. Take for instance the theme of deception. Desdemona deceived her father by eloping with Othello. Brabantio warns him:

> Look to her, Moor, have a quick eye to see:
> She has deceiv'd her father, may do thee.

> (I.iii.292–293)

Othello answers:

> My life upon her faith; honest Iago . . .

Much later, in act III, scene iii, Othello is desperately fending off Iago's talk of jealousy by saying

> Nor from mine own weak merits will I draw
> The smallest fear, or doubt of her revolt,
> For she had eyes, and chose me. No, Iago,
> I'll see before I doubt . . .

> (III.iii.191–194)

Iago takes up the theme of eyes:

> Look to your wife, observe her well with Cassio;
> Wear your eye thus, not jealous, nor secure.

> (III.iii.201–202)

and he reminds Othello of Brabantio's experience:

> She did deceive her father, marrying you;
> And when she seem'd to shake and fear your looks,
> She lov'd them most.

It's not clear when Desdemona shook and feared Othello's looks. Nothing of this is shown. Maybe we are to assume that Othello told the story of his life so histrionically that he made Desdemona quake. Whatever the case, he agrees with Iago: "And so she did." Then by way of acoustic associations, Iago keeps up the talk of seeing, going through "seeming" to sealing:

> She that so young could give out such a seeming,
> To seal her father's eyes up, close as oak,
> He thought 'twas witchcraft . . .

(III.iii.279–281)

And in next to no time Othello is talking of Desdemona's conduct as "nature erring from itself" and of adultery in women as inevitable:

> 'Tis destiny, unshunnable, like death:
> Even then this forked plague is fated to us,
> When we do quicken.

(III.iii.279–281)

In this sequence, several "symbolic structures" have been undermined, thrown into mobility such that any one of them might by caprice or ill luck rush ahead and act.

Often, too, this subversive mobility is made to occur in one word. Think of the words "follow," "blest," "think," "know," "indeed," and—a word Empson wrestles with in *The Structure of Complex Words*—"honest." Think how they are turned into equivocations. "Follow" starts out innocuously when Rode-rigo protests to Iago that if he hates the Moor he shouldn't follow him, shouldn't be one of his company. Within twenty lines, Iago has loosed the word from its duty by speaking it twice, and has diverted it from its stability to the point at which he can truthfully claim, "In following him, I follow but myself." In this play, one has only to repeat a word or hover upon it or say it—like "honest"—fifty-two times, and the earth seems to tremble under one's feet.

Improvisation as absorption is harder to document, though Othello falls victim to it easily. The process by which a "symbolic structure is taken into the ego so completely that it ceases to exist as an external phenomenon" is rife in him because his mind is hopelessly susceptible to certain images and analogies; mainly of the pomp of war, and of natural forces challenging him to rival them. In act III, scene iii, when he is working himself up to an oath of vengeance and Iago keeps him going by interrupting, "Patience, I say, your mind perhaps may change," Othello drowns the possibility of change by correlating his violence with the Pontic sea:

> Never, Iago. Like to the Pontic sea,
> Whose icy current, and compulsive course,
> Ne'er feels retiring ebb, but keeps due on
> To the Propontic, and the Hellespont:
> Even so my bloody thoughts, with violent pace
> Shall ne'er look back, ne'er ebb to humble love,
> Till that a capable and wide revenge
> Swallow them up.
>
>   (III.iii.460–467)

The specious logic of that "Even so" is enforced by the personifications—"ne'er look back" and "ne'er ebb"—till the transferred epithet "wide" makes "Swallow them up" inevitable.

Absorption includes, too, the process by which the primary meaning of a word yields to one of its secondary meanings, to the point at which nothing of the old meaning survives. The most appalling instance is the word "lie." In act III, scene iv, Desdemona and the Clown have a bit of foolery with its innocent meaning: to lie, to lodge. "Do you know, sirrah, where the Lieutenant Cassio lies?" she asks him, and he pretends to think she means telling lies. Desdemona then removes the equivocation by saying "lodges," but the Clown continues fooling with lies. But the foolery is innocuous, since it veers only between lodging and telling lies, and no one has accused Cassio of telling lies. But in the next scene Othello asks Iago whether Cassio said anything, and as soon as "lie" is spoken, Othello catches the sinister meaning and drives himself into every bewilderment the word allows:

> IAGO: He hath, my lord, but be you well assur'd,
> No more than he'll unswear.
> OTHELLO: What hath he said?
> IAGO: Faith, that he did . . . I know not what he did.

OTHELLO: But what?

IAGO: Lie.

OTHELLO: With her?

IAGO: With her, on her, what you will.

OTHELLO: Lie with her, lie on her! We say lie on her, when they belie her. Lie
with her! That's fulsome—handkerchief—confessions—handkerchief!—To
confess, and be hanged for his labour;—first, to be hanged, and then to
confess.—I tremble at it. Nature would not invest herself in such shadowing
passion without some instruction. It is not words that shakes me thus. Pish!
Noses, ears and lips.—Is't possible?—Confess—handkerchief!—O devil!

(IV.i.30–43)

And he falls into a seizure.

"It is not words that shake me thus," Othello says, but we know it is. The
innocent word "lie" and one of its derivations—to belie her, tell lies about
her—can't hold out against the sexual meaning, whether its accompanying
preposition is "with" or "on." The sinister meaning and its imagery of noses,
ears, and lips send Othello into a swoon. In the swoon, his body is smothered
by these images, so introjected it can't breathe. It is an extreme version of the
state of mind Desdemona expresses in act IV, scene ii, when Othello starts
treating their room in the castle as a brothel, Emilia as brothel-keeper, Desdemona as prostitute, and words as if they retained every quality but their sense.
She cries out:

Upon my knees, what doth your speech import?
I understand a fury in your words,
But not the words.

(IV.ii.31–33)

In the end, it is Desdemona who turns the tragedy Greek. She, too, tells a
story, but it does not take part in the improvisations of power. The story of
her mother's maid Barbary is as near to pure narrative as one could imagine; it
has an air of balladry about it, as if its wisdom came from afar. It is also, in
effect, the story of Desdemona and Othello, but no one is meant to be op-
pressed by it:

My mother had a maid call'd Barbary,
She was in love, and he she lov'd prov'd mad,

And did forsake her; she had a song of "willow,"
An old thing 'twas, but it express'd her fortune,
And she died singing it; that song to-night
Will not go from my mind.

(IV.iii.26–31)

The translucent style here tells of stability of reference, achieved over several generations, the willow song and those forsaken women.

In the end, but too late, this Greek translucency is restored to the play. When Othello warns Desdemona of perjury and demands that she confess her sins, I am inclined to think better of Greenblatt's interpretation of the play in this respect. Othello's extravagance seems to call for an explanation. But the play soon resolves matters on secular considerations. Emilia comes to understand what has happened, why Iago took the handkerchief, why he placed it in Cassio's room, and how he set the whole tragedy in motion. The truth comes out. Othello asks Cassio to forgive him, and because he will not speak further to Iago he turns aside to Cassio or someone else and, in a question of heartbreaking indirectness, asks:

Will you, I pray, demand that demi-devil
Why he hath thus ensnar'd my soul and body?

(V.ii.302–303)

The decorum, the patrician hesitation over the interpolated "I pray," and then the change of tone in "demand that demi-devil"—"pray" and "demand" being cognate verbs but abrupt thereafter in their difference of tone—are proof yet again of Shakespeare's genius with word and gesture. Cassio explains the handkerchief, Lodovico announces Othello's arrest, Cassio is to take charge in Cyprus, Iago is to be tortured into truth, Othello kills himself in an act that at once punishes him and, with emphatic ceremony, recalls his heroic deeds on behalf of Venice. He dies, falling on the marital bed:

I kiss'd thee ere I kill'd thee, no way but this,
Killing myself, to die upon a kiss.

(V.ii.359–360)

Lodovico has the last word, handing over authority to Gratiano, while he prepares to sail to Venice and report with heavy heart what has occurred. The truth available to observation, enhanced by justice, has been restored. Words are to serve again, giving up their claim to autonomy.

So what happens in *Othello?* There has been much debate about the marriage, its status in Venice, and when and where we are to assume it was consummated, if it was. I agree with those who say that it was consummated in Cyprus, and that Shakespeare's reason for changing the story of a settled marriage, as it appears in Cinthio's version, was to make it plausible that Desdemona and Othello should elope in high passion but that they should not know each other very well. Otherwise Iago would have great difficulty pouring the poison of suspicion into Othello's ears. Othello is not a fool, though we are permitted to think that he might be. I don't agree with those who say that the marriage was never consummated and that Othello's sexual frustration caused the catastrophe.

I take seriously, as a possible answer to the question—What happens in *Othello?*—the passage in chapter 9 of *Ulysses,* set in the National Library in Dublin, where Stephen Dedalus says of Shakespeare, with *Hamlet* and several other plays in mind: "In *Cymbeline,* in *Othello* he is bawd and cuckold. He acts and is acted on. Lover of an ideal or a perversion, like José he kills the real Carmen. His unremitting intellect is the hornmad Iago ceaselessly willing that the moor in him shall suffer."[17] The Othello in Iago is presumably the man of a constant, loving nature as Iago described him in act II, scene i. Iago is indeed hornmad, just as much given to sexual jealousy as the maddened Othello becomes: he thinks, on no evidence, that his wife has slept with Othello and with Cassio. He has himself been in love with Desdemona. So it is conceivable that he should punish the Othello he feels in himself and use Cassio and Desdemona as means of punishment. This motive, too, can be recognized as a conflict of styles. Iago's common style, his improvisations of power by way of language, are inevitably turned upon Othello's style, the "Othello music" so richly appreciated by G. Wilson Knight—

> If it were now to die,
> 'Twere now to be most happy; for I fear
> My soul hath her content so absolute
> That not another comfort like to this
> Succeeds in unknown fate.

(II.i.218–222)

It is also much to the point that Iago on one occasion speaks in Othello's style, when he promises himself the pleasure of knowing that Othello will never again be at peace:

> Look where he comes, not poppy, nor mandragora,
> Nor all the drowsy syrups of the world,
> Shall ever medicine thee to that sweet sleep
> Which thou owedst yesterday.
>
> (III.iii.335–338)

If I were permitted the conceit of saying that one style may hate another and especially when it feels the other as an alien element in itself, I would point to the reductive, worldly tone as characterizing Iago's style and to the high, noble, epic style as Othello's. Othello's style would then be a scandal to Iago, a disgusting sign of grandeur, all the more repellent if he had to hear it in himself. Iago's cynical style would appear to Othello and everyone else as sign of honesty, befitting a good fellow ready on all occasions to be the best of company, a man of the world. Othello's style has a posthumous air about it; the values it celebrates are already defunct: he is, as R. P. Blackmur said of Irving Babbitt, a praiser of gone times because he has none of his own. Iago is in full though sordid possession of his own. That is why, when he is finished with his time, he refuses to speak:

> Demand me nothing: what you know, you know:
> From this time forth I never will speak word.
>
> (V.ii.303–304)

His refusal corresponds, in the low style, to Othello's terminal eloquence, the self-deluding extravagance of his high style.

So what happens? A modern, low style sets out to destroy an ancient style that it discerns in itself; achieves this aim; but is destroyed in turn by the ceremony of the play, the force that makes for integrity and truth and finds its true voice of feeling in Desdemona. So in a production of the play I would like to see emphasized the scene (act IV, scene iii) in which Desdemona and Emilia talk Greek truth about men and women and the ways of the world. Emilia speaks the narrow truth of Shylock[18]:

> . . . and have not we affections,
> Desires for sport, and frailty, as men have?

> Then let them use us well: else let them know,
> The ills we do, their ills instruct us so.
>
> (IV.iii.103–104)

But Desdemona rhymes a better ethic:

> Good night, good night: heaven me such uses send,
> Not to pick bad from bad, but by bad mend!
>
> (IV.iii.105–106)

Reading *Gulliver's Travels*

Houses of decay, mine, his and all. You told the Clongowes
gentry you had an uncle a judge and an uncle a general in
the army. Come out of them, Stephen. Beauty is not there.
Nor in the stagnant bay of Marsh's library where you read
the fading prophecies of Joachim Abbas. For whom? The
hundredheaded rabble of the cathedral close. A hater of his
kind ran from them to the wood of madness, his mane
foaming in the moon, his eyeballs stars. Houyhnhnm,
horsenostrilled. The oval equine faces, Temple, Buck
Mulligan, Foxy Campbell, Lanternjaws. Abbas father,
furious dean, what offence laid fire to their brains? Paff!
Descende, calve, ut ne amplius decalveris.
—*James Joyce,* Ulysses

On October 28, 1726, the London printer Benjamin
Motte issued the first volume of *Travels into Several Remote
Nations of the World* by Lemuel Gulliver, "first a surgeon,
and then a captain of several ships." A few readers knew that
the real author was Jonathan Swift, dean of St. Patrick's
Cathedral—"the cathedral close"—in Dublin. Presumably
they took the book as a squib thrown off from the dean's

official life, or a satire on those in power in London who had banished him to Dublin in 1714. The book was an immediate success: two further printings were required in 1726, and two more in 1727. John Gay wrote to Swift on November 17, 1726, to report that "from the highest to the lowest it is universally read, from the cabinet-council to the nursery." Some readers enjoyed it as an attack on Whiggery in general and Sir Robert Walpole in particular. Those who brought it into the nursery read it as a yarn populated by big men and little men. Bolingbroke was evidently the first reader to interpret it as an offensive book, a "design of evil consequence to depreciate human nature," as Gay reported to Swift.[1] That sense of the book became common twenty-five or thirty years later: *Gulliver's Travels* is not innocent, a "pleasant humorous book" or "such a merry work," as Swift's friend Arbuthnot called it, but a libel on mankind.[2]

It is essential to the character of *Gulliver's Travels* that it allows readers to mistake it for something else which in certain respects it resembles: a serious travel book, a parody travel book, a philosophical allegory like *Candide,* a vision of Utopia, like More's book. The book is a simulacrum, inserted in the space between whatever at first it may appear to be and what on second thought it may otherwise appear to be. It has lasted for 250 years, mainly because readers can't be certain that they know what kind of book they're reading, even if they know that a trick of impersonation is somehow being played on them. The book is as bizarre in its way as, in quite another way, *A Tale of a Tub.* Many readers have read both books and decided, like the scholars in Brobdingnag who examine Gulliver, that the object of attention is *Relplum Scalcath,* or *Lusus Naturae,* a freak of nature.

The most useful preliminary description of *Gulliver's Travels* that I have seen is Northrop Frye's account of the genre it embodies. I refer to his essay "The Four Forms of Prose Fiction," according to which the forms are novel, confession, romance, and anatomy. Most people, Frye says, would call *Gulliver's Travels* fiction but not a novel: "It must then be another form of fiction, as it certainly has a form, and we feel that we are turning from the novel to this form, whatever it is, when we turn from Rousseau's *Emile* to Voltaire's *Candide,* or from Butler's *The Way of All Flesh* to the Erewhon books, or from Huxley's *Point Counter Point* to *Brave New World.* The form thus has its own traditions, and, as the examples of Butler and Huxley show, has preserved some integrity even under the ascendancy of the novel. Its existence is easy enough to demonstrate, and no one will challenge the statement that the literary ancestry of *Gulliver's Travels* and *Candide* runs through Rabelais and Erasmus to Lucian."[3] *Gulliver's Travels*, then, is an anatomy, as in Burton's *Anatomy of Melancholy*, where anatomy means dissection or analysis. Frye calls it Menippean satire, too, a type of fiction that "deals less with people as such than with mental attitudes." In this respect it differs from the novel. In the anatomy, "pedants, bigots, cranks, parvenus, virtuosi, enthusiasts, rapacious and incompetent men of all kinds are handled in terms of the 'humor' or ruling passion, their occupational approach to life as distinct from their social behavior." It is a feature of the anatomy that characterization is stylized rather than realistic: people are presented as mouthpieces of the ideas or prejudices they hold. In an anatomy the chief character is often a pedant, a lunatic of one idea. Reading *Gulliver's Travels*, one is bemused to find Gulliver keeping on doing the same thing, getting himself into the same predicament, like Charlie Chaplin or Buster Keaton. A constant theme in the anatomy, Frye remarks, is ridicule of the *philosophus gloriosus*. Lucian ridicules the Greek philosophers, Rabelais and Erasmus the scholastics, Swift the Cartesians and the Royal Society, Voltaire the Leibnitzians, Peacock the Romantics, Samuel Butler the Darwinists, Huxley the behaviorists. The reason for this is "that, while the novelist sees evil and folly as social diseases, the Menippean satirist sees them as diseases of the intellect, as a kind of maddened pedantry which the *philosophus gloriosus* at once symbolizes and defines." The anatomy, finally, "presents us with a vision of the world in terms of a single intellectual pattern." It often achieves this pattern by imposing upon its image of life a "logical and self-consistent shift of perspective, presenting it as Lilliputian or Brobdingnagian," or by telling the story "from the point of view of an ass, a savage, or a drunk." Or else "it will take the form of a 'marvelous journey' and present a caricature of a familiar society as the logical structure of an imaginary one." Comedy arises from the disjunction between a point of view, maintained with unquestioned lucidity, and our conviction that we, not these lunatics, know what life is really like.

My reference to *A Tale of a Tub* allows me to remark that *Gulliver's Travels*, like the *Tale*, exhibits instances of irony stable and unstable, to use Wayne Booth's distinction in *The Rhetoric of Irony*. In stable irony we have only to take one interpretative step and we find ourselves back on solid ground. When Gulliver offers to make cannon-guns and explosives for use by the king of

Brobdingnag, we have to make only one move to see that Gulliver and the European civilization for which he speaks are being reflected on. But the irony in *Gulliver's Travels* is often unstable: if we make one interpretative move, we find ourselves still on shifting sands, as in the Voyage to the Houyhnhnms. In stable irony there is always an imaginary point from which the world is to be viewed in its entirety. In unstable irony there is no such point. Instead, there is a sequence of equivocations which we bring to an end only arbitrarily, when we have had as much equivocation as we can bear. Nor is the irony Kierkegaardian—that is, propelled by the ironist's desire to feel free, to relish the freedom of having no motive other than his own enjoyment. We have no such impression of *Gulliver's Travels*. Swift's irony in that book is local, opportunistic, and irregular. You may call it negative if, with F. R. Leavis, you construe the book as sustained by no system of values; unlike, say, Pope's *The Dunciad*. If, reading the *Tale*, you are not happy with the serene and peaceful possession of being well deceived, you may choose to be undeceived, with no greater boon of happiness.

It is generally held that the mischief of *Gulliver's Travels* is postponed till the fourth voyage and Gulliver's encounters with the Houyhnhnms and the Yahoos. In fact, it begins with Swift's presentation of Gulliver. Normally, when writers of fiction establish first-person narration, they give their narrators enough capacity to understand their experiences or the events they witness; not necessarily every form of intelligence, but enough to report on the events. Some writers, notably Henry James, can't bear to have their tales told by an idiot, a fool, or a villain. James knew that such people exist and must be acknowledged, but he didn't think they should have the responsibility of delivering the main issues or of being themselves the chief personages of the fiction. He wondered about Fielding's procedure in *Tom Jones* and only reluctantly came to think that it was acceptable: while Tom hasn't a brain in his head, Fielding has enough brains for both of them. While Gulliver is not an idiot, a fool, or a villain, he is barely qualified to take the force and point of his experience. He is given some competence in navigation and in the rudiments of medicine, but he can deal with experience only when it comes to him in a form he can count or measure. As Hugh Kenner has said of him, he is "aware of nothing but incremental evidence."[4] Swift has created one of the most memorable characters in fiction by giving him no character at all, no imagination, no depth of feeling, no resources of inner life beyond the attributes of a hack reporter on a local newspaper. He has no sense of anything beneath the visible surface, no powers of divination, and no inkling of the need of such powers.

We generally assume that each of us sees the world from his or her own point of view. It would be distressing if we found that our sense of the world differed in fundamental respects from everyone else's. Normally we take it for granted that our perceptions don't differ drastically from those of most other people. We assume that things, by and large, are as we see them. We make for ourselves a picture of the world, perhaps a rudimentary diagram, and we act upon it. Up to that point, we don't differ much from Gulliver. But when we say that Gulliver has no imagination, we also mean that he doesn't feel the lack of it because he is so busy reporting events as if they had only to be reckoned, weighed, and counted. He thrives—or at least gets along—on the penury of his interests. So readers must play an unusually active part in constructing the book. We can't take Gulliver's word as the true last word on any subject, though as the first word we have no choice but to rely on it. In matters of judgment, discrimination, and the relation between one thing and another, readers have to do most of the work for themselves. Gulliver has merely indicated that there is work to be done; he reports the occasions that call for judgment. Again a contrast with James's fiction is appropriate. When we read *The Ambassadors* we find that our main task is to keep up with Lambert Strether, rising to his occasions of perception and divination. We have to think and feel with him up and down and all around the town. In the end we may decide that he's not an impeccable interpreter of the events, and that we are justified in trying to go beyond him or think aside from him. But in *Gulliver's Travels* we start with a conviction that Gulliver's sense of life differs from our own and is palpably inadequate to the reality it negotiates.

Swift sends Gulliver voyaging into several remote nations of the world, and he gives him an absurdly small supply of qualifications. He is allowed to bring with him only the attributes normally found adequate in a settled society—a simple frame of reference, modest expectations, and the disposition of a practical man. We begin to suspect that Gulliver is as he is, not because God made him so but because England made him so. If there is an English tradition in politics, education, and morality, it is inscribed in him: it discloses itself in a sense of life that settles comfortably for its constraints and regards as folly and vanity any interests that range beyond a narrow circle. We are to take things one after another, preferably in the order in which our senses encounter them. England has made Gulliver, written a program for him beyond which he does not stray. His duty coincides with his inclination: to station himself in front of events and to report them in the sequence of their impingement on him. Penuriously direct prose is the means of delivery. Someone else, the reader, must act on the information that Gulliver supplies. The comedy of the book arises from the fact that a mind programmed to observe nothing more than ordinary events in England must bring its rudimentary attributes to bear on situations inordinate and bizarre. Trained to observe certain limited constituents of experience, Gulliver's mind has never been instructed in the art of dealing with monsters.

When I say that England made Lemuel Gulliver, I mean to disagree with Terry Eagleton's claim, in *Heathcliff and the Great Hunger,* that *Gulliver's Travels* is about Ireland. Gulliver, according to Eagleton, is an "appropriate figure for an Ascendancy which was both colonized and colonialist." I can't read the book that way. It seems to me a book about the susceptibility of the human mind to the experiences it happens to undergo; it denotes the conditions, mostly demeaning, under which the mind somehow manages to persist. Samuel Johnson said of *Gulliver's Travels* that when once you have thought of big men and little men, it is very easy to do all the rest. It's not at all easy. Or rather: that isn't what's going on. Swift's real achievement is to attract into the orbit of big men and little men a mind somehow capable of surviving experience without understanding it. In the end, Swift darkens the comedy by showing the same mind succumbing to its experience and nearly dying in the event.

In the first three voyages, the comedy is fairly simple: it is the comedy of disproportion that arises from the differences between ends and means, essence and existence, absolutes and relativities, big men and little men, Big Enders and Little Enders, steady states and floating islands. It is part of the rhetoric of the voyage to Lilliput that we are to be impressed by big people and to despise little people. On every occasion on which such words as "little" and "diminutive" appear, we are to feel contempt for the people to whom they refer. Gulliver adopts the grandiloquent style of address so prevalent in Lilliput. When he prevents war between Lilliput and Blefuscu by pulling the ships out of the Blefuscu harbor, he addresses the ruler of Lilliput in a loud voice: "Long live the most puissant Emperor of Lilliput!" When he is leaving Lilliput, and the emperor and his family come out to say goodbye, Gulliver reports that "I lay down on my face to kiss his hand." He is already brainwashed.

The rhythm of brainwashing is worked up more elaborately in the second voyage; appropriately, since Gulliver is now the diminutive one. When the king of Brobdingnag has listened for a while to Gulliver's account of life in England, he "observed, how contemptible a Thing was human Grandeur, which could be mimicked by such diminutive Insects as I." Gulliver is inclined to take offense, but on second thought not:

> But, as I was not in a Condition to resent Injuries, so, upon mature Thoughts, I began to doubt whether I were injured or no. For, after having been accustomed several Months to the Sight and Converse of this People, and observed every Object upon which I cast mine Eyes, to be of proportionable Magnitude; the Horror I had first conceived from their Bulk and Aspect was so far worn off, that if I had then beheld a Company of *English* Lords and Ladies in their Finery and Birth-day Cloaths, acting their several Parts in the most courtly Manner of Strutting, and Bowing and Prating; to say the Truth, I should have been strongly tempted to laugh as much at them as this King and his Grandees did at me. Neither indeed could I forbear smiling at my self, when the Queen used to place me upon her Hand towards a Looking-Glass, by which both our Persons appeared before me in full View together; and there could nothing be more ridiculous than the Comparison: So that I really began to imagine my self dwindled many Degrees below my usual Size.[5]

Gulliver is not in a position to resent injuries, so he becomes accustomed to not resenting them. Behaviorism is at work. He starts doubting whether he has cause of resentment. He has begun—as Hermia says in *A Midsummer Night's Dream*—to "choose love by another's eyes." The queen's eyes, for the time being. She keeps a dwarf for her amusement:

> Nothing angred and mortified me so much as the Queen's Dwarf, who being of the lowest Stature that was ever in that Country, (for I verily think he was not full Thirty Foot high) became so insolent at seeing a Creature so much beneath him, that he would always affect to swagger and look big as he passed by me in the Queen's Antichamber, while I was standing on some Table talking with the Lords or Ladies of the Court; and he seldom failed of a smart Word or two upon my Littleness; against which I could only revenge my self by calling him *Brother*, challenging him to wrestle; and such Repartees as are

usual in the Mouths of *Court Pages.* One Day at Dinner, this malicious little Cubb was so nettled with something I had said to him, that raising himself upon the Frame of her Majesty's Chair, he took me up by the Middle, as I was sitting down, not thinking any Harm, and let me drop into a large Silver Bowl of Cream; and then ran away as fast as he could. (107–108)

Here the ironies persist, but virtually every phrase sends them off in a different direction. Choosing derision by another's eyes, Gulliver affects to despise the dwarf—"of the lowest Stature that was ever in that country." But the idiom he uses is the repartee of court pages: "affect to swagger and look big." Gulliver hardly glances at his own posture—"while I was standing on some Table talking with the Lords or Ladies of the Court"—the word "some" gaining the effect of inattention. The malice of "this malicious little Cubb" is already prepared for by the force of "dwindled," "diminutive," and other such words in earlier passages. The full effect is realized by associating the affected dwarf with the English ladies in their strutting, bowing, and prating.

Forty pages later, when Gulliver has left Brobdingnag and is rescued by the ship, he tells the captain that when he first saw the sailors, he thought them "the most little contemptible Creatures I had ever beheld": "For, indeed, while I was in that Prince's Country, I could never endure to look in a Glass after my Eyes had been accustomed to such prodigious Objects; because the Comparison gave me so despicable a Conceit of my self" (147). In Brobdingnag, Gulliver accepts the local system of values so readily that when he goes to see the chief temple and the tower which was reckoned the "highest in the Kingdom," he comes back disappointed; it is hardly more than three thousand feet high.

But the most thorough brainwashing takes effect in the fourth voyage. Gulliver sees the Yahoos and thinks them hideous brutes. He is still an Englishman. But after a while he comes to see himself as very like a Yahoo and different only in the clothes he wears: they run about naked. The conviction of resemblance makes him loathe the Yahoos even more, because it forces him to see his own nature in a hideous form. When he meets the whinnying horses, he finds them impressively reasonable, and they think him a Yahoo, though notably teachable for such a brute. However, the Houyhnhnms soon decide that while Gulliver's learning ability is good for a Yahoo, and while his personal habits are cleaner than one would expect of a Yahoo, in every other respect he comes out badly from the comparison. Gulliver doesn't defend himself in these adjudications: gradually, he is brainwashed enough to find them convincing. Chapter 7 begins:

> The Reader may be disposed to wonder how I could prevail on my self to give so free a Representation of my own Species, among a Race of Mortals who were already too apt to conceive the vilest Opinion of Human Kind, from that entire Congruity betwixt me and their *Yahoos*. But I must freely confess, that the many Virtues of those excellent *Quadrupeds* placed in opposite View to human Corruptions, had so far opened mine Eyes, and enlarged my Understanding, that I began to view the Actions and Passions of Man in a very different Light; and to think the Honour of my own Kind not worth managing; which, besides, it was impossible for me to do before a Person of so acute a Judgment as my Master, who daily convinced me of a thousand Faults in my self, whereof I had not the least Perception before, and which with us would never be numbered even among human Infirmities. I had likewise learned from his Example an utter Detestation of all Falsehood or Disguise; and *Truth* appeared so amiable to me, that I determined upon sacrificing every thing to it. (258)

"So free a Representation": free, in the sense of unceremonious, regardless of narrow conceptions of duty or loyalty, at the risk of irresponsibility. As in Swift's pamphlet against abolishing Christianity: "Great wits love to be free with the highest objects; and if they cannot be allowed a God to revile or renounce, they will speak evil of dignities." The ironies run to "I must freely confess." Must, because I have come to value truth more than anything, and this puts me under obligation, but it also leaves me free in a way you might not appreciate.

Gradually, Gulliver comes to accept the Houyhnhnm view of things, at whatever cost to his self-esteem. He agrees, for instance, that a being whose eyes are placed directly in front, one on each side of his nose and each of them directed straight ahead, can't look far on either side without turning his head; a disability from which Yahoos are exempt. Gulliver admits the point of these comparisons. A mind brainwashed, to begin with, by the England that made him, and later by the forces he meets on the three early voyages, is ready to be brainwashed again by his new masters. Appropriately, the first sign of this process is that Gulliver comes to think the English language "barbarous" by comparison with the language of the Houyhnhnms. The Houyhnhnms don't accept Gulliver as a rational animal, they speak of "those appearances of reason" in him, and decide that instead of being a rational creature he has merely been taught to imitate one: "He added, how I had endeavoured to persuade him, that in my own and other Countries the *Yahoos* acted as the governing, rational Animal, and held the *Houyhnhnms* in Servitude: That, he observed in me all the Qualities of a *Yahoo,* only a little more civilized by some Tincture of Reason; which however was in a Degree as far inferior to the *Houyhnhnm* Race, as the *Yahoos* of their Country were to me" (272). When a further comparison arises between Gulliver and the Yahoos, the Houyhnhnms conclude that it still tells against him. After Gulliver has given his master a full account of human life in England, his master says that "when a creature pretending to reason could be capable of such enormities, he dreaded, lest the corruption of that faculty might be worse than brutality itself." He seemed therefore confident, Gulliver reports, "that instead of reason, we were only possessed of some quality fitted to increase our natural vices." When a young female Yahoo attempts a sexual assault on the naked Gulliver, he has to accept the obvious conclusion: "For now I could no longer deny that I was a real *Yahoo,* in every Limb and Feature, since the Females had a natural Propensity to me as one of their own Species" (267). A few pages later Gulliver thinks to himself: "For, supposing I should escape with Life by some strange Adventure, how could I think with Temper, of passing my Days among *Yahoos,* and relapsing into my old Corruptions, for want of Examples to lead and keep me within the Paths of Virtue" (280). Before he has spent a year in the country of the Houyhnhnms he has contracted, he says, "such a Love and Veneration for the Inhabitants, that I entered on a firm Resolution never to return to human Kind, but to pass the rest of my Life among these admirable *Houyhnhnms* in the Contemplation and Practice of every Virtue; where I could have no Example or Incitement to Vice." After a while, he comes to think it wonderful that these whinnying horses would condescend to distinguish him from the rest of his species, the Yahoos, and he can't bear to look at the reflection of his body in a lake. He begins to imitate the trotting of the horses and to speak in a whinnying voice. Compelled to leave the country of the Houyhnhnms, he prostrates himself to kiss his master's foot, and thinks it wonderful that his master does him the honor of raising the hoof to his mouth. When he leaves, and it looks as if he will be rescued by a passing ship, he sails off in another direction, choosing rather, as he says, to live with barbarians than with European Yahoos. Befriended by the Portuguese captain Don Pedro de Mendez, Gulliver concludes that he should descend to treat him "like an Animal which had some little Portion of Reason." Brought to Lisbon, Gulliver can walk the streets only if his nose is "well stopped with Rue, or sometimes with Tobacco." When the captain offers to give him his best suit of clothes, Gulliver declines the offer, "abhorring to cover myself with any thing that had been on the Back of a *Yahoo*": "I only desired he would lend me two clean Shirts, which having been washed since he wore them, I believed would not so much defile me. These I changed every second Day, and washed them myself" (288). Restored to his home, Gulliver finds himself loathing the sight of his family: "My Wife and Family received me with great Surprize and Joy, because they concluded me certainly dead; but I must freely confess, the Sight of them filled me only with Hatred, Disgust and Contempt; and the more, by reflecting on the near Alliance I had to them. For, although since my unfortunate Exile from the *Houyhnhnm* Country, I had compelled myself to tolerate the Sight of *Yahoos,* and to converse with Don *Pedro de Mendez;* yet my Memory and Imaginations were perpetually filled with the Virtues and Ideas of those exalted *Houyhnhnms.* And when I began to consider, that by copulating with one of the *Yahoo*-Species, I had become a Parent of more, it struck me with the utmost Shame, Confusion and Horror" (289). The irony enforces itself between "must" and "freely." As soon as Gulliver entered his home, he reports, "my Wife took me in her Arms, and kissed me; at which, having not been used to the Touch of that odious Animal for so many Years, I fell in a Swoon for almost an Hour" (289). His favorite company in England is that of two horses and their groom: "for I feel my Spirits revived by the Smell he contracts in the Stable." Gradually, the effects wear off: the next phase of brainwashing begins. At the end of the book, Gulliver is becoming an Englishman again, though he will remain for a long time incensed by the vanity and pride of his countrymen. "And although it be hard for a Man late in Life to remove old Habits, I am not altogether out of Hopes in some Time to suffer a Neighbour *Yahoo* in my Company, without the Apprehensions I am yet under of his Teeth or his Claws."

II

There are two overlapping contexts in which we may consider the force of brainwashing in *Gulliver's Travels*. So far as the violence is directed against someone's mind, the first context is epistemological, and the philosophy referred to in all but words is Locke's. I agree with those who hold that Swift had little or no interest in philosophy, and that the third voyage shows how ready he was to make fun of merely intellectual pursuits. But he was interested in religion and politics, and he liked to think he knew what he was saying in sermons and pamphlets. He needed to have some notion of knowledge. That is all I am concerned to assume. I would be surprised to find him speculating, beyond local need, on the character of a sense-datum.

In the *Essay upon Human Understanding* Locke argues that the mind, to begin with, is a blank page waiting to be written on. The first stage in mental activity is a sensory event: adverting to an external object or action, the mind responds with certain sensations. The only other capacity the mind certainly has is that of reflecting on those sensations and, finally, on its own processes; like Gulliver lying bound in Lilliput:

> At length, struggling to get loose, I had the Fortune to break the Strings, and wrench out the Pegs that fastened my left Arm to the Ground; for, by lifting it up to my Face, I discovered the Methods they had taken to bind me; and, at the same time, with a violent Pull, which gave me excessive Pain, I a little loosened the Strings that tied down my Hair on the left Side; so that I was just able to turn my Head about two Inches. But the Creatures ran off a second time, before I could seize them; whereupon there was a great Shout in a very shrill Accent; and after it ceased, I heard one of them cry aloud, *Tolgo Phonac;* when in an Instant I felt above an Hundred Arrows discharged on my left Hand, which pricked me like so many Needles; and besides, they shot another Flight into the Air, as we do Bombs in *Europe;* whereof many, I suppose, fell on my Body, (though I felt them not) and some on my Face, which I immediately covered with my left Hand. (22)

Gulliver leaves nothing to be deduced. He must lift his left hand to his face before he can comprehend the methods the Lilliputians used to bind him. He can move his head two inches, an essay in precision on evidence mainly tactile. "Above an Hundred Arrows" is as accurate as he can be, the hand being out of the eye's range. "Many, I suppose, fell on my Body," supposition being necessary because he didn't feel them all. Why not? Because, five lines later, "I had on me a Buff Jerkin, which they could not pierce." "As we do Bombs in *Europe,*" the neatness of the comparison being offered for what it's worth, an

irony shot with force entirely disinterested. Meanwhile Gulliver's mental activity proceeds along impeccably empirical lines; first the event, followed by its
sensory recognition, followed in turn by considerations punctual to the occasion, and all delivered in a style as close to the event as post-Restoration prose
enabled.

My account of Locke's position in epistemology is as bare as Gulliver's in
reportage. The little I have said would need to be explicated further if I were a
professional philosopher, or if Swift were. My few sentences merely point to
what Locke regarded as the basic materials of knowledge and why he thought
that in their possession the mind has no choice. "In this part," as he says, "the
understanding is merely passive; and whether or not it will have these begin-
nings, and as it were materials of knowledge, is not in its own power" (2.1.25).[6]
Against Descartes, Cudworth, and many other philosophers, Locke insists that
there are no "innate notions," as he calls them in the first Book of the *Essay*. He
maintains that if there were innate notions, an infant would be born with the
idea of God and the certainty that God is to be worshipped. There is no reason
to think that a mind is born with any such notion.

Not that Locke's position on that matter was decisive. Leibnitz attacked it
on the grounds that it is impossible to construct knowledge from a tabula rasa
and the exterior world. Contingent understanding, he argued, never builds
from zero. Locke's "savage," the figure he posited as the zero point of knowledge, is not (in Leibnitz's view) a mere form waiting to be written on, but a
figure of decadence: savages are not primitives but men who have forgotten
everything primitive. But the main reason for Locke's opposition to the notion of innate ideas was political or civic rather than epistemological: he saw
that those who believed in innate ideas also claimed the right to say what those
ideas were and to impose them on others: "Nor is it a small power it gives one
man over another to have the authority to be the dictator of principles and
teacher of unquestionable truths, and to make a man swallow that for an
innate principle which may serve to his purpose who teacheth them" (1.4.25).
It was for political reasons, therefore, that Locke attacked the assumption that
there are innate notions or ideas. Toleration was more important to him than
any other consideration. In the *Letter to a Young Clergyman* some scholars
have found Swift criticizing Locke for his stand against innate notions. It
seems to me clearer in the sermon "On the Testimony of Conscience" where

Swift defines conscience as "that Knowledge which a Man hath within himself of his own Thoughts and Actions." God, he says, "hath placed Conscience in us to be our Director only in those Actions which Scripture and Reason plainly tell us to be good or evil."[7] Clearly if God placed Conscience in us, Conscience is innate. But nothing in Locke's account of sensation and reflection allows for conscience or a moral sense. In Swift's view the denial of Conscience as an innate power would undermine religion. Locke refused to give any credence to innate ideas, but he had no hesitation in saying that there are innate capacities: precisely, the powers of sensory perception and reflection. Only the provocative objects and events had to be supplied by experience. These powers would assure you that you could act in certain ways, but they wouldn't compel you to act in any particular way. Nor would they establish a moral propensity in the midst of their capacities.

But Locke recognized an acute problem in the chapter on the Association of Ideas. His aim was to take the control of our thinking away from passion or any other authority and to allow us to think for ourselves and take responsibility for our actions. We are to step aside from our spontaneous interests and try to understand our processes of thinking. The mind, according to Locke, has a "power to suspend the execution of any of its desires; and so all, one after another; is at liberty to consider the objects of them, examine them on all sides, and weigh them with others" (2.21.53). So Locke included in the power of reflection what we normally call "will." In that respect one's thinking should be a declaration of independence. But in the chapter on the Association of Ideas he meets a difficulty in distinguishing between associations that form customs—which are good—and those that form habits—which are bad. He refers at one point to the "Empire of Habit." Clearly, he thinks that associations of ideas that set up bad habits are the very definition of madness; for one thing, they veto the act of reflection by preventing the mind from feeling inclined to it. Hans Aarsleff has noted, in his *From Locke to Saussure*, that Locke didn't work out this problem; he left to Condillac's *Essay on the Origin of Human Knowledge* (1746) the development of the notion that the association of ideas was somehow innate, or might be.

One of the aims of *Gulliver's Travels*, then, is to make dark fun of Locke's epistemology; to show how vulnerable the mind is if it has no capacities but those of sensation and reflection; if its entire life begins with external events and objects, and depends on them. Gulliver is a parody of Locke's empiricism, a tilt against any philosophy that considers the mind to be the slave of its contents. That is what Yeats had in view, I assume, when he wrote:

> Locke sank into a swoon;
> The Garden died;
> God took the spinning jenny
> Out of his side.[8]

The swoon is passivity: the mind, in Locke's account, depends upon the contingency of the events and objects that impinge on it. Yeats thought that Pound and Joyce, too, capitulated to this wretched assumption. Swift feared that Locke might be right, and he dealt with his fear by parodying it. Assume that Locke is right: then if you change the things a mind encounters, you change the quality of the mind. This is brainwashing, in effect. Swift is demonstrating in Gulliver what Locke's empire of habit comes to: the mind is held captive by enforced associations of ideas. Such an imperial force constrains the act of reflection, upon which Locke's philosophy relies.

III

The second context also involves Locke, but this time the issue is moral philosophy rather than epistemology. Charles Taylor has outlined the situation so clearly in *Sources of the Self* (1989) that I can give the gist of the dispute in his terms. In Swift's time there were two relevant traditions in moral philosophy. One of them was represented by Hobbes and Locke: it expressed a naturalistic transposition of the doctrine of Original Sin. According to this tradition, God's law is doubly external to us as fallen creatures: first, because we cannot identify the good with the bent of our own natures, and second, because the law of God—if we could discover what it is—runs against the grain of our depraved wills. We cannot, therefore, deduce a morality from the natural world, so we do well to regard Nature as neutral. All we can manage is to be as self-aware as possible and to act responsibly under the auspices of tolerance.

The other tradition of moral philosophy is represented by the Cambridge Platonists—especially by Henry More, Ralph Cudworth, Benjamin

Whichcote, and John Smith. They saw human beings as intrinsically attuned to God, hence they spoke with assurance of our "inward Nature," according to which we are in harmony with the universe. This philosophy of benevolence was clear enough in Bolingbroke and Pope, but it was most fully articulated by Shaftesbury and Hutcheson. "I must love whatever happens," Shaftesbury says in his *Philosophic Regimen*, "and see it all as fitted to me and orderly with respect to the whole, even 'the sack of cities and the ruin of mankind.' "⁹ Whereas Locke found the source of morality in the dignity of a disengaged subject confronting a neutral nature, Shaftesbury ascribed it to the benevolent soul participating in the divine harmony of the universe. His crucial phrase is "natural affection," by which he means the sentiment that prompts us to love the whole world and everyone in it. Taylor refers to Shaftesbury's internaliza-tion of a teleological ethic of nature, and to his transformation of the ap-pearances of harmony, order, and equilibrium into an ethic of benevolence. Hutcheson developed this philosophy further in his *Inquiry into the Original of Our Ideas of Beauty and Virtue*. He had Locke in his sights, and attacked the assumption, common to Hobbes, Locke, and La Rochefoucauld, that the distinction between good and bad is founded on self-love, self-interest, and nothing else. Hutcheson's first act in this dispute is to posit in each of us a moral sense. "Some actions have to men an immediate goodness," he says, and by "immediate" he means spontaneous, innately delivered, not the result of reflection and training. Taylor remarks that this is a risky assumption, espe-cially as Hutcheson acknowledges that God could have given us an entirely different moral sense, or none at all. The fact that God gave us the particular moral sense we have is one of Hutcheson's proofs of His benign providence, but he doesn't see that he has opened the door wide to relativism. It is hard to claim at once that our moral sense is primordially given by God, and that God in His absolute freedom could have made a different choice.

In the *Essay on the Nature and Conduct of the Passions and Affections* Hutcheson renews his attack on Locke and the skeptical or misanthropic tra-dition. Some people, he says, might think the passions "too subtle for com-mon Apprehension, and consequently not necessary for the instruction of men in morals, which are the common business of mankind." But in fact cer-tain notions are already current about the passions "to the great detriment of many a natural temper; since many have been discouraged from all attempts of cultivating kind generous affections in themselves, by a previous notion that there are no such affections in Nature, and that all Pretence to them was only Dissimulation, Affectation, or at best some unnatural Enthusiasm."

On the question of moral philosophy—but not of epistemology—Swift is of Locke's party, except that he gives far greater allowance to Revelation and Conscience than Locke did. His general sense of human life in its moral bearing puts him with Hobbes, Mandeville, and La Rochefoucauld in his belief that moral and social life is mainly propelled by self-love. The only mitigations of this dark vision that Swift is willing to concede are religion and the common decencies of friendship and common sense. His religion was that of the Church of Ireland, unexactingly interpreted, but it was not merely a matter of morals. Faith was crucial, though Swift gave a prosaic account of it and cheerfully set aside the hard theological mysteries. "By God's great mercy," as he said with evident relief, "those difficult Points [of Divinity] are never of absolute necessity to our salvation."[10] Swift thought the Christianity of Anglicanism a good enough basis for personal and social life, but he was not theologically insistent beyond the basic articles of faith and practice. As for the decencies: his moral philosophy was mostly negative and pessimistic, but he allowed for exceptional instances of merit. Taylor says of Locke that in his philosophy we take our place in the order of nature and society through the exercise of disengaged reason. As I have suggested, Swift thought this a risky position to adopt, because the mind is appallingly susceptible to what it merely happens to encounter. But his relation to the tradition of benevolence, as in Shaftesbury and Hutcheson, was severe if not dismissive: this is clear from his presentation of the Houyhnhnms, who live as if every virtue were innate, a practice that enchants Gulliver even though it hardly adds up to life at all. As Leavis said, the Houyhnhnms have all the virtue, but the Yahoos have all the life.

Brainwashing embodies the belief that "the reason of the Stronger is always the best." The *Oxford English Dictionary* defines it as the "systematic and often forcible elimination from a person's mind of all established ideas, especially political ideas, so that another set may take their place." The earliest recorded use of the word dates from 1950, during the Cold War, a time we associate with the trial of Cardinal Stepinac and the publication of Richard Condon's novel of brainwashing, *The Manchurian Candidate* (1959). More recently we have seen the case of Patty Hearst, which featured brainwashing, at least in its early stages. The OED also says that brainwashing is "a kind of coercive conversion practised by certain totalitarian states on political dissidents." But the degree of coercion depends on the degree of resistance offered by the victim. The U-2 pilot Gary Powers didn't offer as much as Cardinal Stepinac. Gulliver offers little or no resistance. Nothing about him is more revealing than his willingness to have his brain washed by new masters. If the book appeals to our sense of humor, and to our sense of discrepancy and disproportion, it touches us also in our sense of imprisonment; not imprisonment in a concentration camp, but in any system of ideas and values that is imposed on us. Under those conditions the enforced system becomes our second nature and prevents us from seeing our first.

Any system can become a prison: a tradition we have inherited, a style we have adopted, an official terminology that tells us what to think. These days, we often refer to it as ideology, a system of assumptions on which people are persuaded to live; the more it seems self-evidently valid, the more powerful it becomes. *Gulliver's Travels* is only superficially about big men and little men: it is really about entrapment; and the most disturbing episode in the book deals with the Struldbrugs, those people in Luggnagg who are immortal in the appalling sense that they get older but can't die. They can't leave the system. In Greek mythology Tithonus is the figure whose fate speaks to us most touchingly in this regard. He was loved by Eos, goddess of the dawn. She asked Zeus to grant him immortality, but she neglected to ask that he also be granted eternal youth. Immortal, he withered away and at last became a grasshopper. Tennyson's "Tithonus" begins:

> The woods decay, the woods decay and fall,
> The vapours weep their burthen to the ground,
> Man comes and tills the field and lies beneath,
> And after many a summer dies the swan.
> Me only cruel immortality
> Consumes: I wither slowly in thine arms,
> Here at the quiet limit of the world,
> A white-haired shadow roaming like a dream
> The ever-silent spaces of the East,
> Far-folded mists, and gleaming halls of morn.

The pathos of the poem is that Tithonus speaks to Eos, not to Zeus, and asks
her to take back the gift. But even the gods can't do that, can't undo what they
have done:

> Yet hold me not for ever in thine East:
> How can my nature longer mix with thine?
> Coldly, thy rosy shadows bathe me, cold
> Are all thy lights, and cold my wrinkled feet
> Upon thy glimmering thresholds, when the steam
> Floats up from those dim fields about the homes
> Of happy men that have the power to die,
> And grassy barrows of the happier dead.
> Release me, and restore me to the ground;
> Thou seest all things, thou wilt see my grave:
> Thou wilt renew thy beauty morn by morn;
> I earth in earth forget these empty courts,
> And thee returning on thy silver wheels.[11]

The Struldbrugs are Swift's imagining of the same fate. They are the most
terrible emblems of such a thing. But they are only an extreme manifestation
of Gulliver's fate, to be imprisoned in one system of forces after another.

As long as Gulliver is inside a system, he doesn't bring any irony to bear on
it. Irony is the counterforce to brainwashing: it brings to bear on a given
system other values antithetical to those in place; it holds out against the
official blandishments. Gulliver doesn't. That is shown with particular clarity
in a passage in the fourth voyage, in which he describes the certitude of
reasoning among the Houyhnhnms:

> As these noble *Houyhnhnms* are endowed by Nature with a general Disposi-
> tion to all Virtues, and have no Conceptions or Ideas of what is evil in a ra-
> tional Creature; so their grand Maxim is, to cultivate *Reason,* and to be
> wholly governed by it. Neither is *Reason* among them a Point problematical
> as with us, where Men can argue with Plausibility on both Sides of a Ques-
> tion; but strikes you with immediate Conviction; as it must needs do where
> it is not mingled, obscured, or discoloured by Passion and Interest. I re-
> member it was with extreme Difficulty that I could bring my Master to
> understand the Meaning of the word *Opinion,* or how a Point could be dis-
> putable; because *Reason* taught us to affirm or deny only where we are

> certain; and beyond our Knowledge we cannot do either. So that Controver-
> sies, Wranglings, Disputes, and Positiveness in false or dubious Proposi-
> tions, are Evils unknown among the *Houyhnhnms*.[12]

The irony here is turned upon the Houyhnhnms, who have such a boring life
of certitude that there is nothing to be discussed or questioned. But the
sentence about Controversies, Wranglings, Disputes, and Positiveness doesn't
offer a value to be set against the blankness of intellectual and moral life
among the Houyhnhnms. It refers to a pedagogical tradition, practiced by the
Sophists, in which children were trained to argue, interchangeably, on one
side of a proposition or the other. The long-term result was the faction-
fighting that Swift professed to loathe. Gulliver can't stand aside from his local
experience to the extent of imagining what the proper form of reasoning
might be. Swift appears to be saying: if you send the human mind into the
world without the benefit of Revelation, religious belief, and an innate conscience, it will succumb to every force it meets.

IV

There is a passage in Andrei Sinyavsky's book *A Voice from the Chorus* in which
the Russian writer, imprisoned in Lefortovo in 1966, recalls certain books he
had read as a child, among them *Gulliver's Travels*. Sinyavsky makes the point
that Gulliver is well fitted to represent mankind in general, precisely because
he has no personality, no permanent qualities: everything depends on the
circumstances in which he is placed. As Sinyavsky has it: "he is short or tall,
clean or unclean only by comparison; he is a man by comparison and a non-
man by comparison; he is a giant among Lilliputians, a Lilliputian among
giants, an animal among the Houyhnhnms, a horse among men."[13] Sinyavsky
thinks that Swift is saying that man is a fiction, a sham. But there is another way of phrasing the conclusion. Man is a function of his environment,
trapped in a structure that determines him so long as it holds him there. The
only escape is into another structure, where the brainwashing begins all over
again, according to another set of ideas and principles, equally arbitrary. The
grim comedy of *Gulliver's Travels* arises from the discrepancy between our
vaguely acquired sense of what it means to be human and our more pressing
fear that "being human" depends—more than we care to realize—on favorable

local circumstances. When circumstances change, being human is the last thing we can be assured of being. *Gulliver's Travels* has become a dauntingly "modern" book again in the past thirty or forty years because it presents as fiction what many people are worried about as fact.

These worries are provoked by ideas of mind and society. Marx said that social existence determines consciousness, but he allowed for a dynamic relation between mind and environment. One of the major axioms of Structuralism went far beyond Marx to say that we are determined by the codes we have been given. We don't hear much of Structuralism these days, but none of its successors has claimed that the human mind is autonomous. It is now regularly assumed that reality and knowledge are socially constructed and that sociologists of knowledge are fully equipped to understand the processes of this construction. In *The Social Construction of Reality* (1966), Peter L. Berger and Thomas Luckmann define reality as "a quality appertaining to phenomena that we recognize as having a being independent of our own volition (we cannot 'wish them away')"; and they define knowledge as "the certainty that phenomena are real and that they possess specific characteristics."[14] This is old-style positivism translated into sociology: it allows no place for metaphysical, religious, or visionary values. More to the point, it hands over to "society," by which Berger and Luckmann appear to mean the accredited social institutions that happen to be in place at this moment, the right to decide what constitutes knowledge in any particular. I don't see how this sociology of knowledge differs from the brainwashing I've been describing in *Gulliver's Travels*.

Gulliver's Travels touches on another issue, close to the one I've just described but perhaps distinguishable from it, because it adverts to the possibility that man may not be the son of God but identical with something he resembles—an artifact, a machine, a gadget made like any other to perform a few rudimentary operations. Kenner has examined this motif in *The Counterfeiters*, which he subtitles *An Historical Comedy* presumably because one source of comedy, according to Bergson, is a sense of discrepancy between axioms of life as organism and appearances of life as gadgetry. The normal optimistic answer to this sense of discrepancy is the assertion that if man is a machine, he is a machine with a difference, and that this difference makes all the difference. We say, for instance, that man is an animal with the further distinguishing power of reason or symbolic action: he can reflect on his experience and represent it in symbolic terms. If we think the difference exhilarating, we conclude that man's perfection in his kind enables him to transcend his kind: he is not a mere animal at all. This optimism depends on our emphasizing in man's favor a spiritual dimension, a particular quality or aura that makes men and women what they are.

Gulliver's Travels incites us to think or to fear that this optimism is false; that the x factor is a delusion, merely yet another manifestation of pride. Hazlitt said that Swift took a new view of human nature, "such as a being of a higher sphere might take of it." Precisely: because it is a matter of perspective. Swift presents in Gulliver a man bereft of spiritual radiance; he is merely the sum of his attributes, and these are few. He is someone to whom certain things happen. This is Swift's main satiric device: to present every ostensibly spiritual quality in a material form, reducing qualities to quantities and counters. And if an optimistic reader declares that man is more than the sum of a few attributes, Swift accepts the challenge. We can almost hear him say: "Prove it."

In the end, Gulliver is restored to himself. But what is the self to which he is restored? Is it that of the true-born Englishman, the ideologically propelled figure projected after the Restoration and the Glorious Revolution by an England desperately anxious to avoid another civil war and the execution of another king? Something like that. Gulliver is an empiricist without memory or the need of it, a man restored to sanity who does not know that he has been mad. He is as close as possible to being "a man without qualities."

ELEVEN

On a Word in Wordsworth

The word is "uncertain," as it appears in "The Boy of Winander":

There was a Boy, ye knew him well, ye Cliffs
And Islands of Winander! many a time
At evening, when the stars had just begun
To move along the edges of the hills,
Rising or setting, would he stand alone
Beneath the trees, or by the glimmering Lake,
And there, with fingers interwoven, both hands
Press'd closely, palm to palm, and to his mouth
Uplifted, he, as through an instrument,
Blew mimic hootings to the silent owls
That they might answer him.—And they would shout
Across the watry Vale, and shout again,
Responsive to his call, with quivering peals,
And long halloos, and screams, and echoes loud
Redoubled and redoubled; concourse wild
Of mirth and jocund din! And when it chanced
That pauses of deep silence mock'd his skill,
Then sometimes, in that silence, while he hung
Listening, a gentle shock of mild surprize

Has carried far into his heart the voice
Of mountain torrents; or the visible scene
Would enter unawares into his mind
With all its solemn imagery, its rocks,
Its woods, and that uncertain Heaven, receiv'd
Into the bosom of the steady Lake.
This Boy was taken from his Mates, and died
In childhood, ere he was full ten years old.
—Fair are the woods, and beauteous is the spot,
The Vale where he was born; the Churchyard hangs
Upon a Slope above the Village School,
And there, along that bank, when I have pass'd
At evening, I believe that oftentimes
A full half-hour together I have stood
Mute—Looking at the Grave in which he lies.[1]

I have quoted the poem in the text of 1805–6.

Wordsworth wrote "The Boy of Winander" between October 6 and late November or early December 1798. That first version starts in the third person and stays there—"his" and "him"—till the owls respond to the mimic hootings, when it changes to the first person singular—"my call" and "my skill" and "I hung"—and remains autobiographical till it ends with the line "Into the bosom of the steady Lake."[2] When Wordsworth published the poem in the second volume of *Lyrical Ballads* (1800), he maintained the third person throughout and ended with the boy's death.[3] He included it again in *The Prelude* (1805) and in *Poems* (1815), where it stands first among the group called "Poems of the Imagination." The version in *The Prelude* of 1850 has some textual changes. In the preface to *Poems* (1815), Wordsworth commented on the poem in the context of his mettlesome claim to have exerted the imagination upon its worthiest objects:

> I shall declare . . . that I have given in these unfavourable times, evidence of exertions of this faculty upon its worthiest objects, the external universe, the moral and religious sentiments of Man, his natural affections, and his acquired passions; which have the same ennobling tendency as the productions of men, in this kind, worthy to be holden in undying remembrance.
>
> I dismiss this subject with observing—that, in the series of Poems placed under the head of Imagination, I have begun with one of the earliest pro-

cesses of Nature in the development of this faculty. Guided by one of my own primary consciousnesses, I have represented a commutation and transfer of internal feelings, co-operating with external accidents, to plant, for immortality, images of sound and sight, in the celestial soil of the Imagination. The Boy, there introduced, is listening, with something of a feverish and restless anxiety, for the recurrence of the riotous sounds which he had previously excited; and, at the moment when the intenseness of his mind is beginning to remit, he is surprised into a perception of the solemn and tranquillizing images which the Poem describes.[4]

Wordsworth sent the first version of the poem to Coleridge, who replied in a letter of December 10, 1798:

The blank lines gave me as much direct pleasure as was possible in the general bustle of pleasure with which I received and read your letter. I observed, I remember, that the "fingers interwoven" etc. only puzzled me; and though I liked the twelve or fourteen first lines very well, yet I liked the remainder much better. Well, now I have read them again, they are very beautiful, and leave an affecting impression. That

>   Uncertain heaven received
>   Into the bosom of the steady Lake

I should have recognis'd any where; and had I met these lines running wild in the deserts of Arabia, I should have instantly screamed out "Wordsworth!"[5]

In chapter 20 of *Biographia Literaria* Coleridge quoted a passage of fifteen lines from "The Boy of Winander"—from "mimic hootings" to "the steady Lake"—and italicized the lines from "Then sometimes in that silence" to "the steady Lake" to illustrate the distinctiveness of Wordsworth's poetry; that it exhibits not the perfection of a common style but the individuality of a style peculiar to him. Would any but a poet, Coleridge exclaimed, "have represented the reflection of the sky in the water, as *"That uncertain heaven received into the bosom of the steady lake"*?[6]

I

In the first line, Wordsworth starts the process of commutation, the exchange and substitution of feelings between the boy and the valley. The personification of the cliffs and islands of Winander sets up a to-and-fro of familiarity:

"ye knew him well" because he knew ye well. This cadence anticipates the to-and-fro of the boy's hootings and the replies of the owls, till then silent. It is daring and not at all naive on Wordsworth's part to present the owls as shouting, responsive to the boy's call—"That they might answer him." The force of the boy's desire is allowed to supervene upon the naivete of its apparent fulfillment. In the preface to *Poems* Wordsworth says that the boy's feelings cooperate "with external accidents." No "pathetic fallacy" is entailed: if an ornithologist were to insist that the noise the owls made was not a shout or a response to the boy's hooting, Wordsworth would reply that the noises seemed to the boy to be shouts in response to his call, and that this seeming makes all the difference. In such seemings all things are, as Stevens says.

The crisis of the poem comes with the failure of the boy's hootings: owls, too, get tired of singsong. "Mock'd his skill" is not objective reporting; it gives the situation as the disappointed boy sees it. The pauses of silence are then correlated with the boy's hanging listening as if he might coax further responses from the owls but was prepared to be disappointed. The stance—"while he hung / Listening"—is like the "tiptoe" effect in many of Keats's poems, an incipiently dynamic gesture held back from its outcome, suspended between act and act. The effect is embodied in the suspending of the verb—"hung"—before it is resolved, across the break of line and the delay of syntax, in "Listening." The repetition of "silence" from one line to the next is strikingly Wordsworthian: a poet less confident of his powers would have replaced one of the silences. The second silence may prefigure the boy's death, but if so the force of it is modified as the poem goes on. "A gentle shock of mild surprize": the adjectives go together without being quite the same; the nouns are further apart but in the same scene of impressions. The shock is mitigated into surprise. Thomas de Quincey thought the word "far," in its context, a remarkable stroke of Wordsworth's sublime style: physically, it can't be "far" into the boy's heart, but it feels far by being deep as deep can be, so decisive that it can't be forgotten. It's not clear whether this is what the boy feels or what the narrative voice is made to feel in his behalf. "Far" is more likely to be what the omniscient narrator divines rather than what the boy feels. "The voice of mountain torrents": the noise is assimilated to the boy's idiom of call-and-response, a partial resumption of his communication with the owls. Geoffrey Hartman interprets this passage as showing the boy moved "gently and unhurt toward the consciousness of nature's separate life."[7] True, but "the voice / Of mountain torrents" shows that the separateness is not complete: the relation of man and the natural world continues, despite the shock the boy has felt when the owls have fallen silent. The only consideration that seems to work against this reading is that the next sentence, beginning with "or the visible scene," specifies that the new experience comes to the boy "unawares," which may imply that the first one was a conscious experience from start to finish and depended on that consciousness. But "or" really has the effect of "and," so the evidence is weak. Besides, "unawares" implies that the educative effect of the natural world upon the boy may be all the greater for his being unaware of its action. The visible scene "would enter," as if it knew where it intended to go.

Coleridge disapproved of the word "scene" in this passage because it is used in a vague rather than a strict sense. He maintained that it should always be used, as it is by Shakespeare and Milton, with a clear reference, "proper or metaphorical, to the theatre." The word can be "preserved from *obscurity* only by keeping the original signification full in the mind."[8] But the complaint doesn't hold. The boy perceives the scene as dramatic, potentially theatrical, with its solemn imagery: it wouldn't be called imagery if it weren't like a stage and ready to be the place where a dramatic action would occur. As it does: the boy's death. I grant that it's not as specifically theatrical as Milton's

> Cedar, and pine, and fir, and branching palm,
> A sylvan scene, and as the ranks ascend
> Shade above shade, a woody theatre
> Of stateliest view . . .

—Coleridge's instance of the proper use of the word.[9]

Coleridge doesn't say what he found especially Wordsworthian about the lines

> and that uncertain Heaven, receiv'd
> Into the bosom of the steady Lake.

Presumably he felt in them an unembarrassed movement between the literal and the metaphorical, a distinctive tone of confidence declared in the clarity of "receiv'd," as if it fulfilled the pointedness of "and that uncertain Heaven." Perhaps, too, he had in mind Wordsworth's tendency to indicate the relation between objects more definitely than the mere visibility of the objects.

Wordsworth's talent in the delineation of objects was not remarkable: his sister Dorothy looked at things more closely and saw them more vividly than he did. Wordsworth's genius consisted in imagining or divining relations between things, the things themselves being seen only sufficiently to make the relations hold. He intuited relations and faced the crisis of their failing. In the quoted passage, "receiv'd / Into the bosom of the steady Lake" denotes a relation between things that is apprehended more clearly than the things seen. The natural world is intuited as a mother, and, by extension, it may be relied on to care for the boy as a mother cares. It is not merely seen.

Wordsworth's procedure in this respect is compatible with one of Coleridge's emphases in the *Logic:*

> First, words, that in their proper and primary sense express relations of space, are likewise used sometimes *for* and sometimes inclusive of the relations of time. The language of *sight* is transferred to the affections and objects of the other senses, and of the inward experience. . . . In disciplining his [the poet's] mind one of the first rules should be to lose no opportunity of tracing words to their origin, one good consequence of which will be that he will be able to use the *language* of sight without being enslaved by its affections. He will at least secure himself from the delusive notion that what is not *imageable* is likewise not *conceivable.* To emancipate the mind from the despotism of the eye is the first step towards its emancipation from the influences and intrusions of the senses, sensations, and passions generally. Thus most effectually is the power of abstraction to be called forth.[10]

It was Wordsworth's practice to see things as if the power of abstraction were active simultaneously with the seeing.

"Uncertain Heaven" means what Coleridge took it to mean, the reflection of the sky in the lake; uncertain, presumably, because of clouds moving about. To interpret the phrase as a metaphysical giveaway, a shudder of spiritual insecurity, is to be desperate for novelty. It is also to refuse the intimations of the remaining words of the sentence, which emphasize the quasi-maternal strength the boy feels in the steadiness of the lake.

The gap between this first part of the poem and the remainder anticipates the abrupt disclosure of the boy's death. The death is not accounted for. Recalling that the first version of the poem was autobiographical, we can say that Wordsworth killed the boy off to justify his own conviction, even between

1798 and 1800, that he had lost something of his early poetic faculty. Even if he has gained something, the loss remains. It may seem strange that Wordsworth uses the verb "hangs" so soon again, in the lines about the churchyard, but the effect of the repetition is to humanize the churchyard in its relation to the "Slope above the Village School." The second use recalls the first. Besides, "hangs" was a verb of particular interest to Wordsworth, as another passage in the preface to *Poems* shows:

Imagination, in the sense of the word as giving title to a class of the follow-ing Poems, has no reference to images that are merely a faithful copy, exist-ing in the mind, of absent external objects; but is a word of higher import, denoting operations of the mind upon those objects, and processes of cre-ation or of composition, governed by certain fixed laws. I proceed to illus-trate my meaning by instances. A parrot *hangs* from the wires of his cage by his beak or by his claws; or a monkey from the bough of a tree by his paws or his tail. Each creature does so literally and actually. In the first Eclogue of Virgil, the shepherd, thinking of the time when he is to take leave of his farm, thus addresses his goats—
   "Non ego vos posthac viridi projectus in antro
   Dumosa *pendere* procul de rupe videbo"
      —"half way down
      Hangs one who gathers samphire,"
is the well-known expression of Shakespeare, delineating an ordinary image upon the cliffs of Dover. In these two instances is a slight exertion of the fac-ulty which I denominate imagination, in the use of one word: neither the goats nor the samphire-gatherer do literally hang, as does the parrot or the monkey; but, presenting to the senses something of such an appearance, the mind in its activity, for its own gratification, contemplates them as hanging:
   As when far off at sea a fleet descried
   Hangs in the clouds, by equinoctial winds
   Close sailing from Bengala, or the isles
   Of Ternate or Tidore, whence merchants bring
   Their spicy drugs; they on the trading floor
   Through the wide Ethiopian to the Cape
   Ply, stemming nightly toward the Pole: so seemed
   Far off the flying Fiend.
Here is the full strength of the imagination involved in the word *hangs,* and exerted upon the whole image: First, the fleet, an aggregate of many ships, is

represented as one mighty person, whose track, we know and feel, is upon the waters; but, taking advantage of its appearance to the senses, the Poet dares to represent it as *hanging in the clouds,* both for the gratification of the mind in contemplating the image itself, and in reference to the motion and appearance of the sublime object to which it is compared.[11]

Not that Wordsworth avoids using the verb "to hang" in a literal sense, as in the two-part *Prelude:*

> Oh, when I have hung
> Above the raven's nest, by knots of grass,
> Or half-inch fissures in the slipp'ry rock . . .[12]

But in the metaphorical use of the verb the poet's mind is gratified not by the things it sees or even by the act of seeing them but by the relations it imagines between those things. All that the sense of sight is asked to do is not to get in the way of the imagination. "The Churchyard hangs / Upon a Slope above the Village School." And so it does, since Wordsworth's imagination, like Virgil's, Shakespeare's, and Milton's, chooses to see it hanging—the relation a domestic and familiar one—and the sensory evidence doesn't contradict the choice. It is an instance of "seeing as" rather than "seeing that." The relation between what the eye sees and what the imagination chooses to represent is antinomian, as if the imagination were to say to the eye, "I see what you see, but I'll exercise my distinctive capacity by presenting it differently." There is no need to labor the metaphor to the extremity of thinking that the churchyard hung upon the slope as Gertrude, according to Hamlet, hung upon her first husband, "As if increase of appetite had grown / By what it fed on." The genre and tone of Wordsworth's poem set decent limits on interpretation.

The poem ends, in this version, with another meditative silence:

> And there, along that bank, when I have pass'd
> At evening, I believe that oftentimes
> A full half-hour together I have stood
> Mute—looking at the Grave in which he lies.

"I believe": he has not been consulting his watch. "I have stood": another version of the meditative "hanging," a different one—the boy's "hung" is kinetic, hoping without assurance; the second one, the churchyard's "hangs," is constant, a settling of the ground beside other ground; this third one, "stood /

Mute," is hoping without a stated ground of hope. What is the "I" thinking of? We can only surmise, prompted by the drift of Wordsworth's other poems of the period and by his "Essays upon Epitaphs"; by this passage, for instance: "If, then, in a creature endowed with the faculties of foresight and reason, the social affections could not have unfolded themselves uncountenanced by the faith that Man is an immortal being; and if, consequently, neither could the individual dying have had a desire to survive in the remembrance of his fellows, nor on their side could they have felt a wish to preserve for future times vestiges of the departed; it follows, as a final inference, that without the belief in immortality, wherein these several desires originate, neither monuments nor epitaphs, in affectionate or laudatory commemoration of the deceased, could have existed in the world."[13] In that spirit, "The Boy of Winander" begins as a lyrical ballad and turns aside to become an epitaph—"Pause, Traveller!" The boy has died, like Wordsworth's earlier self, but vestiges of the deceased remain in the remembrance of the mature poet.

II

Wordsworth's poetry, like Stevens's, negotiates two simultaneous values. Stevens called them Imagination and Reality. Wordsworth often called them Consciousness and Nature, but he also referred to Mind and Imagination as synonyms for Consciousness. We may freely settle for Imagination and Nature, treating Society as an emanation from the consanguinities of the natural world or a denial of them. In any event we have two values, and therefore the risk of favoring one at the expense of the other. A materialist favors the natural world by calling it matter, an idealist favors imagination by regarding the natural world as nothing or, in another mood, as a function of the imagination. Stevens mostly favors the imagination and has difficulty acknowledging that the world may remain opaque, impermeable.

There is also the possibility of deeming the two values most fruitful for the relations between them. This is Wordsworth's way as reader of his own poems and other poems. In the use of "hangs" in Virgil, Shakespeare, and Milton, the decencies of sensory perception are observed simultaneously with the gratification of the imagination. Not that the relation between sense and imagination was always straightforward: there are passages in *The Prelude* that show it confounded or otherwise opaque. But we may say, without gross simplification, that most of Wordsworth's nineteenth-century readers, when they got over the rural oddity—which often seemed rural idiocy—of the *Lyrical Ballads*, valued his poems for certifying humane relations between imagination and the ordinary universe. Those poems appeared to indicate that people may consider themselves at home in the world, despite every evidence of sorrow and pain; they are not thrown arbitrarily upon the planet. This was the consolatory emphasis that appealed to John Stuart Mill, Matthew Arnold, and—in our own time—René Wellek and M. H. Abrams. Indeed, Arnold went so far as to say that Wordsworth had no style: he didn't need one, Nature wrote the poems for him.

But there is another way of reading Wordsworth's poems, or some of them. It is possible to regard the natural world as a nuisance, an impediment thwarting the creative imagination. If we take this attitude, we deem the imagination to be the sole value, and we claim heroic status for our regarding the world as well lost in a greater cause. Blake is the clearest exemplar of this stance. In his annotations—written in 1826—to Wordsworth's *Poems* (1815) he insisted that "One Power alone makes a Poet: Imagination, The Divine Vision." "I see in Wordsworth," he writes, "the Natural Man rising up against the Spiritual Man Continually, & then he is No Poet but a Heathen Philosopher at Enmity against all true Poetry or Inspiration." Commenting on Wordsworth's reference to the influence of natural objects in calling forth and strengthening the Imagination in boyhood and early youth—the theme of "The Boy of Winander"—Blake says that "Natural Objects always did & now do weaken, deaden & obliterate Imagination in Me." Wordsworth must know, Blake asserts, "that what he Writes Valuable is Not to be found in Nature."[14] For the same reason, Blake denied the poetic value of memory, another impediment thwarting the work of genius or vision.

Much the same attitude as Blake's is also found in Hazlitt, Keats, Pater, Hopkins and—among the modern critics—Willard Sperry, Geoffrey Hartman, Harold Bloom, and Paul de Man. The gist of it is: when Wordsworth knew himself, he was a poet not of Nature but of the subjective or peremptory imagination. He had an interest in the natural world consistent with the determination to sublime it away: his own vision was sole authority—what Keats called "the wordsworthian or egotistical sublime."

I don't claim that this attitude is held without difference or nuance by these several writers. In the "Retrospect 1971" to the second edition of *Wordsworth's*

Poetry, 1787–1814, Hartman protested against a critic who had "reduced the book to the interesting if bloody-minded argument that Wordsworth needed to kill or violate nature in order to achieve his moments of visionary poetry." The book argued, according to Hartman, "almost the reverse: that Wordsworth, deeply wary of visionary poetry of Milton's kind, foresaw a new type of consciousness, satisfied with nature, or at least not obliged to violate it in imagination."[15] I sympathize with the critic who read Hartman's book otherwise, but I concede that Hartman allows for at least two possibilities in saying that "something too strong in the imagination, or too weak in nature, or vice versa, frustrates the consummation for which his poetry is a 'spousal verse.' "[16] That "vice versa" saves the argument, but Hartman's endorsement of Sperry, Bloom, and de Man a page or two later shows the limit beyond which the vice versa is not allowed to go.

The origin of the post-Blakean interpretation of Wordsworth is clear enough: it involves reading the poems under Milton's sign rather than Shakespeare's. Or rather: under the sign of Satan in *Paradise Lost.* Some critics find the thrill of Satan's eloquence exemplified again in Byron's Cain. The particular moment of satanism that is found irresistible comes in Book V of *Paradise Lost* when Satan, who has evidently been reading Stevens, rounds upon Abdiel, who has been insisting that Christ was God's agent in the Creation. As always, Satan is a spoiled brat:

> That we were formed then say'st thou? and the work
> Of secondary hands, by task transferred
> From Father to his Son? Strange point and new!
> Doctrine which we would know whence learnt: who saw
> When this creation was? Remember'st thou
> Thy making, while the Maker gave thee being?
> We know no time when we were not as now;
> Know none before us, self-begot, self-raised
> By our own quick'ning power, when fatal course
> Had circled his full orb, the birth mature
> Of this our native heav'n, ethereal sons.
> Our puissance is our own.[17]

Satan's claim to have begotten himself is nonsense. Adam deals with it adequately and silently when he tells of his own birth and addresses the sun:

> Tell, if ye saw, how came I thus, how here?
> Not of myself; by some great Maker then,
> In goodness and in power preeminent.[18]

But Blake, Hazlitt, and a formidable rout of critics have sent themselves into an *altitudo* of eloquence under the sway of Satan's vanity. Harold Bloom is the most susceptible of these critics, and in *Ruin the Sacred Truths* and *The Western Canon* he quotes Satan's boast as if it should be taken seriously. Bloom and his associates in this line of interpretation are the bad angels of criticism, exhibiting their own forms of angelism, the desire to transcend the human scale of experience in a rage for essence. They want to be rid of the world of fact, the opaque burdens of history and society, and to fly upon wings of their own devising. As critics, they thrive on weightlessness.

III

The most extreme of the bad angels, Paul de Man, considered "The Boy of Winander" on at least three occasions, in "Heaven and Earth in Wordsworth and Hölderlin" (1965), "Wordsworth and Hölderlin" (1966), and "Time and History in Wordsworth" (1967). The last of these is his most elaborate account of the poem, so I will concentrate on that.[19]

De Man's reading of the first part of the poem is uncontroversial; it is in keeping with Wordsworth's statement, added to the preface for the 1802 edition of *Lyrical Ballads,* that the poet "considers man and nature as essentially adapted to each other, and the mind of man as naturally the mirror of the fairest and most interesting qualities of nature."[20] But the clearest quality of De Man's reading is that this part of the poem doesn't interest him: he thinks Wordsworth is protesting too much that the scene is joyous. But the main reason for de Man's indifference is that in this passage he finds it hard to discover darkness behind the light. He becomes more engaged by the poem when the owls break off their answering shouts and silence falls:

> Yet certainly, by the time we come to "*uncertain* Heaven," we must realize that we have entered a precarious world in which the relationship between noun and epithet can be quite surprising. . . . The line is indeed bound to engender wonder and meditation. The movements of the stars, in the opening lines, had seemed "certain" enough, and their reflection in the lake was

hardly needed to steady the majesty of their imperceptible motion. But the precariousness that is here being introduced had been announced before, as when, a little earlier, in lines 18 and 19, it was said that when "pauses of deep silence mock'd his skill, / Then, sometimes, in that silence, while he [the boy] *hung* / Listening, a gentle shock of mild surprize . . . " We would have expected "stood listening" instead of the unusual "hung / Listening."[21]

But "stood listening" is quite different from what is there; it lacks the felt experience of the boy's waiting in hope of further sounds from the owls, what I have called in relation to Keats the tiptoe effect. "Stood / Mute" is entirely different; the boy is now dead. De Man continues:

> This word "hung" plays an important part in the poem. It reappears in the second part, when it is said that the graveyard in which the boy is buried "*hangs* / Upon a Slope above the Village School." It establishes the thematic link between the two parts and names a central Wordsworthian experience. At the moment when the analogical correspondence with nature no longer asserts itself, we discover that the earth under our feet is not the stable base in which we can believe ourselves to be anchored. It is as if the solidity of earth were suddenly pulled away from under our feet and we were left "hanging" from the sky instead of standing on the ground. The fundamental spatial perspective is reversed; instead of being centered on the earth, we are suddenly related to a sky that has its own movements, alien to those of earth and its creatures. (79)

This is factitious. In neither part of the poem does the verb "to hang" remove us from earth to heaven. Even in Milton's passage about the fleet descried hanging in the clouds, there is no such removal; the "as if" is firmly in place. Wordsworth's churchyard is imagined as hanging upon a slope, not as suspended from the sky:

> In the second part of the poem, we are told, without any embellishment or preparation, that the boy died, and we now understand that the moment of silence, when the analogical stability of a world in which mind and nature reflect each other was shattered, was in fact a prefiguration of his death. The turning away of his mind from a responsive nature toward a nature that is not quite "of earth" and that ultimately is called an "uncertain heaven" is in fact an orientation of his consciousness toward a preknowledge of his mortality. The spatial heaven of the first five lines with its orderly moving stars

has become the temporal heaven of line 24, "uncertain" and precarious since it appears in the form of a preconsciousness of death. (80)

De Man concedes, reluctantly, that the "uncertain Heaven" is received into the bosom of the steady lake; the anxiety, if that is what it has been, is relieved. But he speaks of this line as representing "appeasement," as if that word denoted bad faith.

At this stage in de Man's reading of the poem it becomes clear why he wants to direct our minds away from the earth and point them toward a heaven uncertain and therefore precarious. It is not because an event on earth may correspond to an event among the stars, but because de Man interprets "that uncertain Heaven" as testifying to the most radical of all anxieties, fear of our inevitable death. That anxiety is in the mode of time rather than of place. It follows that de Man wants to delete Wordsworth's concern with the relation between mind and the steady natural world so that he can say that the "key to an understanding of Wordsworth lies in the relationship between the imagination and time, not in the relationship between imagination and nature" (92). In "Heaven and Earth in Wordsworth and Hölderlin" de Man says that for Wordsworth, as for Hölderlin, the analogy between mind and nature "is an inauthentic covering up of the barrenness of our condition."[22] Wordsworth's work shows "a persistent deepening of self-insight represented as a movement that begins in a contact with nature, then grows beyond nature to become a contact with time":[23] "The contact, the relationship with time is, however, always a negative one for us, for the relationship between the self and time is necessarily mediated by death; it is the experience of mortality that awakens within us a consciousness of time that is more than merely natural. This negativity is so powerful that no language could ever name time for what it is; time itself lies beyond language and beyond the reach of imagination. Wordsworth can only describe the outward movement of time's manifestation, and this outward movement is necessarily one of dissolution, the 'deathward progressing' of which Keats speaks in *The Fall of Hyperion*."[24] It is true that no language could name time for what it is, but many languages from Augustine to Wordsworth, Proust, Eliot, and Nabokov have described one's sense of time, the burden and dread of it. That is not enough for de Man; he must drive further and not stop until he crashes against an impasse. The first requirement is to move "from the eternalistic world of analogical thought into the temporal world of the imagination." The next one is this: "When memory dispels the false image of time as mere succession—an illusion of physical continuity borrowed from the geometrical world of space—the poetic imagination can come into play. This is not a reconciliation between mind and nature, but a passing alliance between the self and time. The mind asserts its priority over nature while at the same time asserting its unbreachable separation from Being. That Wordsworth would still have to use the same word, *Nature,* to designate what he moves beyond as well as what he can never reach indicates the hold that an analogical ontology has over our minds and vocabulary. The entire *Prelude* strives toward establishing the distinction between Nature and Being."[25] This is what de Man means by the "transformation of an echo language into a language of the imagination by way of the mediation of a poetic understanding of mutability."[26] The echo is specious, a trivial illusion. The only authentic relation is between the poetic imagination, mutability, and death; and the only thing the imagination can do is assert "the possibility of reflection in the face of the most radical dissolution, personal or historical."[27] That is: the imagination can think upon its own decay. When nature and history have failed, there are still the imagination and language. With that, de Man is at last content. He has produced a reading of "The Boy of Winander" and other poems in keeping with Heidegger's *Sein und Zeit.* His is a Wordsworth-after-Heidegger. It follows that it is inauthentic to cultivate a relation with the natural world; it is impossible for the mind to gain access to Being.

De Man's way of reading "The Boy of Winander" is formidable but perverse. I have to remind myself that Wordsworth, this victim of analogical ontology, wrote some of the most moving poems in the language—"Michael," "Resolution and Independence," "Surprised by Joy," "Ode: Intimations of Immortality," "Lines Written above Tintern Abbey," and parts of *The Prelude* in its three versions.

IV

The most powerful reading of "The Boy of Winander" because it is the most antithetical to it, is Robert Frost's poem "The Most of It":

He thought he kept the universe alone;
For all the voice in answer he could wake

Was but the mocking echo of its own
From some tree-hidden cliff across the lake.
Some morning from the boulder-broken beach
He would cry out on life, that what it wants
Is not its own love back in copy speech,
But counter-love, original response.
And nothing ever came of what he cried
Unless it was the embodiment that crashed
In the cliff's talus on the other side,
And then in the far distant water splashed,
But after a time allowed for it to swim,
Instead of proving human when it neared
And someone else additional to him,
As a great buck it powerfully appeared,
Pushing the crumpled water up ahead,
And landed pouring like a waterfall,
And stumbled through the rocks with horny tread,
And forced the underbrush—and that was all.[28]

This takes "The Boy of Winander" as read and for granted, but chiefly to reject its structure of hopes and fears: it is antithetical to Wordsworth mainly in its denying a presumed relation between human life and natural life. In spirit it is close to Aldous Huxley's argument, in "Wordsworth in the Tropics," that Nature can be felt as "divine and morally uplifting" only in the neighborhood of latitude fifty north. Even in the temperate zone, Huxley insists, Nature is "always alien and inhuman, and occasionally diabolic." A few weeks in Borneo or Malaya would have undeceived Wordsworth.[29]

The differences between "The Most of It" and "The Boy of Winander" start with Frost's first line. "Kept" indicates a more demanding relation to the universe than any posited by Wordsworth; it means possessed, held on to, with the responsibility that goes with that, as in Frost's "An Old Man's Winter Night." He thought he kept the universe alone; as in "keeping house," holding on to it and maintaining it in good order. Frost's Wordsworthian words—voice, answer, echo, response, mocking—are therefore in an ironic relation to the corresponding words in "The Boy of Winander." The issue is not ontology but getting by in the world. Getting by, by love, as in Frost's "Birches":

> Earth's the right place for love:
> I don't know where it's likely to go better.[30]

It is not surprising that the visible scene in "The Most of It" is far barer than in Wordsworth's poem: the starkness of the need is not alleviated by solemn imagery, rocks, woods, or sky. The "he" is not to be placated by copy speech, as the boy of Winander evidently was: the speech that Frost's guardian of the universe wants is an independent one, a counterstatement, not an echo of his own. But still a response. "Cry out on life" is odd, followed by "it," as if he undertook to speak in behalf of life, as he does, and not merely for himself. "Embodiment": embodiment of what? Presumably of his desire for a response from one of his own kind. It is a further irony that the embodiment turns out to be a body but one of a different species and therefore only technically "additional to him." In the last five lines the relentlessness of a life other than human life is insisted upon by the thrust of the sentences, especially in the collateral lines each beginning with "And," the last one enforcing the separateness of species by an additional "and"—"and that was all." The difference of tone is partly a difference between Wordsworth's blank verse and Frost's rhyming quatrains.

But the main difference between the two poems is that Frost's poem clears away Wordsworth's enhancing imagery. There are no familiarities between cliffs, islands, lakes, and the person who lives among them; no commutations of feeling or mood. Instead of the "bosom of the steady Lake" we have water "crumpled" by force of the great buck. Wordsworth's lines—

> and that uncertain Heaven, receiv'd
> Into the bosom of the steady Lake

—depend on two figures, one of them explicit, the other not: one, the lake as nurturing mother, receiving her child; the other, the lake as a mirror, receiving an image of something at large in the world. The first depends on the consanguinity of "receiv'd" and "bosom," the second on the fact that a mirror receives an image with equanimity. The first works not by resemblance—a mother's bosom does not resemble the surface of a lake—but by plenitude of connotation; the second works by a different sense of "receiv'd." A mirror, as Jean-Joseph Goux has remarked, "has the marvelous power of separating form from matter": it conveys an illusion of presence, the presence of the scene it mirrors, but the substance, the matter, is not given.[31] The destiny of the substance is to end up, resolved, as form: there if not elsewhere the uncertainty is removed. This interchange of metaphors, explicit and implied, is typical of Wordsworth. But not of Frost. Wordsworth's "that uncertain Heaven" is not even adverted to in "The Most of It." Frost's witness looks across the lake but neither up nor down. It is as if the diffuse anxiety in Wordsworth's poem—conceding for a moment that such a mood darkens the word "uncertain"—were now taken for granted, inscribed upon a scene that doesn't have to be further delineated. There is no uncertainty, because there has never been certainty. Frost's revision of "The Boy of Winander" is achieved with the help of Darwin, Nietzsche, and William James. His response to the blankness of isolation is that, like Hardy, he never expected much.

TWELVE

The Antinomian Pater

In the first chapter of *Studies in the History of the Renaissance* Walter Pater speaks of a Renaissance in France at the end of the twelfth and the beginning of the thirteenth century, "a Renaissance within the limits of the middle age itself—a brilliant but in part abortive effort to do for human life and the human mind what was afterwards done in the fifteenth."[1] A few pages later he ascribes to this medieval Renaissance a certain force of conviction: "One of the strongest characteristics of that outbreak of the reason and the imagination, of that assertion of the liberty of the heart, in the middle age, which I have termed a medieval Renaissance, was its antinomianism, its spirit of rebellion and revolt against the moral and religious ideas of the time. In their search after the pleasures of the senses and the imagination, in their care for beauty, in their worship of the body, people were impelled beyond the bounds of the Christian ideal; and their love became sometimes a strange idolatry, a strange rival religion."[2] Pater explains this assertion of the liberty of the heart by reference to one of his favorite motifs, the survival of the pagan gods, an idea he received from Heine's essay "Les Dieux en exil" (1853). In *The Renaissance* he speaks of the "return of that ancient Venus, not dead, but only hidden for a time in the caves of the Venusberg, of those old pagan gods still going to and fro on the earth, under all sorts of disguises."[3] The survival of the pagan gods in an otherwise Christian world accounts, he says, for the love of Abelard and Eloise, the legend of Tannhäuser, the Albigensian heresy, the Order of St. Francis, and the prophetic writings of Joachim di Fiore. Only the survival of the old gods could account for these; explain Joachim's Everlasting Gospel, for instance, according to which a third and final dispensation will come about in which Law, imposed by the Father, and Discipline, by the Son, will be super-seded by Love, the Freedom lavished by the Holy Spirit. Largely through Pater, Yeats wrote of "the coming among us of the dead."[4]

Pater chose rather casually these examples of the survival of the old gods. There is no evidence that he studied forms of antinomianism closer to home, the Muggletonianism that E. P. Thompson has described in *Witness against the Beast: William Blake and the Moral Law* (1993) or the other English forms of dissent discussed by A. L. Morton in *The Everlasting Gospel* (1958) and *The World of the Ranters* (1970) and by Christopher Hill in *The World Turned Upside Down* (1972). Nor did Pater show any interest in the theological bearing of antinomianism, the claim of "free grace" that its adepts advanced, or the sanction they found in St. Paul's Epistle to the Galatians 3.24–25: "The law was our schoolmaster to bring us unto Christ, that we might be justified by faith. But after that faith is come, we are no longer under a schoolmaster."[5] It was sufficient for Pater that he divined a spirit of antinomianism at large in the medieval Renaissance: he was not under a scholarly obligation to trace its sources.

Pater noted that the forms of antinomianism he had in mind were in rebellion against Christian doctrine, but he was reluctant to leave the matter there. He disliked presenting a conflict as if it were fixed in that character: it was a mark of his temper to see conflicts as mostly unnecessary. In this respect he was Wordsworthian: in one of the "Essays upon Epitaphs" Wordsworth spoke of "the best feelings of our nature; feelings which, though they seem opposite to each other, have another and a finer connection than that of contrast." It is a connection, Wordsworth said, "formed through the subtle progress by which, both in the natural and in the moral world, qualities pass insensibly into their contraries, and things revolve upon each other."[6] Pater thought that strong institutions should find it in their power to admit dissent even to the degree of heresy and to be liberal on principle. "Theories which bring into connexion with each other," he says, "modes of thought and feeling, periods of taste, forms of art and poetry, which the narrowness of men's minds constantly tends to oppose to each other, have a great stimulus for the intellect."[7] Pater's feeling for the Renaissance is largely his pleasure in finding such oppositions mitigated. The student of the Renaissance, he says,

> has this advantage over the student of the emancipation of the human mind
> in the Reformation, or the French Revolution, that in tracing the footsteps
> of humanity to higher levels, he is not beset at every turn by the inflexi-
> bilities and antagonisms of some well-recognised controversy, with rigidly
> defined opposites, exhausting the intelligence and limiting one's sympathies.
> The opposition of the professional defenders of a mere system to that more
> sincere and generous play of the forces of human mind and character, which
> I have noted as the secret of Abelard's struggle, is indeed always powerful.
> But the incompatibility with one another of souls really "fair" is not essen-
> tial; and within the enchanted region of the Renaissance, one needs not be
> for ever on one's guard. Here there are no fixed parties, no exclusions: all
> breathes of that unity of culture in which "whatsoever things are comely"
> are reconciled, for the elevation and adorning of our spirits.[8]

It is typical of Pater to assume that antinomian values are spiritually and aesthetically superior to the law they oppose: they exhibit "that more sincere and generous play of the forces of human mind and character," and they attract one's sympathy by being fair and comely. It follows that Pater, unusually sensitive to transitions and processes, does whatever he can to make the objects of his attention quietly give up their insistence: he is never pleased to see a force or an institution maintain its privilege. If the terminology of conflict seems unavoidable, he likes to separate the rival parties and to give the antinomian one its due if minor independence; ascribing to it the perfection of standing aside. In the chapter from which I've been quoting, he incurs the risk of contradicting himself for the sake of saying that Abelard "prefigures the character of the Renaissance, that movement in which, in various ways, the human mind wins for itself a new kingdom of feeling and sensation and thought, not opposed to but only beyond and independent of the spiritual system then actually realised."[9] Abelard "reaches out towards, he attains, modes of ideal living, beyond the prescribed limits of that system, though in essential germ, it may be, contained within it."[10] "Ideal" and "essential germ" in that sentence have much work to do: they have to suggest that those men who were in charge of the system could not imagine a culture finer than their own and therefore had an inadequate sense of the system as it might and should be. Pater warms to the antinomian motives not as lost causes he knows to be lost—that is the obvious way of dealing with them—but as values more refined than those of the system they rebelled against. In a passage found only in the first two editions of *The Renaissance* he writes: "The perfection of culture is not rebellion but peace; only when it has realised a deep moral stillness has it really reached its end. But often on the way to that end there is room for a noble antinomianism."[11] Pater recognizes that in any society there is likely to be a body of law, whether we call it power, Christianity, the state, or whatever other institution defines reality and demands that it be obeyed. And there are likely to be forces in conflict with the law and planning to oppose it. But he is especially tender to those feelings that do not attack the law directly but turn aside from it and hold quietly, if they can, to their independence. He thinks these feelings are likely to be the most refined, the most beautiful. So we recognize in Pater's temper a triple rhythm, a desire to move from power through conflict to stillness; from an apparently low degree of refinement to a higher and then an even higher one. I will try to clarify this rhythm in the movement of two essays.

The first is "Diaphaneitè," an essay he first gave as a talk to the Old Mortality in July 1864. He did not publish it, but he retained much of its spirit and several of its sentences for the essay on Winckelmann and the last chapter of *Studies in the History of the Renaissance*. The essay was published post-humously in *Miscellaneous Studies* (1895), the book prepared for the publisher by his friend Charles Shadwell.

Pater did not invent the word "diaphaneitè," he merely interfered with it by displacing the grave accent, a gesture that Shadwell allowed to stand. The word came into French in the fourteenth century and English in the seventeenth; in both languages it means the state of being pervious to light. Air, crystal, and shallow water are instances of it. David de Laura has shown that Pater's "Diaphaneitè" is much indebted to Arnold's *Essays in Criticism:* each marks an attempt to develop a concept of culture toward certain images of its embodi-ment. But Pater is more inventive than Arnold in this respect. Arnold appeals to one's best self as a moral quality independent of one's social class. Pater does not ask people to aspire toward their best or ideal selves in any moral sense: he is concerned with spiritual quality and is willing to let morals look out for themselves.

In "Diaphaneitè" he distinguishes three human types. The first is worldly; it coincides with material interests and enjoys their success. Thriving on fixity and definition, this type has the quality of men who govern. Or, extending the type toward Yeats's discrimination of literary types in "The Tragic Generation," it marks the type of writer who enjoys the companionship of his fellows by sharing a common sense of reality. Pater's second type is alien to the first, but related to it by this alienation: it is exemplified by the saint, the artist, and the sage. People of this second type are "out of the world's order," but they work "in and by means of the main current of the world's energy." Their right to live is easily conceded. Such people are useful to the world: "as if dimly conscious of some great sickness and weariness of heart in itself, it turns readily to those who theorise about its unsoundness." The second type speaks for the conscience of the first and is intermittently allowed to be audible. If it presented a serious risk of undermining the first type, it would have to be suppressed, but there is no risk. Similarly, the writers of Yeats's "tragic generation" are given space in which to express themselves and to run amok if they must. Pater says of these two types that in each "a breadth and generality of character is required," presumably because one type governs the world and the other lives by the irony of rebuking the vulgarity of that empire. The two are related by contrast and conflict, statement and counter-statement, assertion and denial.

Pater's third type is neither broad nor general but rare: "It does not take the eye by breadth of colour; rather it is that fine edge of light, where the elements of our moral nature refine themselves to the burning point. It crosses rather than follows the main currents of the world's life."[12] This is male homosexual code. The subject of the first sentence, "It," refers back to "another type of character." But the clarifying sentence—"rather"—doesn't continue describing the type, it identifies it with "that fine edge of light, where the elements of our moral nature refine themselves to the burning point." "Refine themselves," not "are refined," as if this self-refining were spontaneous, in the course of such a type. The type is as elemental as light and is indistinguishable from its supreme property, "that fine edge of light." Nothing is yet described. The light is not in landscape; it comes into general nature when the elements of our moral nature refine themselves to the burning point. Every detail from "that fine edge of light" through "refine themselves" to "the burning point" would be recognized by Pater's Oxford friends as an allusion to the flame of male homosexual love in Plato's *Symposium*. The type is recommended by being associated not with nature but with the free grace of an ideal nature.

The sentences I have quoted are the earliest version of Pater's most famous motif, that of burning with a hard, gemlike flame. In "Diaphaneitè" he protects the exemplars of this third type by saying that the world "has no sense fine enough for those evanescent shades"; it cannot classify them or engage with them as it engages with saints, artists, and sages. In the essay on Winckelmann "that fine edge of light" becomes "a sharp edge of light" and is attributed not to the few but to the "supreme Hellenic culture."

This third type may seem to be merely the embodiment of Arnoldian disinterestedness. Not so. Disinterestedness in Arnold's account is a quality of one's attention to images and objects at large. As in criticism: a good critic silences the dialogue of his mind with itself while he judges particular objects and actions in the light of the best ideas he can find. The critic should raise his mind above the bias of his standard interests and especially above his preoccupation with himself. He should pay attention to each object as he comes upon it, and he should discriminate one object from another. Disinterestedness is the quality of one who is alert in the world, conscientious, morally responsible. But Pater's third or diaphanous type does not observe this duty: such a person is not concerned with the world, he hardly prefers one part of the world's life to another. He looks to a higher consideration than any implied by such words as culture, society, and civility: he "seeks to value everything at its eternal world," and quietly claims to be the most sensitive judge of that. But "seeks" is misleading. The distinctive quality of this third type is simplicity; it is a happy gift of nature, such that it appears to issue from the higher order of grace, it comes "without any struggle at all." A person of this type treats life in the spirit of art and finds that as he comes nearer to the perfection of the type—with Pater it is always "he," not "she"—"the veil of an outer life not simply expressive of the inward becomes thinner and thinner." Such a person lives a transparent life, indifferent, beyond confusion, as if exempt from the exacerbation of meeting qualities in the world different from his own.

"Diaphaneitè" is a difficult essay, because it affronts one's common sense according to which more is good: the more life, the better. In Pater's sense of life, more is likely to be crass. A life is better the more refined it is, the more it dispenses with what the mob deems enrichments. Pater takes a common adjective of plenitude, cancels it, and presents its trace as supreme value. He lavishes praise upon one's willingness to do without. So we have his choice words: "colourless," "unclassified," "sexless," "impotence," "ineffectual," each of which acknowledges a temptation to plenitude, only to set it aside. Pater urges his fellows to live in the emptied space between "neither" and "nor." He speaks tenderly of reserve, the tact of omission, and even of the ultimate reserve, death.

Diaphaneity is exemplified first by Dante's Beatrice, then by Raphael, "who in the midst of the Reformation and the Renaissance, himself lighted up by them, yielded himself to neither, but stood still to live upon himself." It is also embodied in the hermaphrodites of Greek sculpture: "the statues of the gods had the least traces of sex." But the strangest instance of the type is Charlotte Corday. Pater recalls Carlyle's description of her in *The French Revolution*. It is hard to see Corday as diaphanous, but Carlyle presents her as complete, her energy "the spirit that will prompt one to sacrifice himself for his country." More to Pater's point, Carlyle describes Corday as "still": "of beautiful still countenance." Pater quotes the first part of this passage: "What if she, this fair young Charlotte, had emerged from her secluded stillness, suddenly like a Star; cruel-lovely, with half-angelic, half-daemonic splendour; to gleam for a moment, and in a moment be extinguished: to be held in memory, so bright complete was she, through long centuries!—Quitting Cimmerian Coalitions without, and the dim-simmering Twenty-five millions within, History will look fixedly at this one fair Apparition of a Charlotte Corday; will note whither Charlotte moves, how the little Life burns forth so radiant, then vanishes swallowed of the Night."[13] Marat's assassin, brought out for execution, "wears the same still smile." Pater shows no interest in the deed, or its moral quality, but he invokes Corday in Carlyle's image of her: entirely still, complete, self-possessed, her momentary gleam, her extinction, the after-image of her in our mind. She appears to be the cause of herself.

The main source of "Diaphaneitè" is clear. Gerald Monsman has emphasized the bearing of Fichte's transcendental idealism on this aspect of Pater's early work. To the idealist, as Fichte says in the "Second Introduction to the

Science of Knowledge," the only positive quality is freedom, "existence, for him, is a mere negation of freedom." The self begins with an "absolute posit- ing of its own existence."[14] To posit oneself and to be are one and the same. Fichte then declares that the self's mode of existence in the world is moral—in this he differs from Pater—and that its duty is to participate as finite being in the Absolute or Divine Idea. As if he anticipated Arnold's concept of culture and proposed an alternative to it, Fichte says, "In every age, that kind of edu- cation and spiritual culture by means of which the age hopes to lead mankind to the knowledge of the ascertained part of the Divine Idea, is the Learned Culture of the age; and every man who partakes in this culture is a Scholar of the age. . . . The true-minded Scholar will not admit of any life and activity within him except the immediate life and activity of the Divine Idea; . . . he suffers no emotion within him that is not the direct emotion and life of the Divine Idea which has taken possession of him. . . . His person, and all personality in the world, have long since vanished from before him, and entirely disappeared in his effort after the realization of the Idea."[15] This doesn't seem to differ much from Arnold's appeal, in *Culture and Anarchy,* to one's best self, but it does, because "best" in Arnold always means the best that public, historical life has produced; it refers to an accredited value, though one that is often ignored. Fichte does not appeal to a civic or accredited value: his Divine Idea has no more veridical existence than Wallace Stevens's Supreme Fiction; each is a name for the extreme reach of an idealist desire. Pater, too, derives his values, in "Diaphaneitè," from within: not the best but the most transparent self. But he does not invoke a Divine Idea in any sense distinct from the self at a given moment. He places the Divine Idea within the self and declares its realization to be the achievement of diaphaneity. "Simplicity in purpose and act," Pater says, "is a kind of determinate expression in dexterous outline of one's personality." "Determinate" is Fichte's word: *Bestimmtheit.* Simplicity is the mark of one's self-culture. Pater speaks of a "mind of taste lighted up by some spiritual ray within." The diaphanous person recognizes by instinct those elements in the world which are his, and will have nothing to do with any other: "It is just this sort of entire transparency of nature that lets through unconsciously all that is really lifegiving in the established order of things; it detects without difficulty all sorts of affinities between its own elements, and the nobler elements in that order."[16] Pater's "really" is always his answer to Arnold's claim in using the same word, that he knows the difference between appearance and reality. "Nobler" introduces a rival principle of choosing the things in the world that should concern the scholar, in Fichte's sense of scholar. Arnold is again alluded to and refuted, the Arnold of *Essays in Criticism* and "The Scholar Gypsy." Pater uses a phrase from the poem without naming it or its author. Having described the fulfillment of diaphaneity, he says that "this intellectual throne is rarely won." In "The Scholar Gypsy," Arnold writes:

> And then we suffer! and amongst us one,
>   Who most has suffered, takes dejectedly
> His seat upon the intellectual throne.

Arnold urges the gypsy, who has sequestered himself "with powers / Fresh, undiverted to the world without," to remain apart from that world, "with its sick hurry, its divided aims." Pater's diaphanous type is his version of the scholar gypsy—Arnold, sublimed by Fichte—with this difference, that he calls on him to come into the world and to maintain his autonomy there, as the perfection of standing still. The virtue to be practiced is always stillness, held against the force of circumstance and "one's own confusion and intransparency." It is Pater's highest tribute to Raphael that he "stood still to live upon himself." Hence "the heroism, the insight, the passion, of this clear crystal nature." Nearly thirty years later, in a lecture at Oxford on August 2, 1892, Pater thought it worthwhile to note that in the Blenheim Madonna in London Raphael has given the Baptist a "staff of transparent crystal."[17] Charlotte Corday, too, stood still in her being. It appears not to matter that Raphael painted masterpieces and Corday knifed Marat to death.

But the most complete exemplar of diaphaneity is not mentioned in Pater's essay. When he came to read Winckelmann in the light of Hegel and Goethe, he observed the signs of his diaphaneity, his sense of affinity to Plato, his "happy, unperplexed dexterity," his "transparent nature, with its simplicity as of the earlier world." But the clearest proof of Winckelmann's diaphaneity was the instinctive certitude with which he knew himself. As if to prepare the reader to recognize Winckelmann as a Fichtean scholar, Pater quotes Corday's words before the Convention: "On exécute mal ce qu'on n'pas conçu soi-même."[18] Twenty pages later Pater says of Winckelmann: "To the criticism of that consummate Greek modelling he brought not only his culture but his temperament. We have seen how definite was the leading motive of that culture; how, like some central root-fibre, it maintained the well-rounded unity of his life through a thousand distractions. Interests not his, not meant for him, never disturbed him. In morals, as in criticism, he followed the clue of instinct, of an unerring instinct."[19] The source of Winckelmann's instinct is nature, the root-fibre: the "motive," according to the second sentence in that passage, is the force of nature, the certainty of its affiliation to Winckelmann. There is no need to enquire further. Not only Winckelmann but his interests and the sculpture to which he felt such destined kinship speak of diaphaneity: the Panathenaic frieze as "the highest expression of the indifference which lies beyond all that is relative or partial." Indifference is another word for antinomian completeness. Pater speaks of the Hellenistic bronze in Berlin, the "Boy Praying": "Fresh, unperplexed, it is the image of man as he springs first from the sleep of nature, his white light taking no colour from any one-sided experience." The boy is "characterless, so far as *character* involves subjection to the accidental influences of life."[20]

The claim that Pater makes for diaphanous people could hardly be larger: the world has no use for them till it needs a scapegoat, hero, or sacrificial victim: "Poetry and poetical history have dreamed of a crisis, where it must needs be that some human victim be sent down into the grave. These are they whom in its profound emotion humanity might choose to send."[21] The essay ends with a prophetic conceit as wild as Joachim's: "People have often tried to find a type of life that might serve as a basement type. The philosopher, the saint, the artist, neither of them can be this type; the order of nature itself makes them exceptional. It cannot be the pedant, or the conservative, or anything rash and irreverent. Also the type must be one discontented with society as it is. The nature here indicated alone is worthy to be this type. A majority of such would be the regeneration of the world."[22] No writer is on oath in his last paragraph, but Pater can hardly expect to see a society founded on diaphaneity. Yeats's equivalent of that quality, the *sprezzatura* he found described in Castiglione's *Il Cortegiano*, variously translated as recklessness or nonchalance, is attributed to a few heroes, aristocratic free spirits, notably Kevin O'Higgins and Robert Gregory:

> Some burn damp faggots, others may consume
> The entire combustible world in one small room
> As though dried straw, and if we turn about

The bare chimney is gone black out
Because the work had finished in that flare.[23]

It is a typically theatrical version of Pater's flame, transforming "character" into "personality." But Yeats never envisaged those heroes as exemplars of a basement type of life. What can Pater have had in mind but a vision of human life beginning again, founding itself on the order of nature as a diaphanous person would interpret it, free of Adam and Eve, guilt, confusion, and opacity?

"Diaphaneitè" anticipates the essay on Winckelmann, Pater's most eloquent vision of a new life based on superior instinct, the companionship of comely young men, Hellenic in every tone, each self its own posited, assured divinity. But the essay may also be read in more general terms. Edward Thomas says of Pater that he "has no sense but vision, and he can adapt to it all things presented to him."[24] Thomas evidently means vision in a spiritual sense, but it is possible to adapt his sentence to a literal purpose. In this light, Pater's three types correspond to three experiences of seeing. In the first, it is gratifying to find the eye brought to temporary rest by seeing an object, opaque, unquestionable. This is a worldly pleasure, the rhetoric of realism, a procedure legitimized by its power of reference and stability. In the second, the eye sees an object, but equivocally: the relation between them is indeterminate. This may entail the rhetoric of irony, which claims to be superior, however belatedly, to what it sees. Irony takes pleasure not in objects seen but in itself, the mind in its distancing stance, gathering its force. In the third experience, the order ascending it may be in spirituality, the eye is gratified by ensuring that the object seen will have little or no authority, offer little or no resistance to the eye or the mind's eye. The mind sees through the object, as if the object were air, blue sky, crystal, or shallow water. In "In Memory of Robert Gregory" Yeats claims that the mind by that act of vision returns to itself with doubled might, presumably because it has found its power verified yet again.

In effect, Pater's essay is a plea to young men—Shadwell, preeminently—to remain young, childlike, transparent, free in a world that resents their freedom. Diaphaneity is an aesthete's word for freedom of mind and body, as if Emersonian self-reliance were to become indistinguishable from flesh and blood. It is also Pater's word for ideal passion leading to what the broad-backed world calls sin. In that respect "Diaphaneitè" is the beginning of Pater's thought as "The Child in the House" is the first expression of his desire.

The difference between "Diaphaneitè" and its development in *The Renaissance* is that in the first, Pater assumes with Fichte that unity of experience follows from the inaugural act of the self, its self-positing: in *The Renaissance* he finds not unity of experience but the flow of dispersal and recuperation. Subject and object are vulnerable now. We have no choice, we must take the mind as it appears to be, for the moment, and the object is forever dissolving in our gaze. "Natural laws we shall never modify," Pater writes in the essay on Winckelmann, "embarrass us as they may; but there is still something in the nobler or less noble attitude with which we watch their fatal combinations."[25] "Something" is not further explained, except that each of us may find it in himself and account it noble. I take "something" as Pater's euphemism for diaphaneity: it does not specify an object or a quality, but it is not nothing, it marks the site of a self-engendering, despite those natural laws. Meanwhile the pathos of "watch" is allowed to sigh. The supreme value is experience, whatever one makes of that.

Pater does not consider, in "Diaphaneitè" or elsewhere, the social and political consequences of Fichtean self-positing. One of the lessons learned from *The Origin of Species* was that values could not be simply deduced from a biological narrative of species. But Darwin's figures of development, progress, and refinement could be "translated inward," ascribed to a mind or a spirit considered to some extent free of body and matter. Progress could be attributed to one's desire, as a spiritual being, even if not to one's wisdom. One could desire finer feelings, and seek occasions for them. Pater found in the history of art, not in politics or social life, instances of self-positing, as in those visionary artists—Botticelli, for one—who are not content to transcribe the data before their eyes, they insist on the privilege of their own vision. For a politics of self-positing we go to Yeats in one of his moods; with this difference, that Yeats is moved by the energy gathered up in an act of self-positing rather than by its participation in a Fichtean Absolute Idea. In "The Statues," Yeats's Pearse mobilizes the energy of passion, subject, and will: he is not impelled by an Idea to be appealed to in default of God.

I have been describing a triple rhythm in Pater, his desire to posit a third state beyond the conflict of yea and nay. There are many occasions of this rhythm: indeed it is likely to occur wherever Pater recognizes a choice and prefers not to choose. In the essay on Botticelli, for instance, he is sympathetic to those angels who in the revolt of Lucifer were neither for God nor for His enemies: "So just what Dante scorns as unworthy alike of heaven and hell, Botticelli accepts, that middle world in which men take no side in great conflicts, and decide no great causes, and make great refusals. He thus sets for himself the limits within which art, undisturbed by any moral ambition, does its most sincere and surest work."[26] It is bold of Pater to claim as valid the use of the same adjective—"great"—in equal reference to conflicts, causes, and refusals. It is not surprising that in the essay on Giorgione he sees all the arts constantly aspiring toward the condition of music, the most refined, in performance the most "present," and the least combative mode of expression.

I'll comment more briefly on another instance of Pater's antinomianism, the triple rhythm we find in his essay on William Morris. Pater subsequently divided the essay in two parts, prepared a separate house for each, revised each while failing to note its effrontery, and suppressed each after its first appearance in a book. The part that became "Aesthetic Poetry" in the first edition of *Appreciations* includes Pater's version of art for art's sake. I must say a word or two about Morris and the aesthetic impulse.

Pater's exemplars of aesthetic poetry are Morris and D. G. Rossetti, but Morris even more than Rossetti. In the first stanza of *The Earthly Paradise* Morris acknowledges that "Of Heaven or Hell I have no power to sing." Not only does he lack Dante's genius and Milton's, but he cannot say anything to mitigate the conditions of our lives:

Of Heaven or Hell I have no power to sing,
I cannot ease the burden of your fears,
Or make quick-coming death a little thing,
Or bring again the pleasure of past years,
Nor for my words shall ye forget your tears,
Or hope again for aught that I can say,
The idle singer of an empty day.[27]

We have here the gist of aestheticism. Idle and empty are what the common world calls art. Morris takes the description without much ado. Yeats deals with a similar feeling in "Adam's Curse," defensively, since he knows that poets work their poems by stitching and unstitching, and women their beauty by labor just as hard. "Yet now it seems an idle trade enough." Morris is, I think, Yeats's example of the poet as he is Pater's, quoting precedents out of beautiful old books. If we are genial about this, we take "idle" to mean agreeably detached and "empty" to mean released from the interests commonly accepted as real. An aesthetic poet is one who considers what he can do, what he can feel, by standing aside. What he does has its merit in adversary relation to the Victorian consensus on the moral value of work.

Morris's apology is predicated on a condition nearly universal: there is nothing to be done, except for the little nothings an artist in this condition might attempt in his own terms. But the condition was also particular to Morris and Pater. John Lucas has argued that English writers in the middle of the nineteenth century started finding England, and especially English cities, unknowable. Even those writers who thought they had a strong claim to speak for the whole country started doubting that they could cope with such heterogeneity. *Bleak House* is profoundly concerned with this blankness.[28] Lucas's point might be developed. People in an industrial society have to learn to be indifferent to whatever they don't understand or can't control. Max Weber has described the process by which people in the later years of the nineteenth century started handing over large parts of their lives to experts: bankers, priests, economists, politicians. Most people seem to have done this reluctantly, and they took some of the harm out of necessity by persuading themselves that they still lived their true lives in the privacy of their feelings. Georg Simmel has developed this issue in *The Philosophy of Money,* emphasizing the separation of public and private life. Fortunate people with leisure and a little spare money resorted to experiences of music, literature, and painting to revive their sense of the missing or abandoned parts of their lives, or of forms of life they might still imagine. They convinced themselves that their silences were numinous, to be enjoyed in an art gallery, a library, a concert hall. As late as *Howards End,* the fateful events often happened at a concert or in a garden, while those sensitive people contemplated a distinctive house or old trees. The problem was: how to intuit a sense of the whole while learning to ignore or yield up to others much of what was there. Not that writers calmly gave up the attempt to understand the whole. The realistic novel became the major Victorian genre because novelists had more success than poets or dramatists in developing a relatively flexible language capable of registering the new forces they had to deal with. Aesthetic poetry was one expression of the premonition, sad indeed, that most of life could not now be understood and yet must be lived. Lived, if not ignored or taken on trust. Morris's aestheticism seems hard to square with his socialism, but it expresses the motives his socialism could not use up, his rueful sense that a day ostensibly full was also irrefutably empty. In *The Earthly Paradise* he justifies his singing "of names remembered / Because they, living not, can ne'er be dead." Pater might have made the same claim for *Marius the Epicurean,* but by then English fiction was preoccupied with semblances of living people rather than with sensations and ideas. Other forms of fiction were thought to be romances, sports, or conceits, the sort of thing Poe and Hawthorne wrote. *Marius the Epicurean* should have been a long poem, like *The Ring and the Book* or *Aurora Leigh,* not a work of prose in competition with *Middlemarch.*

Morris's aim in *The Earthly Paradise, The Life and Death of Jason,* and *The Defence of Guinevere*—the books to which Pater referred—was to intuit an alternative world, good while the reading lasted, by singing of fictive names remembered. Pater was delighted with the aim and charmed by the poems. He praised Morris for gathering into the nineteenth century so much of what was essential in Greek mythology and medieval poetry. Morris's poems, according to Pater, embodied a certain sequence in relation to ordinary life. The sequence defines aestheticism and embodies Pater's triple rhythm.

There is, to begin with, the ordinary world of sight and sound. Pater doesn't choose to be subtle about it or even to kick stones to verify it. Above that world there is a secondary state which he finds in poetry: "Greek poetry, medieval or modern poetry, projects above the realities of its time a world in which the forms of things are transfigured."[29] "Above," because the movement is toward more and more spiritual states; "the forms of things" are not allowed to impose themselves. The poet's will is taking command, even though the ordinary world of sight and sound is alluded to. But Pater then posits a third state and finds it in Morris's poetry. That poetry takes possession of the secondary world, "and sublimates beyond it another still fainter and more spectral, which is literally an artificial or 'earthly paradise.'" This third creation, Pater says, "is a finer ideal, extracted from what in relation to any actual world is already an ideal."[30] Morris begins with his apprehension of actual life, transcends it in a secondary universe, then creates an even finer one, chemically purer than the other. This third state, Pater says, is like some strange flowering after date, and "it renews on a more delicate type the poetry of a past age, but must not be confounded with it." The type has issued not from nature but from a formal anticipation of itself.

Pater's essay recites many versions of this triple rhythm. One of them involves Christianity, which starts from the ordinary world of sight and sound only to withdraw from it and to deny its authority. Pater regards the cloister as this secondary place, the monk its exemplar. But he thinks, by a remarkably brash prejudice, that a further reach is possible; that it is the supreme felicity of a religion, however monastic in its bearing, to spiritualize its doctrines and develop into an art. "Who knows whether, when the simple belief in them has faded away, the most cherished sacred writings may not for the first time exercise their highest influence as the most delicate amorous poetry in the world?" As an art, religion returns to the world, but now it is the world imagined, in Pater's terms as in Stevens's, "the ultimate good." The monk becomes a pagan not because he has given up his faith but because he has sublimed it beyond the letter of its law. Pater deduces this bizarre possibility from Morris's poems:

> The *Defence of Guinevere* was published in 1858; the *Life and Death of Jason* in 1867; and the change of manner wrought in the interval is entire, it is almost a revolt. Here there is no delirium or illusion, no experiences of mere soul while the body and the bodily senses sleep or wake with convulsed intensity at the prompting of imaginative love; but rather the great primary passions under broad daylight as of the pagan Veronese. This simplification interests us not merely for the sake of an individual poet—full of charm as he is—but chiefly because it explains through him a transition which, under many forms, is one law of the life of the human spirit, and of which what we call the Renaissance is only a supreme instance. Just so the monk in his cloister, through the "open vision," open only to the spirit, divined, aspired to and at last apprehended a better daylight, but earthly, open only to the senses. Complex and subtle interests, which the mind spins for itself may occupy art and poetry or our own spirits for a time; but sooner or later they come back with a sharp rebound to the simple elementary passions—anger, desire, regret, pity and fear—and what corresponds to them in the sensuous world—bare, abstract fire, water, air, tears, sleep, silence—and what De Quincey has called the "glory of motion."[31]

This is strange, unless we make much of the fact that to come back to the elementary passions is not the same experience as that of never having left them. Pater is imagining a post-monastic state, still in keeping with his triple rhythm. He imagines opening his eyes to daylight, but it is a "better daylight," after a night of dream or delirium. According to this vision, the "late" condition feels like a new first one: "Everywhere there is an impression of surprise, as of people first waking from the golden age, at fire, snow, wine, the touch of water as one swims, the salt taste of the sea. And this simplicity at first hand is a strange contrast to the sought-out simplicity of Wordsworth. Desire here is towards the body of nature for its own sake, not because a soul is divined through it."[32] This third state is a kind of "firstness," but it is the firstness of a newly created or posited world: it is not to be reached by nostalgia. We are to begin with a new Creation, if only this time to fail better. It is a world, Pater says, "in which the centaur and the ram with the fleece of gold are conceivable." In a gorgeous sentence: "The song sung always claims to be sung for the first time."

But my reference to a post-monastic state will not do. Pater places it more specifically. According to his essay on Morris, aesthetic poetry speaks of Courtly Love, its place is the chateau, its voice the fleshly lover's: "Hence a love defined by the absence of the beloved, choosing to be without hope, protesting against all lower uses of love, barren, extravagant, antinomian."[33] The adjectives refer to Provençal passion, not to mundane love. Lateness is all. "Barren," as in Yeats's "for a barren passion's sake"; extravagant, of course; antinomian, because its sprezzatura is autonomous, a choice of quietude, it scorns worldly success. Such love, Pater says, is "incompatible with marriage," it is love of the absent chevalier, "of the serf for the chatelaine, the rose for the nightingale, of Rudel for the Lady of Tripoli." Provençal poetry sings of vassalage: "To be the servant of love, to have offended, to taste the subtle luxury of chastisement, of reconciliation—the religious spirit, too, knows that, and meets just there, as in Rousseau, the delicacies of the earthly love. Here, under this strange complex of conditions, as in some medicated air, exotic flowers of sentiment expand, among people of a remote and unaccustomed beauty, somnambulistic, frail, androgynous, the light almost shining through them, as the flame of a little taper shows through the Host. Such loves were too fragile and adventurous to last more than for a moment."[34] These poets of Provence make a rival religion with a new cultus. "Coloured through and through with Christian sentiment, they are rebels against it." Like Abelard and Eloise.

So we have, finally, yet another triad in the figures of love: husband, monk, and courtly lover, the last of these doomed by office and definition, doomed in every respect but the transparency of his love.

THIRTEEN

On a Chapter of *Ulysses*

"What is the first half of 'Nausicaa,'" Hugh Kenner asks, "but Gerty MacDowell's very self and voice, caught up into the narrative machinery?"[1] Much of what I have to say arises from Kenner's rhetorical question and my doubts about it. But before I start disagreeing, I should indicate the aspects of "Nausicaa"—Chapter 13—that are uncontested.

I

Everyone agrees that the chapter is written, as Joyce told Frank Budgen, "in a namby-pamby jammy marmalady drawersy (alto la!) style with effects of incense, mariolatry, masturbation, stewed cockles, painter's palette, chitchat, circumlocutions, etc. etc."[2] It is also agreed that the story "Nausicaa" tells—such as it is—is drawn from several sources, including the following. First, the episode in the *Odyssey,* beginning with book 6, in which Nausicaa, beautiful daughter of King Alcinous and Queen Arete, is dreaming of her wedding. Attended by two handmaids, she goes to the beach for a picnic, plays ball, and sings with her companions: "and white-armed Nausicaa was leader in the song." "The much-enduring, goodly Odysseus" awakes to find the girls running free. Nausicaa befriends him, guides him to her father's court "in the city of the Phaeacians," and imagines that he might be her future husband: "Before, he seemed to me uncouth, but now he is like the gods, who hold broad heaven. Would that a man such as he might be called my husband, dwelling here, and that it might please him here to remain."[3] This episode gives the outline of "Nausicaa" and leaves Joyce free to gain effects of piquancy and pathos by having Gerty and Bloom communicate only by eyes and gestures: in the *Odyssey* their precursors speak to each other, but in *Ulysses* not a word. Nor is Joyce under obligation to allude to the episode in deferential or heroic terms; he can reduce its grandeur—if grandeur it has—as much as he likes. It is common nowadays to dismiss the Homeric story in its bearing on *Ulysses*, as if it were scaffolding, useful to Joyce but of no account to his readers. This seems vain to me, a trivial reaction to Eliot's praise of Joyce's "mythical method." Joyce took the Homeric story seriously enough, but he held himself free to take it opportunistically, too. As here in "Nausicaa."

The second and more immediate source, as Margot Norris has shown, is the Judgment of Paris.[4] The story begins with the exclusion of Eris, the goddess of discord, from the marriage feast of Peleus and Thetis. In revenge, Eris throws a golden apple labeled "For the Fairest" among the wedding guests. Three goddesses, Athena, Hera, and Aphrodite, fight for it. They submit their dispute to Paris of Troy for judgment, but each of them offers him a bribe for his favor. Paris awards the apple to Aphrodite, who promises him in return the most beautiful woman in the world, Helen of Troy, wife of Menelaus. In "Nausicaa" the judgment is alluded to only once—"the apple of discord" (42)—but the jealousy between the three girls is clear, and at one point the competition is explicit.[5] Cissy Caffrey asks Bloom to throw the ball to her. He throws it in her direction, but it rolls down the slope and stops "right under Gerty's skirt near the little pool by the rock" (355). "But the ball rolled down to her as if it understood," Bloom muses: "Every bullet has its billet" (950–951).

The third source is Satan tempting Eve in the Garden. One of Gerty's monologues has this divination of Bloom: "He was eying her as a snake eyes its prey. Her woman's instinct told her that she had raised the devil in him and at the thought a burning scarlet swept from throat to brow till the lovely colour of her face became a glorious rose" (517–520). The fourth source is the ritual of Christianity. The apposition of Gerty and the Virgin Mary inscribes throughout the chapter discrepancies of fantasy and desire. Finally, if we observe that we are reading a book of several chapters, there is whatever we remember of "Proteus" in which, several hours ago, Stephen Dedalus walked on Sandymount Strand and lay, for relief similar to Bloom's, on the same weedgrown rocks.

These are the forces of myth at work in the chapter. It is common, these days, to be hard on myth, as Frank Kermode is in *The Sense of an Ending*. According to Kermode, myth is what fiction becomes in the mode of its degradation. When we forget that our structures are fictive, devices to know by but not to act on, we let our fictions congeal into myths. *King Lear* is a fiction, anti-Semitism is a myth. But it is possible to think of myths more agreeably, as Northrop Frye did, and take them as stories told for the benefit of the community to which they are addressed. No harm in that. Even the community from which Kermode comes has its myths, the more insidious because it conceals them by calling them common sense. Besides, if a community told itself stories but insisted on their fictive character, they would soon lose their force and become constituents of the weightlessness from which many communities suffer. The myths of "Nausicaa"—Homer, the Judgment of Paris, Satan, the Virgin Mary—have the force of such stability and bearing as we grant them. They are not merely or equally residual. Taken for the moment together, they are emblems of a culture in some degree classical, Christian, and Irish. Joyce can present the Benediction ironically through Gerty's mind, but that doesn't mean that the Blessed Virgin and the Benediction are inauthentic. I have heard the Litany of the Blessed Virgin mumbled as rote, but I have also heard it recited devoutly—in Dublin, too—as if every invocation counted, and in that spirit it does. Buck Mulligan mocks the Mass with his shaving bowl, mirror, and razor, but the Mass survives his mockery, as we know when we take due part in its celebration.

It is also generally granted that in "Nausicaa" Joyce acted upon procedures he learned from Flaubert, especially the technique of cutting from one situation to another to enforce ironic discrepancy, as in the chapter of *Madame Bovary* in which fragments of speeches from the agricultural show at Yonville are heard at the same time as the love-talk of Emma and Rodolphe. In "Nausicaa" the main cutting is from the scene on the beach to the service of

Benediction in the Church of the Star of the Sea. These are simultaneously present in Gerty's mind. Joyce also learned from Flaubert how to deploy clichés, as in *Bouvard et Pécuchet*. Both procedures are evident in this passage from "Nausicaa":

> As per usual somebody's nose was out of joint about the boy that had the bicycle off the London bridge road always riding up and down in front of her window. Only now his father kept him in in the evenings studying hard to get an exhibition in the intermediate that was on and he was going to go to Trinity college to study for a doctor when he left the high school like his brother W. E. Wylie who was racing in the bicycle races in Trinity college university. Little recked he perhaps for what she felt, that dull aching void in her heart sometimes, piercing to the core. Yet he was young and perchance he might learn to love her in time. They were protestants in his family and of course Gerty knew Who came first and after Him the Blessed Virgin and then Saint Joseph. But he was undeniably handsome with an exquisite nose and . . . (129–141)

The passage is an epitome of the chapter, giving the gist of its themes and tones, romantic, religious, and sexual. The idling of Gerty's mind from brother to brother, bicycle to bicycle races, Trinity college to Trinity college university, is effected by a remarkably undemanding use of the word "like." It is enough to keep the wheels spinning downhill.

II

Coming back to Kenner's question about Gerty MacDowell: he asks it in *Joyce's Voices*, where he expounds the "Uncle Charles Principle," as he calls it, a narrative method by which "the normally neutral narrative vocabulary" is pervaded "by a little cloud of idioms which a character might use if he were managing the narrative." If you were to ask Uncle Charles what he did in the morning, he would say that he creased and brushed his hair, brushed and put on his tall hat, and repaired to the outhouse to smoke his tobacco, a brand of black twist he found very cool and mollifying. So we read: "Every morning, therefore, uncle Charles repaired to his outhouse but not before he had creased and brushed scrupulously his back hair and brushed and put on his tall hat."[6] The Uncle Charles Principle, in Kenner's version, is this: "the narrative idiom need not be the narrator's."[7] The principle is sometimes called *style indirect libre,* presumably because it is free to appropriate a particular character's vocabulary and to posit as real, for the time being, only what that character would designate as real.

Kenner works on two large assumptions, that there is always a narrator and that normally the narrator employs a neutral vocabulary. I can't see how a vocabulary could be neutral unless it restricted itself to indications of number and location on the advice of Alain Robbe-Grillet. There were two cats on the mat. Taking Kenner's second assumption first, I put it to the test by consulting *The Wings of the Dove.* The scene is the one, near the beginning of the novel, in which Kate Croy's father after unconscionable delay presents himself to her: "When her father at last appeared she became, as usual, instantly aware of the futility of any effort to hold him to anything. He had written her he was ill, too ill to leave his room, and that he must see her without delay; and if this had been, as was probable, the sketch of a design he was indifferent even to the moderate finish required for deception. He had clearly wanted, for the perversities he called his reasons, to see her, just as she herself had sharpened for a talk; but she now again felt, in the inevitability of the freedom he used with her, all the old ache, her poor mother's very own, that he couldn't touch you ever so lightly without setting up. No relation with him could be so short or so superficial as not to be somehow to your hurt."[8] There is indeed a narrator, on the evidence of there being a narrative voice that recites the episode. But the narration is not neutral. The tone of the sentences is continuously sympathetic to Kate. We are invited to believe in her sense of the issue at hand, her father's alleged falsity, his refusal to be straight when he might be crooked. But there is no reason to think that Kate, if she were managing the narrative, would use these words. She would not bring forward the metaphor traced in "sketch," "design," and "finish." She would not refer to the "perversities he calls his reasons." Henry James or the narrator is thinking for Kate, completing in his terms what she might have started with her own. The narrative voice surrounds Kate but does not defer to the consideration of what precisely she might say in her own behalf.

Kenner's first assumption, that there is always a narrator, is also questionable. In many works of fiction it is convenient to refer to the narrative voice, as if the voice issued from a person who might be thought of as producible even if not visibly present in a particular scene. But the invention of the printing press has made it possible to confound this assumption, and to thwart the expectations attendant upon the words "author" and "narrator." Fracture and anonymity are aspects of the narrative just as coercive as acoustic recognition and other intimations of continuity. It is impossible to say who wrote the editorials in this morning's *New York Times,* which enforce the notion that a certain corporate stance, a system of political attitudes, issues in those sentences. An anonymous journalist wrote them. Or a team of journalists. It is hard to give up the notion that words on a page have been spoken by a person ready to take responsibility for them, but the machinery of print has made it commonplace to dislodge words from any quasi-personal quality and to deploy them in the mode of simulation. Critics of *Ulysses* regularly invoke a narrator and, for one of its chapters, an arranger, but in some chapters we do well to abandon the mystification of thinking that we hear a voice and therefore a person speaking. We still have to learn how to read such chapters.

III

"Nausicaa" begins: "The summer evening had begun to fold the world in its mysterious embrace. Far away in the west the sun was setting and the last glow of all too fleeting day lingered lovingly on sea and strand, on the proud promontory of dear old Howth guarding as ever the waters of the bay, on the weedgrown rocks along Sandymount shore and, last but not least, on the quiet church whence there streamed forth at times upon the stillness the voice of prayer to her who is in her pure radiance a beacon ever to the stormtossed heart of man, Mary, star of the sea" (1–8). Not omniscient narration: this passage comes from knowledge local and partial, the "collective assemblage" that Gilles Deleuze and Félix Guattari describe in *A Thousand Plateaus* as the source of anything that may be said in a given society. The sentences do not describe Sandymount strand in any objective sense, even though the references to Howth and the Church of the Star of the Sea have the force of being verifiable. You can take a bus or a train to Howth, you can pray in the Church of the Star of the Sea. The paragraph "sets the scene" in accordance with what Kenneth Burke calls, in *A Grammar of Motives,* "the scene-agent ratio": that is, a scene is described such that its quality will be apposite to the agents or characters who will be featured in it. What is implicit in the scene will be explicit in the characters, especially Gerty MacDowell.

Hence the characteristic diction of the paragraph. After the anfractuosities of "Cyclops" we have the melting of mood into mood, the idiom of felicity construed as a scene, at once natural and cultural, of embracings and foldings, the sun falling with universal benevolence on sea, strand, Howth, and rocks alike, and—not least—on the church devoted to the Blessed Virgin—a "beacon ever to the stormtossed heart of man." If the paragraph implies a voice, as in "dear old Howth," it is the communal voice of Dublin, Irish, and Catholic, speaking of consonance and warmth, nature and nurture at one. The tempo of the paragraph is continuously *lento,* the mood *cantabile.* The gravity appropriate to the church is achieved by a delaying phrase—"last but not least"— and by the formality of "whence" and "streamed." Local conflicts will develop between Gerty and her friends, but they will be resolved by the affiliation of nature and society, landscape and the correspondingly emollient feelings.

The first paragraph does not anticipate the complications of the story, the contest between the girls, Bloom's masturbation, and Gerty's erotic fantasies, but it suffuses them and appeases their transgressions in the end. With so much begun, the narration moves to accommodate Gerty and her friends. Gerty is not named yet, being reserved for loftier registrations: "The three girl friends were seated on the rocks, enjoying the evening scene and the air which was fresh but not too chilly. Many a time and oft were they wont to come there to that favourite nook to have a cosy chat beside the sparkling waves and discuss matters feminine, Cissy Caffrey and Edy Boardman with the baby in the pushcar and Tommy and Jacky Caffrey, two little curlyheaded boys, dressed in sailor suits with caps to match and the name *H. M. S. Belleisle* printed on both" (9–15). Not quite the Uncle Charles Principle: none of these girls would report that they were "seated on the rocks," or use a tag from Shakespeare. None of them would discriminate between "fresh but not too chilly," or say "wont to come," "the sparkling waves," and "matters feminine." It is stereotypical narration, designed to intuit the type of recreation and contentment that Dublin girls of a certain social class enjoyed, rather than to distinguish—as yet—between these three. The phrases denote a cultural formation unquestioningly familial, literate up to a point soon reached, and repetitively at one with its simple pleasures.

When it comes to a difference between Gerty and her two friends, the narration notes the difference as a quality of her syntax: "But Gerty's crowning glory was her wealth of wonderful hair. It was dark brown with a natural wave in it. She had cut it that very morning on account of the new moon and it nestled about her pretty head in a profusion of luxuriant clusters and pared her nails too, Thursday for wealth" (115–119). Kenner says of the last sentence: "So eager is the second 'and' to join 'pared' with 'cut'—Gerty has performed the due rituals, has observed the moon and the Thursday—that it crumples syntax (was it hair that pared?) in flushed impetuosity."[9] I would call the sentence an instance of imitative form and note Gerty's redundant emphasis— "that very morning"—and the syntax that Kenner describes. But the rest of the sentence gives us not what Gerty would say of herself, but what she yearns to have someone say of her, that her hair nestled about her pretty head in a profusion of luxuriant clusters. Her impetuosity is not so flushed that it can't wait for a grand flourish of appreciation offered between Gerty's obeisance to the moon and the propriety of the manicure, Thursday for wealth. Margot Norris is driven to posit "a phantom narrator constructed by Gerty's imagination to produce the language of her desire, the hypothetical discourse of her praises that she fears no one will ever utter."[10]

Several pages later, after the masturbation, Gerty and Bloom exchange the discourse of eyes and silence:

> Then all melted away dewily in the grey air: all was silent. Ah! She glanced at him as she bent forward quickly, a pathetic little glance of piteous protest, of shy reproach under which he coloured like a girl. He was leaning back against the rock behind. Leopold Bloom (for it is he) stands silent, with bowed head before those young guileless eyes. What a brute he had been! At it again? A fair unsullied soul had called to him and, wretch that he was, how had he answered? An utter cad he had been! He of all men! But there was an infinite store of mercy in those eyes, for him too a word of pardon even though he had erred and sinned and wandered. Should a girl tell? No, a thousand times no. That was their secret, only theirs, alone in the hiding twilight and there was none to know or tell save the little bat that flew so softly through the evening to and fro and little bats don't tell. (741–753).

Kenner refers to "Gerty MacDowell's very self and voice," apparently intending no irony: he assumes that the three emphatic words coincide with her. Fritz Senn thinks it "a triumph of indirect characterization" that "through such a melange of set pieces and trash" does Gerty "emerge as a person in her own right."[11] What does it mean to ascribe to Gerty a very self and voice, or to claim that she emerges as a person in her own right?

Take the passage I've just quoted. It reads like the stage directions for a scene of Victorian melodrama, with Bloom as the cad who has taken advantage of the innocent maiden. Not that Bloom sees himself in that role. In the second half of the chapter we find that he's not at all dismayed by his having used the image of Gerty's legs and thighs for masturbation; he thinks it a matter of no account. The paragraph presents Bloom in one of the many ways in which he might be seen, but not as he sees himself. Gerty sees herself for the time being as the Blessed Virgin with an infinite store of mercy, forgiving the poor sinner. But also as the heroine of a tragedy, her silence approved by the "hiding twilight." She is a bovaryste, according to Jules de Gaultier's description of that form of cognition: bovarysme is the power given to human beings to see themselves as other than they are.[12] Homais in *Madame Bovary* and Regimbard in *L'Education Sentimentale* are cases in point. In *Mensonge romantique et vérité romanesque* René Girard extended de Gaultier's essay into a theory of the mimetic or triangular structure of desire. My desire for another person is mediated through a third: the one I really desire is the mediator. But what I crave is to appropriate the mediator, whom I see as my rival. My desire is mimetic, it seeks to take the place of the mediator. The worst thing that can happen to me as a desiring subject is to see my imitation brought into the open.[13] Paolo and Francesca fall in love after they have been reading the story of Lancelot and Guinevere. The "real" kiss follows and imitates the imaginary one, as Renato Poggioli says.[14]

In "Nausicaa," desire is the form in which Gerty sees herself as she is not. But the desire, and the vicarious image in which Gerty sees herself, are never spontaneous. Senn makes the point that "Gerty's mind is almost incapable of recognizing an identity." There is always a "preexisting classification to which phenomena have to conform, and she, herself, seems predetermined: 'she was more a Giltrap than a MacDowell.' "[15] But she seems predetermined not by being enslaved to a single fate but by having only a few paradigms of desire available to her. The Blessed Virgin is the main one. There is no evidence that in taking the Blessed Virgin as mediator, the rival third, between herself and Bloom, she knows what she is doing. But her desire may still be mimetic in Girard's sense: she may take the Blessed Virgin as mediator, the supreme form of herself as she sees it, and wish to take Mary's place in that capacity.

What then of her "very self and voice," of her emerging as a "person in her own right"? This is a difficult issue: much depends on the scale of the claim. Everyone agrees that the materials that have constituted Gerty as a person are mostly degraded; a put-upon, snuff-snorting mother, a warm-hearted but drunken and rough father, the lore of women's magazines and novelettes, the narcissistic rigmarole of fashion, low paradigms of romance. There is also the ritual of Catholicism, a structure of beliefs and practices that I admire far more than Joyce did. Gerty's devotion to the Blessed Virgin is habitual, and it allows her to see herself in a dramatic light, but it is not null. She may be interpreted as merely the sum of her experiences, in which case there is little further to be said. But Kenner and Senn evidently judge that she is more than that sum, or that she is somehow independent of her experiences. Kenner hasn't provided any reasons; Senn has: "By expressing unmitigated disdain for the cliché, for *kitsch,* and for a victim like Gerty MacDowell (or Bloom's inept endeavors), we also, of course, are adopting a Gertyan pose, pretending to remain perpetually above their inefficacious lure. But the lure affects us too, on and off. Romantic *kitsch* in 'Nausicaa' (or in 'Sirens') also serves to embody the motif of seductiveness, to which most readers are not wholly immune. There is a fascination about that glamour too, an appeal that we hesitate to acknowledge."[16] Senn doesn't say what he means by kitsch. I assume he means what Milan Kundera has in view in the May Day parade described in *The Unbearable Lightness of Being.* Kundera says that the parade expresses not political agreement with Communism but "an agreement with being as such."[17] Kitsch would then mean any cultural manifestation from which even the possibility of misgiving, equivocation, and irony has been removed. Presenting no challenge to your desires, it invites you to be folded in its mysterious embrace. A work of kitsch is always sincere and always pleased with itself, it has no quarrel with reality. What it expresses is agreement with the malleability of the world, its susceptibility to the expression of one's desires and aspirations, its readiness to take beautiful forms. If that, or something like it, is what Senn has in mind by kitsch, I agree with him. Of course Joyce is mocking the cheap mellifluousness of the culture in which Gerty lives, but he is not merely mocking it. He is allowing it to hold on to a certain withered charm. Margot Norris's conclusion on this issue is unnecessarily censorious: "By earning from his contemporaries praise for his use of myth, Joyce further dramatizes modernism's blind eye to the cruelties of its own elitism, the libidinal impulses behind its attacks on what is poor, mean, squalid, and cheap in the culture, and the dishonesties of its own pretensions."[18] Those of us who have been schooled to admire high culture are often moved to tears by middlebrow and lowbrow forms. We are embarrassed to find ourselves moved. The impact of sentimental films—the first *Brief Encounter,* for example, in which steam from the train engine separated the lovers—is hard to understand, but irrefutable. I approve of Senn's implication that the materials of Gerty's experience are not merely or entirely degraded; there is true life in them, as well as false. Clichés are not merely moribund discourse, they harbor life as well as death. Perhaps these considerations amount to Gerty's being a person in her own right. She still seems to me, to cite a distinction proposed by Yeats, a character rather than a personality; she is more the result of her cultural conditions than the self-willed author of new experience. But we have been instructed to modify our claims to autonomy, especially if de Gaultier and Girard are right. My own reading of Gerty emphasizes the attribute she doesn't mention—her limp, and the resilience with which she suffers it. Joyce seems to me to be tender rather than scathing in this chapter. I can't see where in "Nausicaa" he attacks what is poor, mean, squalid, and cheap in Gerty's culture; perhaps because her sentimentalities are close to those he enjoyed in nineteenth-century Romantic opera and song.

But if Gerty is a person in her own right, it means that Joyce has given her the boon of a life to some extent independent of its material conditions. In *The Philosophy of Money,* Georg Simmel indicated the factors in nineteenth-century economics and politics that had the effect of splitting one's private life from one's material or public life. It became common to regard one's private life as the sole form of one's authenticity, by comparison with which one's life among the given social and economic forces was felt to be specious, however necessary. This could be deemed a blessing or a catastrophe. But it was one of the chief goals of capitalism, as John Carlos Rowe has pointed out: "Capitalism lays special claim to the individual subject as the figure capable of affirming, expressing, and reproducing itself in and through a capitalist economy. This may well be the fundamental irony of capitalism; it is in fact the great artistic *achievement* of capitalism: to turn into a philosophical origin and end the very individual that capitalist economic practices seem intent upon destroying. By now, the 'solution' to this apparent paradox is familiar enough.

Alienating workers from the coherent processes and products of their own labor-power, capitalism invents a philosophical and idealist 'category' of the 'subject' that defines itself just insofar as it can distinguish itself from its material circumstances."[19] The "subject"—Gerty MacDowell, Leopold Bloom, Molly Bloom, and other characters in the novel—may not know enough to make this distinction, but Joyce may give them the enjoyment of it nonethless. That is the main reason for the attacks on Joyce which have been made in recent years by Fredric Jameson, Leo Bersani, and other critics: they deem it a scandal that Joyce, ostensibly an avant-garde writer, gives his characters the old nineteenth-century privilege of appearing to be more than the sum of their conditions. In Bersani's view, Beckett—not Joyce—is the truly avant-garde writer, because he shows his figures—Watt, Molloy, and the rest—not unified but dispersed among their attributes.

IV

When Gerty gets up to join the girls and the children at the bottom of the strand, Bloom notices her limp: "Tight boots? No. She's lame! O!" (771): "Mr Bloom watched her as she limped away. Poor girl! That's why she's left on the shelf and the others did a sprint. Thought something was wrong by the cut of her jib. Jilted beauty. A defect is ten times worse in a woman. But makes them polite. Glad I didn't know it when she was on show. Hot little devil all the same. I wouldn't mind" (772–776). Bloom's syntax differs from Gerty's. He has had his tumescence. Now one image is displaced without delay or fuss by another. A reference to Gerty—"Jilted beauty"—leads to a rough generalization—"A defect is ten times worse in a woman." Then to another one, callous indeed—"But makes them polite." Bloom doesn't even linger over an erotic image, being quite willing to see it yield to a commonplace one: "Still she was game. Lord, I am wet. Devil you are. Swell of her calf. Transparent stockings, stretched to breaking point. Not like that frump today. A. E. Rumpled stockings. Or the one in Grafton street. White. Wow! Beef to the heel" (928–932). He knows about bovarysme though he doesn't call it that. Nor is he a victim of it, his desires being cooler than Gerty's:

> Mr Bloom with careful hand recomposed his wet shirt. O Lord, that little limping devil. Begins to feel cold and clammy. Aftereffect not pleasant. Still

you have to get rid of it someway. They don't care. Complimented perhaps. Go home to nicey bread and milky and say night prayers with the kiddies. Well, aren't they? See her as she is spoil all. Must have the stage setting, the rouge, costume, position, music. The name too. *Amours* of actresses. Nell Gwynn, Mrs Bracegirdle, Maud Branscombe. Curtain up. Moonlight silver effulgence. Maiden discovered with pensive bosom. Little sweetheart come and kiss me. Still, I feel. The strength it gives a man. That's the secret of it. Good job I let off there behind the wall coming out of Dignam's. Cider that was. Otherwise I couldn't have. Makes you want to sing after. *Lacaus esant taratara.* (851–863)

Bloom is not entirely the victim of this rhetoric. He knows he is at the opera or the music-hall, he doesn't mistake this venue for reality. So he lets his mind ramble disinterestedly over many themes: menstruation, women's clothes, masturbation, prostitutes, perfume, magnetism, priests, Bailey Lighthouse on Howth Head, the flying bat, and smells, including his own: "Mr Bloom inserted his nose. Hm. Into the. Hm. Opening of his waistcoat. Almonds or. No. Lemons it is. Ah no, that's the soap" (1042–1043). Some themes can't be fended off, especially if you defer—as Bloom does—to a vaguely understood theory of magnetic force. Did Bloom's watch stop at 4:30 because that was the moment at which Blazes Boylan entered Molly? "Was that just when he, she? . . . O, he did. Into her. She did. Done . . . Ah!" (849–850).

V

There are far more styles in "Nausicaa" than I have annotated. Senn has examined some of them. But perhaps I have said enough to draw further attention to styles as such, and to Joyce's typical ways with them. Rowe has argued that the guiding motive of modern artists is "to exceed the boundaries and limitations of modern society and its discursive formulations": "The modern artist stakes his/her claim by insisting upon the figural and connotative variety of literary style. By contrast, the 'language of the marketplace' is simply denotative and suppresses figural play for the sake of useful, literal meanings whose references to things and concepts are established by consensus."[20] I think Rowe has in mind the diverse uses of the demotic in "The Waste Land," Pound's *Cantos,* and Williams's *Paterson.* But the figural and connotative variety of literary style he refers to is not deployed merely to scorn the language of the marketplace. Joyce had no style, but mastery of many styles. In "Oxen of the Sun," "Cyclops," "Nausicaa," and other chapters of *Ulysses* he appropriates old styles, partly to make fun of them, but also to add to the stock of available reality, as R. P. Blackmur said literature is supposed to do.

FOURTEEN

Yeats: The New Political Issue

I

On September 18, 1923, W. B. Yeats wrote the first draft of "Leda and the Swan" and called it "Annunciation." He revised it several times even after he had published it in *The Dial* (June 1924) and *To-Morrow* (August 1924).[1] The definitive text appeared as "Leda" in the first edition of *A Vision* (1925) and as "Leda and the Swan" in *The Tower* (1928). Most editions since 1928 have the date 1923 appended. I'll comment on the poem later.

Yeats died on January 28, 1939. For several years after his death it was commonly thought that there were two aspects of his life and work that came into question and might amount to scandals. The first of these was his commitment to occult and esoteric practices, seances and so forth, the Southern Californian element in him, as Auden called it. T. S. Eliot deplored Yeats's interest in such practices and regarded it as an aberration in a great poet. He was not alone in that sentiment. But I don't think modern readers are much troubled by the occult aspect of Yeats's life. Their attitude seems to be: let him seek communication with spirits if he has a mind to and if it helps him to write his poems. Besides, R. F. Foster has offered a reasonable explanation of this practice. He maintains that Yeats's dealings with the occult are at one with what Foster calls Protestant Magic. In *Paddy and Mr. Punch* and again in the first volume of his biography of Yeats, Foster argues that the condition of beleaguered Irish Protestants from the early nineteenth century was epitomized by the Gothic or "supernatural" fictions of Charles Maturin, Sheridan Le Fanu, and Bram Stoker. Maturin's *Melmoth the Wanderer,* Le Fanu's *Uncle Silas* and *Carmilla,* and Stoker's *Dracula* are the work of Irish Protestants "often living in England but regretting Ireland, stemming from families with strong clerical and professional colorations, whose occult preoccupations surely mirror a sense of displacement, a loss of social and psychological integration, and an escapism motivated by the threat of a takeover by the Catholic middle classes—a threat all the more inexorable because it is being accomplished by peaceful means and with the free legal aid of British governments."[2] By "peaceful means" and "the free legal aid of British governments" Foster has in mind the several Land Acts that British govern-ments passed in the late nineteenth century and early twentieth to bring the land agitation to an end. The crucial acts were those of 1885 and 1903: their aim was to facilitate the transfer of land in Ireland from landowner, usually Protes-tant, to tenant, usually Catholic. It seems reasonable to account for Protestant Magic in terms of such fears, especially when we recall the mixture of contempt and dread that Yeats felt toward Daniel O'Connell. Catholics revered O'Con-nell as the Liberator, hero of Catholic Emancipation. Yeats hoped to remove the specter of O'Connell, the man of the people, by rhetorical appeal to Parnell, the lonely, autonomous hero. I might add that magical practices and the speculations that accompanied them also gave Yeats a relatively clear space for the play of his subjective or neo-Platonic imagination.

The second source of scandal was the increasingly authoritarian insistence of Yeats's political convictions, especially after the assassination of Kevin O'Higgins on July 10, 1927. This rage for images of authority could be regarded as the fantasy of a bitter and powerless man, ash on an old man's sleeve. But in the years leading up to the execution of Mussolini and the death of Hitler, and especially after the discovery of the death camps at Belsen, Buchenwald, and Dachau, the question of Yeats's politics became, in retrospect, a difficult is-sue. It could not be ascribed to his excessively devout reading of Gentile's theories of education. A few of his contemporaries, notably Louis MacNeice and Joseph Hone, had long since adverted to Yeats's quasi-Fascist tendency, but the subject was not closely examined till 1965, when Conor Cruise O'Brien published "Passion and Cunning: An Essay on the Politics of W. B. Yeats." O'Brien's essay was revisionist in its intent, a biographical study of Yeats the public figure, designed to undermine his "myth of himself as 'a foolish passionate man.'" The weight of the evidence suggested to O'Brien that Yeats was "something much more interesting: a cunning passionate man."[3]

O'Brien's themes were the standard ones: Yeats's predicament as an Anglo-Irish Protestant in a country largely Catholic and at least residually Gaelic; his nationalism under the auspices of the old Fenian John O'Leary; the influence of Maud Gonne, which O'Brien thought not as significant as common opinion held; the fall and death of Parnell in 1891; Maud Gonne's marriage to John MacBride in 1903; the Dublin Lock-Out of 1913; the Easter Rising of 1916; the Treaty; the Civil War; the founding of the Irish Free State; the rise of Fascism in Italy and of General O'Duffy's Blueshirts in Ireland; and Yeats's last years. O'Brien interpreted Yeats's part in these episodes as showing that he was not the fragile, wilting poet of early legend but a worldly man who kept his eye on the main chance. In the Lock-Out of 1913, for instance, Yeats took the workers' part not because he felt a rush of sympathy for the urban poor but because he had his own reasons for opposing the powerful newspaper owner William Martin Murphy and his associates, the main representatives of the employers; and because he resented the interference of the Catholic Archbishop of Dublin, who told the workers' wives that if they allowed their children to be brought to England to be fed, they could no longer be held worthy of the name of Catholic mothers.[4]

The part of O'Brien's essay that has been most influential is his documentation of Yeats's authoritarian zeal in the years from 1927 to 1939. He argues that Yeats never modified this zeal, but that he recognized, by the early months of 1934, that Eamon de Valera was too strong for O'Duffy and that the blue of the Blueshirts had faded. The Yeats who began to sneer at the Blueshirts when they proved a flop was not, O'Brien claimed, more "real" than the Yeats "who was excited about them when he thought they might win." It was the same Yeats, "strongly drawn to Fascism, but no lover of hopeless causes."[5]

O'Brien's essay has been much criticized and in many details corrected by Elizabeth Cullingford, Grattan Freyer, and other scholars, but it seems to me to have weathered these interrogations pretty well. I find his biographical account of Yeats convincing on the whole: it doesn't greatly change what we already knew, but it adds concentrated evidence.

II

The most original page of O'Brien's essay is the one on which he describes a quandary we have not been able to resolve. It has to do with a poet's imagination rather than with biographical facts. O'Brien refers to George Orwell's essay on Yeats in which Orwell seeks "some kind of connection between [Yeats's] wayward, even tortured style of writing and his rather sinister vision of life." Orwell finds this connection, O'Brien maintains, "so far as he finds it at all, in Yeats's archaisms, affectations and 'quaintness.' " But the argument, as O'Brien notes, is implausible:

> This does not fit very well, for the "quaintness" was at its height in the 'nine-ties, when Yeats's vision of life was, from either an Orwellian or a Marxist point of view, at its least sinister: when he was identified with the popular cause in his own country and when, in England, he sat at the feet of William Morris and looked on Socialism with a friendly eye. Unfortunately for Or-well's thesis, it was precisely at the moment—after the turning point of 1903—when Yeats's vision of life began to turn "sinister"—aristocratic and proto-Fascist—that he began to purge his style of quaintness, and his great-est poetry was written near the end of his life when his ideas were at their most sinister. A Marxist critique which starts from the assumption that bad politics make for bad style will continue "not to succeed." The opposite as-sumption, though not entirely true, would be nearer to the truth. The poli-tics of the left—any left, even a popular "national movement"—impose, by their emphasis on collective effort and on sacrifice, a constraint on the art-ist, a constraint which may show itself in artificialities of style, vagueness or simple carelessness. Right-wing politics, with their emphasis on the freedom of the *elite,* impose less constraint, require less pretense, allow style to be-come more personal and direct.[6]

The theoretical challenge in this passage has not been taken up. O'Brien doesn't attempt a further answer to it. But he adduces "Leda and the Swan" as evidence that there is an issue to be addressed. He quotes Yeats's note on the poem:

> I wrote "Leda and the Swan" because the editor of a political review asked me for a poem. I thought: "After the individualist, demagogic movement founded by Hobbes and popularized by the Encyclopaedists and the French Revolution, we have a soil so exhausted that it cannot grow that crop again for centuries." Then I thought: "Nothing is now possible but some movement, or birth from above, preceded by some violent annunciation." My fancy began to play with Leda and the Swan for metaphor, and I began this poem; but as I wrote, bird and lady took such possession of the scene that all politics went out of it, and my friend tells me that his "conservative readers would misunderstand the poem."[7]

O'Brien asks the right questions: "How can that patter of Mussolini prose 'produce' such a poem? How can that political ugly duckling be turned into this glorious Swan?" But he can only suggest that the prose and the poem are "cognate expressions of a fundamental force, anterior to both politics and poetry." That force, however, turns out to be entirely political, Yeats's intuition, in his maturity and old age, "of what the First World War had set loose, of what was already moving towards Hitler and the Second World War."[8] It is just as far from that notion to the poem as it is from Yeats's commonplace prose to his imagining of bird and lady.

The question is not: what did Yeats, between 1923 and 1925—when he wrote the several versions of "Leda and the Swan"—think of individualism and the relation between individualism and his philosophy of historical change? The question is: what is the character of Yeats's poetic imagination, such that his idea of individualism and its relation to the philosophy of historical change incited him to write a poem and virtually disappeared among its lines? How did "Leda and the Swan" become a poem about the annunciation of the cycle of civilization that preceded the "rocking cradle" of Christ's birth, just as "The Second Coming" is a poem about the cycle that Yeats imagines will displace the two thousand years of Christianity? We can say only that the political idea somehow recalled the myth of Leda and Zeus, with their fateful offspring Helen, the Dioscuri and Clytemnestra, only to disappear under the more compelling determination of language, myth, figure, and form.

There are two main versions of the Greek myth of Leda and Zeus. In one, Leda was the mother, by her husband Tyndareus, of Castor and Clytemnestra; and, by Zeus who took the form of a swan and raped her, of Pollux and Helen of Troy. In the other, she was the mother, by Zeus in the form of a swan, of two eggs, from one of which came Castor and Clytemnestra, and from the other Polydeuces and Helen. In the final text of *A Vision,* the section called "Dove or Swan" begins with the poem Yeats called "Leda" and goes on nearly at once to the passage in which he meditates on the historical period from 2000 B.C. to the first year of the Christian age: "I imagine the annunciation that founded Greece as made to Leda, remembering that they showed in a Spartan temple, strung up to the roof as a holy relic, an unhatched egg of hers, and that from one of her eggs came Love and from the other War. But all things are from antithesis, and when in my ignorance I try to imagine what older civilisation that annunciation rejected I can but see bird and woman blotting out some corner of the Babylonian mathematical starlight."[9]

III

The first important readings of "Leda and the Swan" were by Leo Spitzer and Giorgio Melchiori. Spitzer was a scholar of Romance literature and a linguist as well as a literary critic. He emphasized the movement in Yeats's poem from the nominal sentence in the present tense of the first words—"A sudden blow"—to the past tense—"Did she put on his knowledge . . . ?" which, "in removing us from the event, concentrates on its meaning." The blow, he says, comes out of nowhere, but it engenders events the meaning of which will become clear only in time with the fall of Troy and the death of Agamemnon. Spitzer notes, too, the correspondence of content and form offered by the construction of the participles, "the broken wall" instead of "the breaking of the wall." In the question "Did she put on . . . ?" Yeats is reminding us of the triumphant passage in St. Paul's Epistle to the Corinthians 1.5:51–54. "Behold, I shew you a mystery. We shall not all sleep, but we shall all be changed . . . for the trumpet shall sound and the dead shall be raised incorruptible, and we shall be changed. For this corruptible must put on incorruption, and this mortal must put on immortality. So when this corruptible shall have put on incorruption, and this mortal shall have put on immortality then shall be brought to pass the saying that is written, Death is swallowed up in victory. O Death, where is thy sting? O grave, where is thy victory?" Spitzer thinks that "when Leda 'dies' to the divine swan, her body conquered in the union, she cannot put on his immortality." The words "put on," as he reads them, point up the difference between the pagan and the Christian worlds. "Before the indifferent beak could let her drop": the word "could" indicates, for Spitzer, "the demoniac compulsion to which the divine bird himself is subject." Spitzer thinks that a negative or at most a doubtful answer is implied to the question: "Did she put on . . . ?" This suggests "the tragic possibility that Leda in the moment of bodily union with the divine had no foreknowledge of the historical consequences of the rape."[10] I can't agree. The difference between paganism and Christianity meant little to Yeats, at least in this poem and when he was concerned with historical change: each of them was merely a turn in the historical gyre. He was far more concerned with the violent annunciation by which one civilization displaced another. Christianity, too, seemed violent to the civilization it ousted, as in "The Second Coming":

> but now I know
> That twenty centuries of stony sleep
> Were vexed to nightmare by a rocking cradle . . . [11]

Besides, in "The Magi," Yeats has the Magi "hoping to find once more, / Being by Calvary's turbulence unsatisfied, / The uncontrollable mystery on the bestial floor."[12] It would be reasonable to hold that Leda had to put on Zeus's knowledge with his power before a new cycle of civilization could come into being. "Could let her drop": if it was an act of fate, the passing on of Zeus's knowledge and his power to Leda and her offspring had to be effected before the indifferent beak could let her drop. I refer to Spitzer's reading now only to note that he indeed read the poem; he moved with Yeats's words. He did not try to turn the poem into something else or give it a different theme.

Melchiori's work on "Leda and the Swan" is mainly an elucidation of Yeats's swan in this poem and elsewhere.[13] He notes the degree to which Yeats invokes a tradition of writing on this myth that includes Spenser, Blake, Pater, Gogarty, and many other writers. He remarks, too, that Yeats's imagining of the sexual congress of god and beast, bird and lady, goes back to *The Player Queen*, a play he worked on between 1907 and 1919. It is unnecessary to recite Melchiori's evidence in detail, or Ian Fletcher's study of the sources of the poem in his *W. B. Yeats and His Contemporaries*. It is enough that I indicate that Spitzer, Melchiori, Fletcher, Ellmann, and other critics have indeed read the poem. Each of these critics has assumed that Yeats's theme is what it appears to be, an imagining of the sexual conjunction of god and human being, bird and lady, embodying forces of historical change, the violent displacement of one form of civilization by another. Melchiori especially emphasizes the annunciation, antithetical to the Christian one, the tidings brought to Mary.

But in more recent work on Yeats's poem, we find many instances of a disabling ideological turn in criticism. Yeats is not allowed to have his theme: he must be writing about something else. What else but Ireland and England? This turn is effected, for the most part, by Irish critics or by visitors to Ireland who feel obliged to interpret Yeats in the murky light of the violence in Northern Ireland since 1968–1969. Edward Said reads "Leda and the Swan" as an essay in decolonization: "[Yeats's] greatest decolonizing works quite literally conceive of the birth of violence, or the violent birth of change, as in 'Leda and the Swan,' instants at which there is a blinding flash of simultaneity presented to his colonial eyes—the girl's rape, and alongside that, the question "did she put on his knowledge with his power / Before the indifferent beak could let her drop?" Yeats situates himself at that juncture where the violence of change is inarguable, but where the results of the violence beseech necessary, if not always sufficient, reason."[14] Said reads the poem as if its theme were: what do you do with your gunmen when the revolution is over? Seamus Deane's *Celtic Revivals* brings Adorno and Horkheimer to bear upon Yeats and other Irish writers, while forgetting Adorno's concern to register the aesthetic character of works of art. David Lloyd's *Anomalous States* reaches for Albert Memmi's *The Colonizer and the Colonized*. I am not claiming that these gestures are futile but that they issue in the production of specious comparisons. Furthermore, these critics appeal to History against Myth, but they negate the detail of local history by putting a stop to its mobility: they set up reified and ahistorical polarities—England and Ireland, Protestant and Catholic, North and South, First World and Third World, colonizer and colonized. In these polarities, each is the other's Other, invulnerable to historical change, cut adrift from its origin and development. In the process, much of Yeats's work is ignored. We hear nothing of his relations with Blake, Shelley, the French Symbolists, the Upanishads, the neo-Platonic tradition, or the Noh theater. He might never have written "Lapis Lazuli." We hear of nothing but Ireland and England. The resultant confusions are dismaying. Said reads "Leda and the Swan" as an act of decolonization and regards Yeats as an inspiring figure in the first phase of liberation. But Deane claims that Yeats's "so-called Fascism is, in fact, an almost pure specimen of the colonialist mentality."[15] Lloyd describes Yeats as one of those "colonizers who refuse," a motif from Memmi's book.[16] But the most elaborately reductive account of Yeats and of "Leda and the Swan" is a feature of Declan Kiberd's *Inventing Ireland.*

Kiberd applies to modern Irish literature and culture—and to "Leda and the Swan"—the postcolonial vocabulary of Fanon's *The Wretched of the Earth.* This procedure might be considered bizarre, but it issues from one of the most disabling prejudices of postcolonial studies, that all empires are the same. Local conditions in Algeria, India, Ireland, South Africa, the Belgian Congo, and other colonies don't affect the paradigm of empire. One theory of hegemony fits all, apparently. So a theory that emanated from Algeria under the French will serve well enough to explain Ireland under the British. The gist of Fanon's theory is that the paradigm of decolonization has three phases. The first is one of incipient revival, a project that entails no serious threat to the empire. Revival is an attribute of colonial occupation in its late stage, when a few alert people intuit a historical past of their own in preference to the one they have been given by their masters. But the typical error of revivalists is that they worship a single past that they are determined to control. They are antiquarians; as Fanon says, drunk on remembrance. So their victories are victories of the father. Sons and daughters do not partake of the feast. Meanwhile, fathers concentrate their zeal on the past, with the approval of the colonist, who is charmed by native culture so long as it is agreed to be a museum of mummies. Fathers do not understand that their heroes are ghosts. Meanwhile, as Sartre remarked in his introduction to *The Wretched of the Earth,* the colonists have the Word, the natives only the use of it.

The second stage of decolonization is nationalism. According to Fanon, nationalists feel that they are making something new, but they are merely miming and repeating categories foisted on them by the colonists. In Ireland, nationalists fasten upon an idea of the nation, unaware of the fact that the idea has been ordained for them by England: the category, and the system of affections and expectations it denotes, are imperial. Kiberd says, following Fanon, that an insurgent nationalism is doomed to define itself in the loaded language set by the colonizer. The stories in Joyce's *Dubliners,* Kiberd maintains, are prophecies of "the failure of a nationalism which would insist on confining its definitions to the categories defined by the colonizer."[17] Kiberd names Michael Collins and, in *Ulysses,* the Citizen, as nationalists, engaged in repetitions that they do not recognize as mimicries.

The third stage, according to Fanon, is liberation, the victory of the son over the father. The son, not content to remember, imagines a future commensurate with his new sense of himself. Like Christy Mahon at the end of *The Playboy of the Western World,* he creates himself when he decides that it is no longer necessary for him to kill his father. He can improvise himself in a future he deems to be open. Kiberd's exemplars of liberation are Padraic Pearse and, in the early *Samhain* essays, Yeats.

Kiberd's account of "Leda and the Swan" has Fanon in mind, and Said's essay, too. I'll quote the long passage with which he brings his commentary to an end:

> At the most obvious level, the poem identifies the swan with the supernatural authority and power of the creative imagination; and so the broken wall and the burning roof are less significant as historic facts than as immortal elements of a poet's epic narrative. Art and image are "engendered" there. At a deeper level, however, these references to one war remind us that Yeats was writing in the year of another: 1923, italicized at the foot of the sonnet. This leads to the possibility of interpreting the swan as the invading English occupier and the girl as a ravished Ireland. The girl is more expert in "feeling," the swan in "knowledge." She is a mere mortal, whereas he comes from an imperial eternity. The debate about her alleged consent recalls vividly those common cliches to the effect that the Irish were colonizable because they secretly wished others to take command of their lives. The poem might then be read as a study of the calamitous effects of the original rape of Ireland and of the equally precipitate British withdrawal. The final question would then be asking: when the Irish took over power from the departing occupier, did they also assume the centuries-honed skills of self-government and control (or "knowledge")? The "indifferent beak" might then be Yeats's judgment on the callous and irresponsible suddenness of an unplanned and ill-prepared British withdrawal. The "Anglo" side of Yeats, a man now in mortal peril himself during the civil war, must have felt the precipitate nature of the withdrawal a hard betrayal, and a betrayal of possibly tragic dimensions, given that the two peoples had seemed in recent years to have come to a forced but real understanding, rather like the uneasy concord between woman and swan in the poem. The "Irish" side of Yeats was just plain angry, an anger palpable in the bitter, bleak monosyllables of the close.
>
> The poem was to have been about one kind of politics, the Russian Revolution and its aftermath, but Yeats explained in a commentary that the lyric

which he eventually wrote was different: bird and lady took possession of the scene, and he claimed that all politics went out of the poem. If politics went out, it returned again in the cited date and in the civil war imagery. The poem which Yeats delivers in his moments of greatness is invariably not the one which he sets out to write, nor even the one which he often thinks he is writing in the early lines. "Leda and the Swan" may indeed be another account of the artistic or even the readerly process: but in teasing out those themes, it has much besides to say on the crisis of a newly independent people.[18]

Where to begin? I have given a substantial excerpt from Kiberd's book lest I be accused of quoting him out of context. It is unpleasant to have to follow him into ideology. Karl Mannheim pointed out, in *Ideology and Utopia,* that political discussion differs from academic discussion in being at once intellectual, social, and existential: "it seeks not only to be in the right but also to demolish the basis of its opponent's social and intellectual existence."[19] I can't find any such motive in myself on this occasion, but I may be wrong. Kiberd's ways of reading literature seem to me blatantly reductive and therefore damaging.

His reading of "Leda and the Swan" is the most perverse interpretation I have come across. Even on its chosen ground—the poem as a political commentary, setting out Yeats's alleged resentment against the British government for its supposedly premature withdrawal from Ireland—it is erroneous. I am not aware that Yeats ever expressed such resentment, or indeed that in any pondered sense he ever thought the British withdrawal premature. Like many other witnesses to the Civil War, he was appalled to find Irishmen killing one another. He may even have asked himself, during that dreadful year, whether it was worthwhile getting rid of the British if the Civil War was the first response to their departure. But by the time he had completed the poem in 1925, the Civil War was more than two years over, and the Irish Free State was exercising its powers with every sign of authority, as Tom Garvin has shown.[20] The civil service was in working order. The courts and the electoral system were fully operative. Yeats himself accepted appointment as a senator in the first Free State government and took his duties seriously. Kiberd's reference to the "invading English occupier" is erroneous. The war in 1921–1922 was not between England and Ireland but between Irishmen and Irishmen; between those who accepted the Anglo-Irish Treaty and those who rejected it. Kiberd makes much of the inscribed date, 1923; but Yeats sometimes gave the date of a poem, sometimes not, and even when he added a date, the date was often fictive or a retroactive opportunism. No principle is at stake. "Nineteen Hundred and Nineteen" is a case in point. Yeats drafted it in that year, worked over it in 1920 and 1921, and published it in *The Dial* (September 1921). When he published it again in *The London Mercury* (November 1921), he called it "Thoughts upon the Present State of the World." He didn't call it "Nineteen Hundred and Nineteen" till he included it in *The Tower* (1928).

The juxtaposition of "feeling" and "knowledge" to which Kiberd refers is not in the poem; the first of these words does not appear. As for a "forced but real understanding . . . between the two peoples," there was no possibility of such an understanding after the execution of the leaders of the Rising in 1916. On the Russian Revolution: Yeats's note on the poem doesn't mention it, and he does not say, here or elsewhere, that "Leda and the Swan" was to deal with that. It is possible that Kiberd has confused "Leda and the Swan" with "Nineteen Hundred and Nineteen," a poem in which the state of the world—not just of Ireland—is reflected on. Presumably we can include the Russian Revolution in our sense of the poem and of that year. Kiberd's reading of "Leda and the Swan"—to stay with that—reduces the poem to an editorial, as if Yeats were saying: "I wish my British friends had stayed on for a few more years so that they could have taught our chaps how to run the show." Where has the poem gone, to be replaced by such an absurdity?

In the face of Kiberd's commentary, it is necessary to remark that "Leda and the Swan" is a poem and to consider what that entails. The implications of this remark have been approached, as a question of reading, in many different ways. I'll mention three, without claiming that they are decisive. First, there is Eliot's preface to the 1928 edition of *The Sacred Wood* in which he maintains that "when we are considering poetry we must consider it primarily as poetry and not another thing . . . [it] is not the inculcation of morals, or the direction of politics, and no more is it religion or an equivalent of religion, except by some monstrous abuse of words . . . a poem, in some sense, has its own life."[21] This passage is heavily qualified by the word "primarily" and the phrase "in some sense," but it holds out against the temptation to treat a poem as merely instrumental or ancillary to the politics, religion, or morals it seems to recommend. The fact that Eliot has to say what poetry is by saying what it is not should not be held against him: no one has done better than Eliot with the description of the intrinsic quality of a work of literature. The second way of approaching the issue is by recourse to the Emersonian distinction between psyche and pneuma, the first of these referring to one's psychological form or constitution, the second to the impersonal or poetic wind that bloweth where it listeth. A theory of genius or inspiration needs such terms. And the third way of approaching the issue is indicated by Blackmur's claim that poetry is life at the remove of form and meaning; not life lived but life framed and identified. I think, too, of Blackmur's observation, with Stevens's poetry in view, that Stevens's great labor has been to allow the reality of what he felt personally to pass into the superior impersonal reality of words. In the end these several reflections are at one.

IV

I have referred to Conor Cruise O'Brien's essay and its aftermath mainly to indicate the terms in which the question of Yeats and politics was examined thirty years ago; but also to say that those terms have now been considerably revised. The revision is mainly the work of Irish critics younger than O'Brien and myself. My emphasis on Irish critics is justifiable, I think, because the new and most emphatic readings of Yeats have constituted a part of Irish political thought since 1968–1969, the years of renewed violence in Northern Ireland. It has been alleged that he must take some responsibility for the murders in the north in the past thirty years, because his poems and plays have given Irish readers a heroic vision of Ireland that could be fulfilled only by young men and women with guns aimed at British soldiers and the police. I read his work otherwise: his poems and plays are not campaign manifestos or calls to arms. But I concede that he felt some misgiving, in his last years, on the question of responsibility. When he wondered, in "Man and the Echo," whether that play of his—*Cathleen ni Houlihan*—sent out "certain men the English shot," he was not taking his work with excessive gravity. In "7 Middagh Street" Paul Muldoon—in Auden's voice—denounces Yeats's question as "crass, rhetorical posturing" and claims that the right answer to it is: "certainly not." But it is certainly not "certainly not." As David Lloyd has remarked, Yeats's writings— plays and poems, especially—played an extraordinary part in forging in Ireland a "mode of subjectivity apt to find its political and ethical realization in sacrifice to the nation yet to be."[22] In the past thirty years many young men and women in Northern Ireland have been prepared to make that sacrifice, and to kill and be killed in its cause.

But Lloyd's book does so much to identify the new political issue in Yeats that I want to speak of it in a more sustained fashion. He starts from an agreed position, that Yeats "devoted three decades of his life to a cultural nationalism whose object was to forge a sense of national identity in Irish subjects such that their own personal identity would be fulfilled only in the creation of the nation."[23] The bardic poet represents the nation-yet-to-be and identifies himself with it in ethical and cultural terms. "The national artist," Lloyd says, "not only deploys symbols, but is a symbol, participating organically in what he represents, that is, the spiritual identity of the nation-yet-to-be."[24] That project occupied Yeats until the Rising of Easter Week 1916. But the militant and sacrificial nationalism of Pearse and his companions appropriated Yeats's symbolism and forced his work to the margin of Ireland. Pearse's symbols were the glorious dead, the martyrs, according to a system of values at once religious and aesthetic. Those symbols, even more dramatically than Yeats's, were consubstantial with the nation they represented: they proclaimed organic continuity from symbolism to nationhood. Lloyd argues that Pearse's declaration of a republic, in the name of the Irish people, was a purely performative act: it marked "the passage from a symbolic nationalism which seeks to develop the nation in continuity with what it posits as its original, self-identical essence to an 'allegorical state' whose relationship to that which it represents is always by appeal to an arbitrary act of constitution."[25] The consequence for Yeats, in turn, was that he had to articulate to its logical extremes "the lesson of an act that threatened to displace him both as a poet whose cultural work becomes redundant and as one of the 'colonizers who refuse.'"

This writing in extremis, as Lloyd describes it, proceeds on four levels which are distinct but interrelated: one, "a refusal of a symbolism founded in an organic model of natural representation, in favor of an allegorical mode"; two, "a wrestling, from the very condition of dislocation, of a language use which depends for its authority on authorial *fiat* alone, being anti-mimetic and performative"; three, "the radical deployment of antinomies which, if posited in pure formality, often gain an extraordinary degree of signifying instability on account of the inorganic arrangements through which their elements produce meaning"; and four, "a sustained reflection on the political significance of violence and death as the condition of any act of foundation."[26]

Lloyd's essay, then, is concerned with the conditions that forced Yeats to abandon his bardic commitment to symbolism and, instead, to have recourse to allegory. He agrees with de Man that Yeats, at some disputed point in his career, ceased to rely on the continuity of nature and sense and resorted instead, for accrued significance, to the plenitude of poetic tradition. But there is a crucial difference between Lloyd's reading of Yeats in this regard and de Man's. Lloyd makes a strict distinction between Yeats's practice of symbolism and of allegory: the change came in 1916. De Man argues that the change came much earlier. Yeats discovered, as early as 1892, another difference, the difference between symbol and emblem. Thereafter, according to de Man, he wrote poems that can be interpreted, superficially perhaps, as symbolic but can be more profoundly interpreted as emblematic. The difference between a symbol and an emblem, as Yeats's "The Philosophy of Shelley's Poetry" indicates, is that a symbol is given by nature, and the sense of it is contiguous to the gift. The moon and the sun are symbols. An emblem is given not by nature but by poetic tradition. Shelley's domes and Milton's lonely tower are emblems— even though Yeats ignores his own distinction when he writes: "I declare this tower is my symbol" and remembers it again when he refers, in "Blood and the Moon," to his setting up a "powerful emblem." It's not clear to me why de Man finds emblems more profound than symbols, unless he resents the common recourse to nature for meanings and senses. He tends to give each of Yeats's poems two readings, one predicated on the image or the symbol, the other on the emblem, and to claim that the poem "declares the absolute superiority of the emblem over the image."[27] Referring to the honey bees in "Meditations in Time of Civil War," de Man says that "the poem uses natural imagery and gains its immediate appeal and effectiveness from this imagery; the true meaning, however, is revealed only if the images are read as emblems, and one is led to believe that it consists of emblems masquerading as images rather than the opposite."[28] In "Adam's Curse," a "striking nature image, 'A moon . . . in the trembling blue-green of the sky,' functions also as an emblem that states the inadequacy and the downfall of precisely that type of natural image."[29]

My own view is that Yeats never abandoned symbolism in favor of allegory—or images and symbols in favor of emblems—but that he used these opportunistically, often in the same poem. In "Coole Park, 1929" the swallows are symbols, their instinct of companionship and flight a gift of nature which we receive with wonder, but on the next page, in "Coole and Ballylee, 1931," water, swans, and horse are used as emblems, their provenance being found now in the poetic tradition rather than in nature. I should try to clarify this.

In the last stanza of "Among School Children," the chestnut tree is a symbol, given by nature: the sense of it is the possibility, even in human life, of organic unity, Unity of Being. Dance and dancer make an emblem, given by culture, the poetic and dramatic tradition. In the first stanza of "Coole and Ballylee, 1931"—one of the poems Lloyd examines—Yeats moves peremptorily from symbol to emblem:

> Under my window-ledge the waters race,
> Otters below and moor-hens on the top,
> Run for a mile undimmed in Heaven's face
> Then darkening through 'dark' Raftery's 'cellar' drop,
> Run underground, rise in a rocky place
> In Coole demesne, and there to finish up
> Spread to a lake and drop into a hole.
> What's water but the generated soul?[30]

It would be reasonable to interpret that stanza as describing a landscape, familiar from Yeats's several poems of Coole Park, appropriate setting for what follows, but the last line enforces another reading. Yeats is referring to a passage in Porphyry's commentary on the Homeric "Cave of the Nymphs," in which the cave is said to represent the descent of the soul into matter by means of the act of generation. Porphyry says that all souls descending into generation are called nymphs, for they are incumbent on water, steeped in moisture. Instructed by that reference, one reads the stanza again and this time emblematically, as de Man does. Then the course of the water, in this stanza, becomes a version of the cave, bounded by the gates of generation and of death. De Man comments: "The successive stages of the river above and below ground mark the different incarnations which according to Yeats's poetic mythology extend the existence of the individual soul over several lives; the subterranean stretches correspond to life on earth, the others presumably to a partly immaterial, purgatorial state. In its final return to the divine principle, the ultimate death of the body, the soul drops into the 'hole' of the lake. The 'moor-hens on the top' are the divine principle, which Yeats generally associates with birds, while the 'otters below' are the animal principle, indicating the composite nature of the generated world."[31] In the third stanza of "Coole and Ballylee, 1931," Yeats, seeing the mounting swan, exclaims: "Another emblem there!" If a reader asks why the swan is an emblem rather than a symbol—since it is given by nature—I think there are two reasons. The swan, as given by nature, could be a symbol of beauty, patience, oneness with the world; unlike the moon, which lends itself to a feeling of transience, or the sun, to intimations of creativity. The swan is associated here with inspiration or the autonomy of the solitary soul only because Plato makes this comparison in the *Phaedo* and because the comparison was taken up by Shelley in *Prometheus Unbound*, Browning in "Pauline," and Yeats in "The Wild Swans at Coole" and other poems. It is also much to the point that there are many paintings and sculptures, by Correggio, Leonardo, Tintoretto, Delvaux, and other artists, on the theme of Leda and the Swan.[32] So the force of the swan comes, on this occasion, from the poetic and aesthetic tradition. In his notes on *Calvary* Yeats claimed that "certain birds, especially as I see things, such lonely birds as the heron, hawk, eagle, and swan, are natural symbols of subjectivity."[33] But they are not natural symbols, they are poetic emblems. De Man says of "Coole and Ballylee, 1931": "The allusion to the *Phaedo* . . . now becomes altogether understandable. In opposition to the generated 'water' of stanza 1, the swan 'But seems a concentration of the sky'—air being an element closer to the sky than water—joyously 'mounting' from the decaying wood of matter toward its true abode."[34]

V

But I should remark that the recourse to symbols and emblems in Yeats's poetry has been sharply questioned. In Canto 83 Pound makes fun of the symbolist poet:

> Le Paradis n'est pas artificiel
> and Uncle William dawdling around Notre Dame
> in search of whatever
>   paused to admire the symbol
> with Notre Dame standing inside it.[35]

Poundian readers, notably Hugh Kenner and Donald Davie, take the same attitude. "When swans get into Yeats's verse," Davie says, "the swan loses all its swanliness except what it needs to symbolize something in the person who observes it: 'Another emblem there!' "[36] "Yeats's incorrigibly symbologizing mind," according to Kenner, "infects much of his verse with significance imposed on materials by an effort of will."[37] This becomes the issue if we read poems under Pound's auspices and think that the health of modern poetry is embodied in its affiliations to Imagism, Vorticism, and Objectivism and that its relation to Symbolism is a mark of Paterian decadence. According to that view, images, symbols, and emblems animate three rival senses of the world. Images are valid: intelligently chosen, they are—in Pound's phrase— "luminous details." A poet who uses an image in that spirit does not impair the objective status of the thing it denotes. The mind that engages those images does not undermine their autonomy. With symbols, a poet begins the process of appropriation; he demands that objects in the world yield up their independence to his need of them. Symbols are called upon to reconcile people to their finite presence in the world by letting them feel that they share in the life of nature. With emblems, poets express their distance from the natural world and their fellowship with one another. Davie was dismayed, reading "In Memory of Major Robert Gregory," by the stanza in which Yeats refers to artists and "their secret discipline," that capacity "wherein the gazing heart doubles her might." According to this passage, Davie says, "we attend to natural landscape, not for the sake of delighting in it, nor for what it may tell us of supernatural purpose or design, but so that the imperious personality, seeing itself there reflected, may become the more conscious of its own power—'the gazing heart doubles her might.' "[38] In that gaze, we may add, the object looked at loses its independence while the poet's mind looks through it.

VI

On the limited issue, I am persuaded by de Man that Lloyd's interpretation of Yeats's career should be modified. It is reasonable to hold that Easter Week 1916 was a turning point and that Yeats had to enter upon a new relation to his art and to Ireland. But there were several turning points. I see one of

them in 1907 when, to ease his mind after the disturbances at the first performance of Synge's *The Playboy of the Western World*, Yeats accompanied
Lady Gregory and her son Robert to northern Italy. The landscapes, towns,
buildings, and works of art he saw in Italy filled his mind with images of
Renaissance splendor, a form of life in which intelligence, beauty, and power
were close kin. When he came back to Dublin he confronted the usual rigmarole of exacerbations, the declension of Ireland from imagined nation to
mere country after all. It was difficult for him to think that he could still be
Ireland's bard.

Lloyd's reading of Yeats pays sustained attention not only to Easter Week
and therefore to Ireland and the British Empire but to Yeats's relation to
Fascism. It would be reasonable to think that Yeats's increased recourse to
performatives in the later poems—"I summon to the winding ancient stair"—
implies a politics of the will and therefore a neo-Fascist impulse. But Lloyd
argues against this conclusion:

> The terror of these poems lies in the relentlessness with which they discover
> death at the heart of culture and at the base of the state. Though their exul-
> tation in violent acts of the will points the way towards a fascist politics, it
> draws that political solution from a desperation by no means capable of of-
> fering the consolatory myths of belonging on which fascism relies for its le-
> gitimation. If, as Walter Benjamin put it, fascism is the "aestheticization of
> politics," Yeats's writings are profoundly antagonistic to the representational
> aesthetics in which fascism finds its legitimation, deriving, for example, the
> power of the leader from his organic symbolic relation to the race. But to
> recognize this is equally to realize the futility of any condemnation of Yeats's
> politics in the name of representative democracy, for it is to the same sym-
> bolic aesthetic that democratic states appeal for their own legitimation.[39]

The effect of this passage is to separate yet again—to use Eliot's terms from
"Tradition and the Individual Talent"—the man who suffered from the mind
that created. Just as Conor Cruise O'Brien pointed to the difference between
"Leda and the Swan" and the commonplace notions that preceded it, so Lloyd
points to the difference between Yeats's later poems and the rant of *On the
Boiler*. I welcome this emphasis and regard it as proposing a new political issue.
It is not the first of its kind. In his study of Wyndham Lewis's style, Fredric
Jameson finds that Lewis's futurism is a "profoundly anti-transcendental,

democratic gesture: the machine as against the luxury furnishings of the great estates, the production of sentences as against the creation of beauty or the masterpiece": "Lewis was of course himself an elitist in politics and an adherent of the genius or great-man theory of history: what I want to suggest at the present is that his artistic practice, on the level of its smallest intelligible units, the sentences and the images themselves, has a quite different inner logic about it, and one which contradicts the spirit of his ideology."[40] Such a distinction, between a writer's ideology and the inner logic of his style, is rarely acknowledged in criticism. It clearly indicates that our descriptions of Yeats and other writers are often reductive, especially when a political vocabulary is dominant. We must give up ascribing to the poems, as works of art that fulfill their own imaginative logic, the convictions we ascribe to Yeats the public man, senator, pamphleteer.

VII

To return to "Leda and the Swan." It is a sonnet. Yeats's performative imagination turns the genre to unusual purpose. Sonnets are normally lyrical or meditative poems of love, desire, and frustration: they confide disheveled feelings to a strict form and therefore to the possibility of a saving grace. Yeats's poem imagines a trajectory of action and passion: it starts with the swan's blow, which takes up the octave, and moves—in the sestet—to the consequences of the rape and back to its significance for Leda and everything she represents in history and culture. The poem enacts the violent transfer of force from Zeus to Leda, so that a new, transformed force may start out in the world. Yeats's procedure is to dissociate each of the participants, the swan and Leda, into its several parts: the effect of this is to present each part as an abstract instrument of force, giving or receiving. "A sudden blow"—it comes as yet from nowhere, without form, personal origin, or syntax. The dissociations follow: "the great wings beating still / Above the staggering girl," the present participles holding the images as if they were indelible, in a painting. The hypothetical unity of bird and lady is dispersed, dismembered: "her thighs caressed," "her nape caught in his bill," "her helpless breast," "his breast," "those terrified vague fingers," "the feathered glory," "her loosening thighs," "that white rush," "the strange heart," "a shudder in the loins," "the broken wall," "the burning roof," "the brute blood of the air," and "the indifferent beak." It is an appalling naming of parts, the whole remaining without a name all the while and throughout the violence. Yeats summons Zeus and Leda from Greek mythology and the store of literature and art. The myth is not in any comprehensive sense incarnated: only its force is registered, and that almost anonymously. The clearest mark of dissociation is the anonymity of "body."

In the second quatrain the movement from the present indicative—"He holds . . . "—to the two rhetorical questions—"How can . . . And how can . . . ?" anticipates the more formidable question with which the poem ends. The first question is a rout of dissociations:

> How can those terrified vague fingers push
> The feathered glory from her loosening thighs?

—where the dismembered fingers retain grotesque agency, set off against the passivity of her loosening thighs. Visualization is not entailed. "The feathered glory" gives the sense of the bird abstracted, as if in an Augustan poem, but not a visual image. Later in the poem, "that white rush" is to be felt for the force of it rather than seen as a picture.

But the most powerful dissociations are effected in the first lines of the sestet. Nothing is given of Zeus but "a shudder in the loins," and the rapidity of the next phrases testifies to the fateful inevitability of these consequences. The whole sequence of events is compacted into one sentence, and "engenders" propels them all. The isolation of "And Agamemnon dead" at the end of the sentence but not at the end of the metrical line crowds every consequence into the sentence but doesn't let one's mind sink to rest upon it. After a pause, we resume the poem with two remarkably distancing past participles—"Being so caught up, So mastered . . . "—before we come to the last question. "Caught up" chimes with "put on." In "the brute blood of the air" nothing is seen; only the violence of dissociated life is given, as if the force of "mastered" were extended, but not diffused, throughout the universe. The last question implies that Leda put on Zeus's power but not necessarily his knowledge; though I take it she put on both. In the fifth Book of *The Prelude* Wordsworth speaks of "knowledge not purchased with the loss of power." We know the other kind of knowledge, a disabling self-consciousness.

So much, so little, by way of commentary on the poem. In *Anni Mirabiles,*

1921–1925 Blackmur quoted "Leda and the Swan" and said of it: "No doubt we have here the annunciation of Greek civilization and the turning of the Great Year, but it was not this that disturbed the churchmen of Dublin when the poem first appeared; the metaphysics was deeper than that of any existing church. It was the staggering, vague blow of the knowledge and power of the central, spreading, sexual quick: the loosening of thought into life and into itself, with a gained life."[41] I don't know that the churchmen of Dublin protested, but they may well have been disturbed. What Blackmur senses in the poem is what more conventional commentary risks becalming, the force of the sublime that works beneath the metaphysics and the doctrine. Postcolonial commentary has no access to this sublime, its chosen terms being merely accusatory and discursive.

FIFTEEN

Teaching *Blood Meridian*

I

Two or three years ago I taught a graduate course at New York University called Aesthetics and Aesthetic Ideology. The main aim I set myself was to examine the impingement of political, social, and moral considerations on the reading of certain works of literature. I did not conceal from myself or from the students the fact that I wished to respect the aesthetic and formal character of literature and that I was dismayed by current attempts to submit works of literature to ideological censorship. Many of those attempts resorted to biographical cartoons and caricatures. Yeats and Pound were Fascists, Eliot was anti-Semitic, Wyndham Lewis was a neo-Nazi, So-and-so was prejudiced against women, So-and-so was homophobic. In the face of such routines, I have found it hard to convince students that a work of literature is not an editorial or a political manifesto and that the experience of reading a novel does not consist in finding one's prejudices confirmed. It is difficult to speak of language, form, style, and tone without appearing decadent, ethically irresponsible.

One of the books I prescribed for the course was Cormac McCarthy's *Blood Meridian*. I chose it because it is a work of remarkable creative power and because this power seems to be at one with McCarthy's refusal to bring in a moral verdict on the characters and actions of the book. I started with a few rudimentary notes on his early fiction, mainly to accustom the students to his themes and preoccupations. *Blood Meridian or The Evening Redness in the West* (1985) is McCarthy's fifth novel. The earlier ones are *The Orchard Keeper* (1965), *Outer Dark* (1968), *Child of God* (1974), and *Suttree* (1979). The more recent ones are *All the Pretty Horses* (1992) and *The Crossing* (1994), the first two volumes of *The Border Trilogy*. Neither of these seems to me as powerful as *Blood Meridian*, though each contains unforgettable episodes. I recited such preliminary notes as these.

II

The Orchard Keeper is set in mountainous Tennessee between 1918 and 1948, by my count. It tells of an old man, Arthur Ownby, living a grim life by himself in a mountain cabin; his dog, Scout; and a boy, John Wesley Rattner, whose father has been killed in a fight with a whiskey bootlegger, Marion Sylder. A country bar burns down, the boy saves a dog from attack by a coon and is befriended by Sylder. There are strong descriptions of weather, snow, six days of rain, and sundry hardships. The book ends with an elegiac passage: "They are gone now. Fled, banished in death or exile, lost, undone. Over the land sun and wind still move to burn and sway the trees, the grasses. No avatar, no scion, no vestige of that people remains. On the lips of the strange race that now dwells there their names are myth, legend, dust."[1] In *Outer Dark* Rinthy Holme has a child by her brother Culla. Culla abandons the child in a local wood where it is found and taken away by a tinker. Rinthy wanders about trying to find child or tinker. Culla goes off to look for work, steals a squire's boots, is pursued by four men, takes a ferryboat to cross a river in high flood and is nearly lost along with a terrified horse. Eventually he comes upon three men and the child—one of his eyes gone—at a campfire. One of the men cuts the child's throat: "The man took hold of the child and lifted it up. It was watching the fire. Holme saw the blade wink in the light like a long cat's eye slant and malevolent and a dark smile erupted on the child's throat and went all broken down the front of it. The child made no sound. It hung there with its one eye glazing over like a wet stone and the black blood pumping down its naked belly."[2] There are further horrors in *Child of God,* the story of Lester Ballard, whose father hanged himself when the boy was nine. Lester grows up a crazed necrophile. "Were there darker provinces of night he would have found them," the narrator says.[3] Lester kills several women, brings them to a cave where he adorns their corpses and makes love to them. This one, for instance: "He would arrange her in different positions and go out and peer in the window at her. After a while he just sat holding her, his hands feeling her body under the new clothes. He undressed her very slowly, talking to her. Then he pulled off his trousers and lay next to her. He spread her loose thighs. You been wantin it, he told her."[4]

The main characters in these three novels are like recently arrived primates, each possessing a spinal column but little or no capacity of mind or consciousness. A few of the minor characters are ethically precocious; that is, they are kind by nature and instinct, like the doctor who helps Rinthy. But most of them, and especially Culla, live on a subsistence level of feeling and cognition. They meet the world without the mediation of law, morality, religion, or politics, and therefore they assume—without putting the assumption in words—that the power of the world is absolute and arbitrary. In *Democracy in America,* Tocqueville says that "the social conditions and institutions of democracy impart certain peculiar tendencies to all the imitative arts: the soul is often left out of the picture which portrays the body only; movement and sensation take the place of feeling and thought; finally realism takes the place of the ideal."[5] McCarthy's first novels imply that these dispositions are innate and incorrigible, as if they were emanations from life itself.

This may explain why McCarthy appears to have little interest in plot, the development or complication of a story. His novels are episodic, rampant with incident, but each of the incidents is placed at the same distance from the reader, as if each came with impersonal authority. The frisson of surprise and suspense is not part of McCarthy's rhetoric. The effect of his procedure is that a scene of violence and bloodshed, excruciating while it is going on, composes itself almost at once into a *nature morte.* It is amazing to see this occur. I am reminded of Freud's account of the work of dreaming in *The Interpretation of Dreams.* Dream-work "does not think, calculate or judge in any way at all; it restricts itself to giving things a new form."[6] The incidents in McCarthy's novels are not discriminated, adjudicated for significance, or pointed toward a climax, a disclosure, or a resolution. The new form they are given is that of being released from observances of ethical or other judgment. In *Child of God* we read of "old buried wanderings, struggles, scenes of death . . . old comings and goings."[7] But we are not encouraged to ask what these might mean or whether they entail a motive other than survival. As Elizabeth Bishop wrote in "Over 2000 Illustrations and a Complete Concordance," "Everything only connected by and and and." Not by "and then and then and then." McCarthy's novels don't make me wonder what is to happen next and whether or not a significant pattern of events is to be disclosed at last. His episodes are produced not to be interrogated but to be sensed, mostly to be seen in the mind's eye. The appalling quality of each deed is its emptiness, as if it were done before anyone thought of a meaning it might have. Conduct is predicated on some primitive energy, and when it is vicious beyond apparent cause it is merely an outbreak of force that knows nothing else to do. Even when the scene is genial we are invited to look at it without thinking beyond the thing seen. As in *The Orchard Keeper:* "Light pale as milk guided the old man's steps over the field to the creek and then to the mountain, stepping into the black wall of pine-shadows and climbing up the lower slopes out into the hardwoods, bearded hickories trailing grapevines, oaks and crooked waterless cottonwoods, a quarter mile from the creek now, past the white chopped butt of a bee tree lately felled, past the little hooked Indian tree and passing silent and catlike up the mountain in the darkness under latticed leaves scudding against the sky in some small wind."[8] This narrative procedure is Dutch rather than Italian, according to a distinction Svetlana Alpers makes in *The Art of Describing.* An Italian painting is narrative, dramatic, theatrical, "a framed surface or pane situated at a certain distance from a viewer who looks through it at a second or substitute world."[9] This second or substitute world is full of imagined actions and sufferings; the spaces exist so that people and their deeds may engross them. But a Dutch painting gives the look of things and assumes that that is enough, it does not incite the mind's eye to go beyond or through the canvas to divine a story behind it. Meaning coincides with what is offered as visible; there is no remainder. In the passage I've quoted from *The Orchard Keeper* the details one might pay attention to, such as the descriptive pressure on "past" . . . "past" . . . and "passing," are points of light and color on the canvas, they are not indications of a prior life—the old man's—to be divined by looking through them or beyond them. The old man lives to the extent to which he is a visible presence on the scene. Each of McCarthy's early novels conveys a multitude of events, affiliated loosely or not at all, and soon we start feeling that the world or life has presented itself in these dire ways without human intervention and is not to be asked why or wherefore. If human action in the world of these novels is arbitrary, occasionally kind but mostly red in tooth and claw, there is no point in looking further for causes and explanations.

But in *Suttree* there is a revision of these assumptions. This book, too, is panoramic, picturesque; one picture gives way to the next. We are not to assume that each object of attention is organically or otherwise related to the next one as a phase in a story being told. But to the spinal column there has been added in at least a few specimens a brain capable of self-consciousness and wit. *Suttree* is set along the banks of the Tennessee River at Knoxville, where Cornelius Suttree, a dropout, has made himself a shantyboat and gets a poor living by selling fish to local eating houses. A friend, Gene Harrogate, survives on odd jobs and the fruit of his wits; robbing telephones boxes, poisoning bats for sale to the authorities, removing the upholstery from wrecked cars (under the seat of one of which he finds a human eye). Most of the characters are derelicts and they get a hard time from sheriffs. People in this book tend to get shot or to turn up dead in the river or to cause mayhem with bottles in the Indian Rock roadhouse. Near the end, Suttree takes to the Gatlinburg mountains, hallucinates, nearly goes mad, but survives to see the world as if it might at least sustain a question or two:

> It seemed to rain all that winter. The few snowfalls turned soon to a gray slush, but the brief white quietude among the Christmas buntings and soft-lit shopwindows seemed a childhood dream of the season and the snow in its soft falling sifting down evoked in the city a surcease nigh to silence. Silent the few strays that entered the Huddle dusting their shoulders and brushing from their hair this winter night's benediction. Suttree by the window watched through the frosted glass. How the snow fell cherry red in the soft neon flush of the beersign like the slow dropping of blood. The clerks and the curious are absent tonight. Blind Richard sits with his wife. The junkman drunk, his mouth working mutely and his neck awry like a hanged man's. A young homosexual alone in the corner crying. Suttree among others, sad children of the fates whose home is the world, all gathered here a little while to forestall the going there.[10]

The amplitude of this passage does not depend on Suttree's particular intelligence but on a comprehensive sense of life which is innate to McCarthy's narrative and dispersed throughout his pages. It is as if people gained this sense of life not by being especially alive but by being "sad children of the fates whose home is the world." They say yes to life without being particularly specific about its constituents. Later Suttree is allowed a soliloquy in which he claims to repent of one deed only: "One thing: I spoke with bitterness about my life and I said that I would take my own part against the slander of oblivion and against the monstrous facelessness of it and that I would stand a stone in the very void where all would read my name. Of that vanity I recant all."[11] *Suttree* is the strongest of McCarthy's early novels because its sense of life is a sense of more life than the other novels imagine. By comparison with *Suttree* the other novels are intense but narrow. *Suttree* is not afraid of its grandeur or of the irony such grandeur attracts: it practices a range of styles such that no narrative perception is too high or too low to be adumbrated. "A surcease nigh to silence" doesn't need the precedent of Faulkner's authority or Conrad's to save it from bombast. Possible bombast is merely the risk nearest to McCarthy's hand, a risk he brushes aside. As here, in one of my favorite passages, when Suttree on a visit to his Aunt Martha looks through her photograph album: "Old distaff kin coughed up out of the vortex, thin and cracked and macled and a bit redundant. The landscapes, old backdrops, redundant too, recurring unchanged as if they inhabited another medium than the dry pilgrims shored up on them. Blind moil in the earth's nap cast up in an eyeblink between becoming and done. I am, I am. An artifact of prior races."[12] The cough recurs, as coughs do, hacking its way through "thin" and "cracked" and "macled" to "the dry pilgrims." Macled, I find, means blurred. I note, too, that the eyeblink doesn't move from "becoming" to its customary affiliate, "being," but closes upon a word of blatant finality, "done," achieved at last but also over and done with.

III

Blood Meridian is a historical novel based on episodes in the history of the Southwest—especially the territory between El Paso and Chihuahua City—in the middle of the nineteenth century. McCarthy's main source is evidently General Samuel E. Chamberlain's *My Confession*. Chamberlain fought in the war with Mexico from 1846 to 1848, then deserted and joined John Joel Glanton as a mercenary. His book was not published till 1956. Other sources include John Woodhouse Audubon's *Audubon's Western Journal, 1849–1850* and—a book read by writers as different as McCarthy and T. S. Eliot—Mayne Reid's *The Scalp-Hunters*.[13]

Northrop Frye has remarked that the "so-called historical novel is generally a romance presenting some kind of historicized myths."[14] When we recall the four forms of prose fiction as Frye delineates them—novel, romance, confession, and anatomy—we are alerted to see that *Blood Meridian* is a romance, closer to Hawthorne, Scott, and Emily Brontë than to George Eliot and Jane Austen: it is akin to the tale and the ballad, with "stylized figures which expand into psychological archetypes."[15] The last thing it needs is what the novel thrives on, a settled society with a complex system of personal and social relations which the novelist negotiates as the substance and pressure of reality. The "historicized myth" to which *Blood Meridian* refers is one in which men acquire the aura of gods or devils by sheer force of will and are recalled with fascination for doing so.

The historical context is well known. In June 1849, Angel Trias, governor of Chihuahua, contracted with Glanton to form a war party to hunt down Apaches who were harassing his people. Glanton was one of many such contractors. Trias agreed to pay $200 for every scalp. This was more money than the army offered to men of similar qualifications, and it attracted many displaced immigrants, ex-soldiers, and gunmen. In *Blood Meridian* a boy called the Kid leaves home, comes to Nacogdoches, Texas, and joins a private army, commanded by Captain White, to fight in Mexico. There are terrible scenes of carnage when they confront a band of Comanches. The Kid survives, joins Glanton, his second-in-command, Judge Holden, and about forty mercenaries to hunt the Apache leader Gomez and to scalp Apaches and other Indians.

Blood Meridian raises an ethical issue mainly by not speaking of it. Most of the events of the novel are barbarous, but they seem to be protected from any ethical comment. Many actions disclose something of the "motiveless malignity" that Coleridge ascribed to Iago. To list a few of these: Near the beginning, Judge Holden bears false witness, as if for fun, against the Reverend Green, a man he has never met till now. Toadvine beats up Old Sydney and sets fire to the hotel he's lodging in. Glanton tries out a new pistol by shooting a cat, some hens, and a goat. One of Glanton's mercenaries kills two infants of the Gilenos. The judge takes up an Apache child, dandles him on his knee, keeps him for a few days, and scalps him. Glanton's men massacre the peaceful Tiguas. The judge buys two dogs, only to drown them. Glanton's men come upon a conducta of 122 mules bearing quicksilver from the mines, and drive them over a ridge to their death. One of Glanton's men, David Brown, sets fire to a young soldier and lets him burn to death. Glanton and a few of his men tie up an alcalde, his wife, and the local grocer and leave them to die. There is more. The only ethical objection to these acts is made by Toadvine when the judge scalps the child: "Goddamn you, Holden." But Toadvine doesn't otherwise speak up for decency. True, there are a few acts of human kindness. The Kid gives the wounded Shelby his supply of water. Yuma women take care of the imbecile James Robert. The judge saves him from drowning. The Diagueons rescue Tobin and the Kid and tend to them. But that is the sum of decency. The dominant impression conveyed by incident after incident is that no ethical, moral, or civic sense is allowed to act upon these characters.

In our class discussions we paid a good deal of attention to a passage in which Glanton's men are looking for the Apaches: "They wandered the borderland for weeks seeking some sign of the Apache. Deployed upon that plain they moved in a constant elision, ordained agents of the actual dividing out the world which they encountered and leaving what had been and what would never be alike extinguished on the ground behind them. Spectre horsemen, pale with dust, anonymous in the crenellated heat. Above all else they appeared wholly at venture, primal, provisional, devoid of order. Like beings provoked out of the absolute rock and set nameless and at no remove from their own loomings to wander ravenous and doomed and mute as gorgons shambling the brutal wastes of Gondwanaland in a time before nomenclature was and each was all."[16] The first surprising phrase is "devoid of order," as if in Glanton's world that were a consideration. But the word has been prepared for by "ordained," which hovers near its referent but doesn't settle on it. Ordained by whom? Not by Glanton, who merely "deployed" the men. They have been ordained, these anti-priests, by some nameless will inseparable from the "absolute rock." "Like beings provoked out of the absolute rock." Provoked, I assume, by the force of things, pressure in the rock itself, and therefore emerging into human being before there was a society, a culture to receive them. "At no remove from their own loomings": at once threatening and impalpable, formless. Before nomenclature: anonymous, and therefore exempt from the name and value of humanity, decency, ethical claim. They are forces of nature, not of nurture; there is no common law of culture to be known, obeyed, respected. They are as innocent and as opaque as the rock. Under some other dispensation each of these figures might be considered an individual, not entirely dispelled in the commonality, but here they are merely disturbances of the landscape, movements of life hardly distinguishable from the rock they may be fancied to have come from after millennia of unanswerable but pointless evolution.

A page or two later, the ethical issue is waived again from the same source, as if murder were in the nature of things: "In the morning they rode out to the south. Little was said, nor were they quarrelsome among themselves. In three days they would fall upon a band of peaceful Tiguas camped on the river and slaughter them every soul. On the eve of that day they crouched about the fire where it hissed in a softly falling rain and they ran balls and cutpatches as if the fate of the aborigines had been cast into shape by some other agency altogether. As if such destinies were prefigured in the very rock for those with eyes to read."[17] More explicitly still, in a passage that negates distinction and enforces the figure of equality as if that, too, were a decision of nature: "They rode on. The horses trudged sullenly the alien ground and the round earth rolled beneath them silently milling the greater void wherein they were contained. In the neuter austerity of that terrain all phenomena were bequeathed a strange equality and no one thing nor spider nor stone nor blade of grass could put forth claim to precedence. The very clarity of these articles belied their familiarity, for the eye predicates the whole on some feature or part and here was nothing more luminous than another and nothing more enshadowed and in the optical democracy of such landscapes all preference is made whimsical and a man and a rock become endowed with unguessed kinships."[18] One of the unguessed kinships is prefigured in the second sentence, where horses and earth are brought together by "trudged" and "rolled" to culminate in "milling" as if a motive for such movements could be thought of, Ptolemaic in its figured husbandry. "Phenomena" holds out the possibility that one article might still be distinguished from another and valued for that consideration, but spider, stone, and blade of glass sink into indiscriminateness, taking their names with them. What remains is the pathos of McCarthy's diction—"luminous" . . . "enshadowed"—as if the world once had use for such distinctions.

Some students thought that the ethical issue in *Blood Meridian* could be set aside by construing the book as a satire against the myth of Manifest Destiny; specifically, against those white men who killed Comanches, Apaches, Yumas, and other Indian tribes without question and thought themselves justified by the mythology of American destiny and progress. One student proposed that we think of *Blood Meridian* as McCarthy's Holocaust fiction, his cry of despair over the bones of native Americans. A few students found this reading attractive, especially as it allowed their ethical sense to protest even when the book didn't: it was pointed out that McCarthy's Comanches and Apaches, unlike the Jews of Germany, Austria, and Poland, were just as vicious as the mercenaries who scalped them. In the end this Holocaust reading failed to convince. The pervasive style of the book holds every consideration at a distance from the events, with the result that a critical or ethical impulse finds itself thwarted at every point. Satire is evidently not the issue.

But the main difficulty of the book—a point the students kept coming back to—is McCarthy's apparent refusal to adjudicate; or rather, his refusal to allow an immediate judgment to be elicited by any deed. The narrative style—"neuter austerity"—makes ethical judgment seem naive to itself and therefore willing to be subsumed in ostensibly larger considerations. But what are the larger considerations? A student remarked that McCarthy's procedures are comparable to Homeric style as Auerbach describes this in the first chapter of *Mimesis*. Auerbach quotes Schiller's observation that what Homer gives us is the "quiet existence and operation of things in accordance with their natures." Homer's method, according to Auerbach, is the "externalization of phenomena in terms perceptible to the senses." The procession of phenomena takes place "in the foreground," that is, "in a local and temporal present which is absolute."[19] Homer does not distinguish between light and shade: he assimilates every event, large or small, to a "nature of things" that is self-evident and therefore undifferentiated. Like McCarthy's "optical democracy."

This comparison seemed worth following up, especially in a passage which describes how the Kid and his company are brought to Chihuahua City under arrest:

> They entered the city in a gantlet of flung offal, driven like cattle through the cobbled streets with shouts going up behind for the soldiery who smiled as became them and nodded among the flowers and proffered cups, herding the tattered fortune-seekers through the plaza where water splashed in a fountain and idlers reclined on carven seats of white porphyry and past the governor's palace and past the cathedral where vultures squatted along the dusty entablatures and among the niches in the carved facade hard by the figures of Christ and the apostles, the birds holding out their own dark vestments in postures of strange benevolence while about them flapped on the wind the dried scalps of slaughtered indians strung on cords, the long dull hair swinging like the filaments of certain seaforms and the dry hides clapping against the stones.[20]

In this remarkable passage no action is ascribed to an individual: groups dominate their members—"they," "the soldiery," "the tattered fortune-seekers," "idlers." Actions are reduced to motions, as if the operation of things according to their natures required no motive or intent—"with shouts going up." Verbs reduce the difference between one action, such as it is, and another: idlers "reclined," vultures "squatted," the scalps "flapped on the wind." The effect is to draw the separate species, living and dead, human and animal, into a middle range of vocabulary, a compromise between their several notional modes of existence. The most daring of these displacements is the fanciful award of something like human status to the vultures, presented like priests, "the birds holding out their own dark vestments in postures of strange benevolence." At the end of the paragraph the word "clapping" hovers between the applause of the people and the impersonal noise of hide against stone, while the reader's mind is led away to the "filaments of certain seaforms." We seem to be in a world such as the one that Nietzsche ascribed, in *The Birth of Tragedy,* to the Olympians, a world of "luxuriant, triumphant *existence,* which defies the good and the bad indifferently."[21] Or a demotic version of such a world.

Another student emphasized the three epigraphs to *Blood Meridian,* the first from Valéry:

> Your ideas are terrifying and your hearts are faint. Your acts of pity and cruelty are absurd, committed with no calm, as if they were irresistible. Finally, you fear blood more and more. Blood and time.

The second is from Boehme:

> It is not to be thought that the life of darkness is sunk in misery and lost as if
> in sorrowing. There is no sorrowing. For sorrow is a thing that is swallowed
> up in death, and death and dying are the very life of the darkness.

The third is from *The Yuma Daily Sun,* June 13, 1982:

> Clark, who led last year's expedition to the Afar region of northern Ethiopia,
> and UC Berkeley colleague Tim D. White, also said that a re-examination of
> a 300,000-year-old fossil skull found in the same region earlier shows evi-
> dence of having been scalped.

The epigraphs have in common a vision of life beyond good and evil, as if the
constitutive principle of life were energy, self-subsistent and unquestionable.

The most remarkable section of *Blood Meridian* is the last sixty pages. The
Yumas attack Glanton's band. Their leader, Caballo en Pelo, kills Glanton with
an axe—he "raised the axe and split the head of John Joel Glanton to the
thrapple." The judge escapes with the imbecile. Toadvine and the Kid also
escape—the Kid is wounded, with an arrow in his leg—and they meet up with
the ex-priest Tobin. One of the most memorable images has the judge and the
imbecile following the Kid and Tobin: "More strangely he carried a parasol
made from rotted scraps of hide stretched over a framework of rib bones
bound with strips of tug. The handle had been the foreleg of some creature
and the judge approaching was clothed in little more than confetti so rent was
his costume to accommodate his figure. Bearing before him that morbid
umbrella with the idiot in its rawhide collar pulling at the lead he seemed
some degenerate entrepreneur fleeing from a medicine show and the outrage
of the citizens who'd sacked it."[22] From here to the end the judge emerges as
McCarthy's most audacious creation, the historical personage transformed
from a name and a few memorable details into a comprehensive force.

Historical evidence of the judge appears only in Chamberlain's book, but it
sounds convincing:

> The second in command, now left in charge of [Glanton's] camp, was a man
> of gigantic size called "Judge" Holden of Texas. Who or what he was no one
> knew but a cooler blooded villain never went unhung; he stood six feet six
> in his moccasins, had a large fleshy frame, a dull tallow colored face destitute

of hair and all expression. His desires was [*sic*] blood and women, and terrible stories were circulated in camp of horrid crimes committed by him when bearing another name, in the Cherokee nation and Texas; and before we left Frontereras a little girl of ten years was found in the chaparral, foully violated and murdered. The mark of a huge hand on her little throat pointed him out as the ravisher as no other man had such a hand, but though all suspected, no one charged him with the crime.

Holden was by far the best educated man in northern Mexico; he conversed with all in their own language, spoke in several Indian lingos, at a fandango would take the Harp or Guitar from the hands of the musicians and charm all with his wonderful performance, and out-waltz any *poblana* of the ball. He was "plum centre" with rifle or revolver, a daring horseman, acquainted with the nature of all the strange plants and their botanical names, great in Geology and Mineralogy, in short another Admirable Crichton, and with all an arrant coward. Not but that he possessed enough courage to fight Indians and Mexicans or anyone where he had the advantage in strength, skill and weapons, but where the combat would be equal, he would avoid it if possible. I hated him at first sight, and he knew it, yet nothing could be more gentle and kind than his deportment towards me; he would often seek conversation with me and speak of Massachusetts and to my astonishment I found he knew more about Boston than I did.[23]

As McCarthy presents him, the judge is a scholar of sorts, a linguist, Darwinian note-taker, amateur biologist, reader of sign, a Nietzschean before he could have read Nietzsche, and so psychologically opaque that he seems a force of nature. Sometimes he sounds like Melville's Ahab or a crazed philosopher of the Enlightenment:

Whatever exists, he said. Whatever in creation exists without my knowledge exists without my consent. He looked about at the dark forest in which they were bivouacked. He nodded toward the specimens he'd collected. These anonymous creatures, he said, may seem little or nothing in the world. Yet the smallest crumb can devour us. Any smallest thing beneath yon rock out of men's knowing. Only nature can enslave man and only when the existence of each last entity is routed out and made to stand naked before him will he be properly suzerain of the earth.

What's a suzerain?

A keeper. A keeper or overlord.

Why not say keeper then?

Because he is a special kind of keeper. A suzerain rules even where there
are other rulers. His authority countermands local judgements.[24]

One might expect this speech to be interrogated, if only by the mercenary to
ask what's a suzerain, but no one in the judge's company is equal to the task.
Indeed, it is the judge whose speech gathers up bits of the Bible and Shakespeare and the lore of Western culture and utters moral values by virtue of
denouncing them: "Moral law is an invention of mankind for the disen-
franchisement of the powerful in favor of the weak. Historical law subverts it
at every turn."[25] This sounds like a passage from Nietzsche's *Human, All Too
Human* or *The Genealogy of Morals;* it expresses similar contempt for the little
Christian virtues, patience, humility, otherworldliness, the disposition of
turning the other cheek. When the judge is quietly and relentlessly pursuing
the Kid across the desert, he calls out to him:

> The priest has led you to this, boy. I know you would not hide. I know too
> that you've not the heart of a common assassin. I've passed before your gun-
> sights twice this hour and will pass a third time. Why not show yourself?
> No assassin, called the judge. And no partisan either. There's a flawed
> place in the fabric of your heart. Do you think I could not know? You alone
> were mutinous. You alone reserved in your soul some corner of clemency
> for the heathen.[26]

Later, when the judge visits the Kid in jail, he persists in this Nietzschean
rebuke: "You came forward, he said, to take part in a work. But you were a
witness against yourself. You sat in judgment on your own deeds. You put
your own allowances before the judgments of history and you broke with the
body of which you were pledged a part and poisoned it in all its enterprise.
Hear me, man. I spoke in the desert for you and you only and you turned a
deaf ear to me. If war is not holy man is nothing but antic clay. Even the cretin
acted in good faith according to his parts. For it was required of no man to
give more than he possessed nor was any man's share compared to another's.
Only each was called upon to empty out his heart into the common and one
did not."[27] This is the gist of the judge's complaint against the Kid: he should
have voided in himself every scruple, every impulse of kinship with the defeated. He should have retained no will but the common will, so far as that was
embodied in the work of war and killing.
 The relation between the judge and the Kid is the point of greatest pressure

in the last section of the book. It is a relation of antithetical principles, but we have to apprehend the Kid's principles by default, he never speaks of them. The judge is all speech, endlessly voluble, the Kid is silence. But the judge divines that the Kid is his adversary, his blood-brother, his brother in blood. "Was it always your idea," he asks him, "that if you did not speak you would not be recognized?" "You seen me," the Kid answers. The judge ignores this naivete or deems it false. "I recognized you when I first saw you," he counters.[28] So far as the novel is explicit, there was never any bad blood between these two. So the antagonism must be reckoned as primordial, one of principles rather than of particles: it is a relation of moral archetypes, and in that regard the conflict must have been developing silently all along. The Kid has no philosophy, except to survive; no moral doctrine, except not to kill unless killing is necessary. He would spare a life if he could. We have to deduce as much from his deeds and the silence in which he commits them. The judge's philosophy is one of will, war, power, blood, game, eloquence, and in the end the order of what he ambiguously calls "the dance."

Years later, in 1878, the Kid is in Texas. He goes into a bar. There is a girl on a rudimentary stage and with her there is a dancing bear. The judge is sitting at a table. One of the drinking men shoots the bear. The judge comes up to the counter and speaks to the Kid:

> The last of the true. The last of the true. I'd say they're all gone under now saving me and thee. Would you not? He tried to see past him. That great corpus enshadowed him from all beyond. He could hear the woman announcing the commencement of dancing in the hall to the rear. And some are not yet born who shall have cause to curse the Dauphin's soul, said the Judge. He turned slightly. Plenty of time for the dance.
>
> I aint studyin no dance.
>
> The judge smiled. . . . You're here for the dance, he said. . . . Drink up, he said. Drink up. This night thy soul may be required of thee.[29]

And so it is required. After a session with a whore the Kid goes out to the jakes and opens the door: "The judge was seated upon the closet. He was naked and he rose up smiling and gathered him in his arms against his immense and terrible flesh and shot the wooden barlatch home behind him."[30] Presumably the judge kills the Kid. McCarthy doesn't say.

I have brought the judge's allusions to Shakespeare's *Henry V* and Luke's

Gospel a little closer together than they are in the novel. The misquotation from *Henry V* (I.ii.287–288)—Henry says

> And some are yet ungotten and unborn
> That shall have cause to curse the Dauphin's scorn

—and Christ's parable of the rich man hoarding his goods are set to a different tune when the judge speaks them. But they remain allusions, and they have something of the force of the fragments of Greek and Chinese that Pound includes in the *Cantos* and the French and Italian phrases that Eliot recalls in his early poems. They say, if nothing else: there have been other times, other voices. If nothing else, the judge's allusions summon up customary knowledge—as Lyotard in *The Postmodern Condition* says it is the work of narrative to do. The fact that such lore is now virtually forgotten is part of its force, the pathos of it: most of what has been known and spoken in the world is now forgotten. The judge's phrases from the Bible, Shakespeare, Vaughan, and many other sources speak of gone times and give them momentary acknowledgment, even though other passages in *Blood Meridian* claim that in McCarthy's Southwest there is no difference between what has been and what will never be, that they are all one in the void. But the judge's tune is his own, or his own choice of an accredited tune. He assimilates his phrases not to Christ's prophecy of eternal life or King Henry's promise to "dazzle all the eyes of France," but to Nietzsche's claim, in *The Birth of Tragedy,* that "only as an aesthetic product can the world be justified to all eternity."[31] No individual life matters except in relation to the provisional orders, forms, and measures which are the best that can be achieved; but even these cannot control the Dionysian violence of blood and heart. What else can the judge mean by "the dance" except the irrefutable force of life itself, before every accredited form of mediation or adjudication?

The book ends, except for the Epilogue:

> And they are dancing, the board floor slamming under the jackboots and
> the fiddlers grinning hideously over their canted pieces. Towering over them
> all is the judge and he is naked dancing, his small feet lively and quick and
> now in doubletime and bowing to the ladies, huge and pale and hairless, like
> an enormous infant. He never sleeps, he says. He says he'll never die. He
> bows to the fiddlers and sashays backwards and throws back his head and
> laughs deep in his throat and he is a great favorite, the judge. He wafts his

hat and the lunar dome of his skull passes palely under the lamps and he
swings about and takes possession of one of the fiddles and he pirouettes
and makes a pass, two passes, dancing and fiddling at once. His feet are light
and nimble. He never sleeps. He says that he will never die. He dances in
light and in shadow and he is a great favorite. He never sleeps, the judge. He
is dancing, dancing. He says that he will never die.[32]

As for the Epilogue: some of my students thought it a nuisance and took it
as McCarthy's last-minute attempt to make *Blood Meridian* mean more than
he has shown it to mean. Others read it as evidence of the Gnostic or Mani-
chean axioms on which the book is apparently based.[33] The Epilogue, merely a
few sentences, is printed in italics:

> *In the dawn there is a man progressing over the plain by means of holes which*
> *he is making in the ground. He uses an implement with two handles and he*
> *chucks it into the hole and he enkindles the stone in the hole with his steel hole*
> *by hole striking the fire out of the rock which God has put there. On the plain*
> *behind him are the wanderers in search of bones and those who do not search*
> *and they move haltingly in the light like mechanisms whose movements are*
> *monitored with escapement and pallet so that they appear restrained by a pru-*
> *dence or reflectiveness which has no inner reality and they cross in their prog-*
> *ress one by one that track of holes that runs to the rim of the visible ground and*
> *which seems less the pursuit of some continuance than the verification of a*
> *principle, a validation of sequence and causality as if each round and perfect*
> *hole owed its existence to the one before it there on that prairie upon which are*
> *the bones and the gatherers of bones and those who do not gather. He strikes fire*
> *in the hole and draws out his steel. Then they all move on again.*[34]

One man, and two groups differing in purpose. The man is a fire-bringer,
Promethean in one tradition, Gnostic in another: whatever else, he is not
Judaeo-Christian. The two groups follow him as in clockwork. Escapement
and pallet are technical terms for instruments that regulate and adjust ratchets
which move at different speeds, as in a watch. One group remembers the past,
the other has forgotten or ignored the bones. A parable, then, but of what? I
read it as a parable of the artist as Promethean, thief of fire on behalf of
humankind, or, if Leo Daughtery is right, as one who releases the *pneuma* or
spark of "the alien divine."[35] That is as much as I can say on that issue.

Who speaks, then, for reality and justice in *Blood Meridian* and the early novels? Yeats said that his occult instructors helped him to hold in a single thought reality and justice. Where is the single thought in McCarthy's novels? I say it is in the narrator; or rather, in the narrative voice, since no character in the stories is given the role of narrator, except for a while in *Child of God*, in which the narrator is a local resident, gossip, and mythmaker. In the other novels we have impersonal narration that recalls the ancient styles, often biblical or epic, that have served a similar genre. As in *Blood Meridian*, a description of Apaches riding across the playa to attack the mercenaries:

> . . . the riders were beginning to appear far out on the lake bed, a thin frieze of mounted archers that trembled and veered in the rising heat. They crossed before the sun and vanished one by one and reappeared again and they were black in the sun and they rode out of that vanished sea like burnt phantoms with the legs of the animals kicking up the spume that was not real and they were lost in the sun and lost in the lake and they shimmered and slurred together and separated again and they augmented by planes in lurid avatars and began to coalesce and there began to appear above them in the dawn-broached sky a hellish likeness of their ranks riding huge and in-verted and the horses' legs incredibly elongate trampling down the high thin cirrus and the howling antiwarriors pendant from their mounts immense and chimeric and the high wild cries carrying that flat and barren pan like the cries of souls broke through some misweave in the weft of things into the world below.[36]

Greek rhetoric includes the figure called parataxis: it is a device for placing one thing beside another without subordination. No relation of cause and conse-quence is proposed: no article requires more attention than another. The effect of this writing is to nullify the force of successiveness and to make the details appear to compose themselves as a picture. Even the words that stand out as fancy writing—"pendant" . . . "elongate" . . . "chimeric"—allow them-selves to be assimilated without fuss to the parataxis. They are subdued to the reign of "and." The governing motif is given as a phrase, itself picturesque: "some misweave in the weft of things."

Some students felt that McCarthy's high style, even with the examples of Melville, Dostoevski, Conrad, and Faulkner to warrant it, is pretentious. They said of a few passages: "That is English or American speech, written as if it were Spanish." Anticipating that someone would mention Gongorism, *gongorismo,* "a style in imitation of the ornate style of Gongora y Argote 1561–1627," as the dictionaries say, I suggested that this would have its own felicity in a writer dealing, as McCarthy does, with Spanish-speaking Mexicans as well as gringos. I defended many, most, nearly all of McCarthy's high passages by noting how much they have to do. They have to speak for characters who cannot speak as eloquently for themselves, as in *All the Pretty Horses:* "He lay on his back in his blankets and looked out where the quartermoon lay cocked over the heel of the mountains. In that false blue dawn the Pleiades seemed to be rising up into the darkness above the world and dragging all the stars away, the great diamond of Orion and Cepella and the signature of Cassiopeia all rising up through the phosphorous dark like a sea-net. He lay a long time listening to the others breathing in their sleep while he contemplated the wildness about him, the wildness within."[37] He didn't contemplate any of these things, McCarthy contemplated them for him: it is a common predicament for novelists who know more than their characters know. Or who have heavier duties. McCarthy's styles have to speak up for values the characters could not express; for regions, places, landscapes, vistas, movements of the seasons, trees, rain, snow, dawn, sunset, outer and inner weather; and for time not our time. For such purposes McCarthy commands many styles and dictions. Reading these novels, I was often lost among unfamiliar words, like the mercenary with suzerain. In *Suttree* alone I was grounded by these and had to go to the dictionaries: mordant (a reagent for fixing dyes), muricate (covered with many short spikes, and therefore used by McCarthy of Christ's crown of thorns), trematode (a kind of worm), soricine (of a shrewmouse), and tribades (lesbians: "the sometime cries of buckled tribades in the hours toward dawn when trade was done") [398]. Most of these are in the third edition of the *American Heritage Dictionary of the English Language,* more useful than the *Oxford English Dictionary* when reading McCarthy's fiction. The hard words are always accurately used, I gather from the dictionaries, and they help McCarthy to control the pace of one's reading and therefore the duration and quality of the attention one pays. A hard word slows you down, keeps you looking.

It may appear that *Blood Meridian* is a post-Nietzschean fiction expressing what Lionel Trilling calls the "bitter line of hostility to civilization" that runs through modern literature. In *Beyond Culture* Trilling comments on the books he chose for a course in modern literature for undergraduates at Columbia College. His choice was perhaps an odd one. He prescribed several books that might be thought of as prologomena to modern literature rather than as exemplifications of it: *The Golden Bough, The Birth of Tragedy, The Genealogy of Morals, Civilization and its Discontents* leading to *Notes from Underground*, "The Death of Ivan Ilyitch," "Disorder and Early Death," and *Heart of Darkness*. Not surprisingly, Trilling claimed that "nothing is more characteristic of modern literature than its discovery and canonization of the primal, non-ethical energies." Referring to Mann's assertion that the chief intention of modern literature is to escape from the middle class, Trilling extended it to cover "freedom from society itself."[38]

It might be thought that *Blood Meridian* would be a fit text for such a course as Trilling's: it appears to give privilege to the primal, nonethical energies, it virtually ignores the values of civilization and society, and it seems to endorse Nietzsche's claim that art rather than ethics constitutes the essential metaphysical activity of man. "The dance" may be thought to be another name for the Dionysian revel. So much is clear. But Nietzsche is Judge Holden's philosopher, not McCarthy's. *Blood Meridian* subsumes far more of western thought than the judge's allusions to Nietzsche would suggest: it invokes mystical, hermetic, and antinomian traditions. Indeed, the only traditions to which it refuses credence are those of the Enlightenment and Christianity.

The experience of reading *Blood Meridian* is likely to be, for most of us, peculiarly intense and yet wayward. The book demands that we imagine forces in the world and in ourselves which the Enlightenment and Christianity, rarely in agreement on other issues, encourage us to think we have outgrown. We have not outgrown them, the book challenges us to admit. These forces are primordial and unregenerate, they have not been assimilated to the consensus of modern culture or to the forms of dissent which that consensus recognizes and to some extent accepts. They are outside the law. The difficult beauty of McCarthy's sentences arises from the conflict between these dire forces and the traditions of epic, tragedy, elegy, and lyric which have been devised to appease them. Or to sequester them, if they cannot be appeased.

Notes

Chapter 1: Curriculum Vitae

1. T. S. Eliot, *The Sacred Wood: Essays on Poetry and Criticism* (New York: Knopf, 1930), pp. viii, ix, 53.
2. T. S. Eliot, *On Poetry and Poets* (New York: Farrar, Straus and Cudahy, 1957), pp. 80–81.
3. R. P. Blackmur, *Outsider at the Heart of Things,* edited by James T. Jones (Urbana: University of Illinois Press, 1989), pp. 66–67.
4. T. S. Eliot, *Selected Essays, 1917–1932* (London: Faber and Faber, 1932), p. 273.
5. Blackmur, *Outsider at the Heart of Things,* p. 67.
6. R. P. Blackmur, *The Double Agent: Essays in Craft and Elucidation* (Gloucester, Mass.: Peter Smith, 1962 reprint), pp. 269–270.
7. R. P. Blackmur, *Henry Adams,* edited by Veronica A. Makowsky (New York: Harcourt Brace Jovanovich, 1980), pp. 315–316.
8. David Lloyd and Paul Thomas, "*Culture and Society* or 'Culture and the State,' " in Christopher Prendergast, editor, *Cultural Materialism: On Raymond Williams* (Minneapolis: University of Minnesota Press, 1995), p. 275.
9. Eliot, *Selected Essays,* p. 289.
10. T. W. Adorno, *Aesthetic Theory,* translated by Robert Hullot-Kentor (Minneapolis: University of Minnesota Press, 1997), pp. 4, 336.
11. Susanne K. Langer, *Feeling and Form* (New York: Scribner, 1953), p. 231.
12. Raymond Williams, *The Country and the City* (New York: Oxford University Press, 1973), pp. 75, 78.
13. John Crowe Ransom, *The World's Body* (Baton Rouge: Louisiana State University Press, 1968 reprint), p. 131.

14. L. S. Vygotsky, *Thought and Language,* translated by Eugenia Hanfmann and Gertrude Vakar (Cambridge, Mass.: MIT Press, 1962), p. 8.

15. Louise M. Rosenblatt, "On the Aesthetic as the Basic Model of the Reading Process," *Bucknell Review* 26, no. 1 (1981):21–22, 24–25.

16. Henry James, *The Figure in the Carpet and Other Stories* (London: Penguin, 1988 reprint), pp. 200–201.

17. Anatole Broyard, *Kafka Was the Rage* (New York: Vintage, 1993), pp. 29–30.

18. Kenneth Burke, *Counter-Statement* (Chicago: University of Chicago Press, 1957 reprint), pp. 29–30.

Chapter 2: Theory, Theories, and Principles

1. Ralph Barton Perry, *Present Philosophical Tendencies* (New York: George Braziller, 1955), pp. 7–8, 21–23.

2. Christopher Ricks, *Essays in Appreciation* (Oxford: Clarendon, 1996), p. 322.

3. Geoffrey Hill, *The Lords of Limit: Essays on Literature and Ideas* (New York: Oxford University Press, 1984), p. 107.

4. Immanuel Kant, *The Conflict of the Faculties/Der Streit der Fakultaten,* translated by Mary J. Gregor (New York: Abaris, 1979), p. 11.

5. Ibid., p. 43.

6. Ibid., p. 55. Quoted in Jacques Derrida, "Mochlos; or, The Conflict of the Faculties," in Richard Rand, editor, *Logomachia: The Conflict of the Faculties* (Lincoln: University of Nebraska Press, 1992), pp. 27–28.

7. Ian Hunter, "The Regimen of Reason: Kant's Defence of the Philosophy Faculty," *Oxford Literary Review* 5, no. 17 (1995):70.

8. Kant, *Conflict of the Faculties,* p. 63.

9. Immanuel Kant, *Religion Within the Limits of Reason Alone* (New York: Harper, 1960), p. 123. Quoted in Hunter, "Regimen of Reason," pp. 73–74.

10. Kant, *Conflict of the Faculties,* p. 119.

11. Hunter, "Regimen of Reason," p. 80.

12. Derrida, "Mochlos," pp. 22–23.

13. Ibid., p. 23.

14. Ibid., p. 202.

15. Friedrich Schelling, *Vorlesungen über die Methode des akademischen Studiums* (Jena: University of Jena, 1802). Quoted in Derrida, "Mochlos," pp. 33–34.

16. Ian Hunter, "Literary Theory in Civil Life," *South Atlantic Quarterly* 95, no. 4 (Fall 1996):1129.

17. Edward Said, *Culture and Imperialism* (New York: Knopf, 1993), pp. 366–367. Quoted in Hunter, "Literary Theory in Civil Life," p. 1108.

18. Said, *Culture and Imperialism,* p. 406.

19. Hunter, "Literary Theory in Civil Life," p. 1124.

20. William Empson, *Some Versions of Pastoral* (New York: New Directions, 1974 reprint), pp. 4–5.

Chapter 3: Three Ways of Reading

1. Catherine Gallagher, "The History of Literary Criticism," *Daedalus* 126, no. 1 (Winter 1997): 150.
2. Ibid., pp. 150–151.
3. Matthew Arnold, "On Translating Homer," in *On the Classical Tradition,* edited by R. H. Super (Ann Arbor: University of Michigan Press, 1960), p. 140.
4. Lionel Trilling, *The Liberal Imagination: Essays on Literature and Society* (New York: Viking, 1950), p. 151.
5. Helen Vendler, *The Music of What Happens: Poems, Poets, Critics* (Cambridge, Mass.: Harvard University Press, 1988), pp. 111foll.
6. William Wordsworth, *Selected Poems and Prefaces,* edited by Jack Stillinger (Boston: Houghton Mifflin, 1965), p. 420.
7. F. R. Leavis, editor, *A Selection from Scrutiny* (Cambridge: Cambridge University Press, 1968), 1:239–240.
8. Donald Davie, *Articulate Energy: An Inquiry into the Syntax of English Poetry* (London: Routledge & Kegan Paul, 1955), p. 75.
9. Walter Pater, *The Renaissance: The 1893 Text,* edited by Donald L. Hill (Berkeley: University of California Press, 1980), pp. 98–99.
10. Wallace Stevens, *The Palm at the End of the Mind,* edited by Holly Stevens (New York: Vintage, 1972), p. 98.
11. Georges Poulet, "Phenomenology of Reading," translated by Richard Macksey, *New Literary History* 1, no. 1 (October 1969):55.
12. Henri Bergson, *Oeuvres,* edited by André Robinet (Paris: Presses universitaires de France, 1959, fifth edition, 1991), p. 1395.
13. Gustave Flaubert, *Madame Bovary* (Paris: Club de l'Honnete homme, 1971 reprint), p. 193.
14. Gustave Flaubert, *Madame Bovary,* translated by Francis Steegmuller (New York: Modern Library, 1957), pp. 181–182.
15. Georges Poulet, *Studies in Human Time,* translated by Elliott Coleman (Westport, Conn.: Greenwood Press, 1979 reprint), p. 251.
16. Flaubert, *Madame Bovary* (Club de l'Honnete Homme edition), p. 193.
17. Flaubert, *Madame Bovary* (Modern Library edition), p. 182.
18. *The Artist as Critic: Critical Writings of Oscar Wilde,* edited by Richard Ellmann (New York: Random House, 1968), pp. 366–369.
19. Quoted in Jules de Gaultier, *Bovarysm,* translated by Gerald M. Spring (New York: Philosophical Library, 1970), p. 11.
20. Ibid., p. 4.

21. Ibid., p. 13.

22. T. S. Eliot, *Selected Essays, 1917–1932* (London: Faber and Faber, 1932), p. 39.

23. Shakespeare, *Othello,* edited by Louis B. Wright and Virginia A. Lamar (Washington: Folger Library, 1971 reprint), p. 127 (V.ii.392–410).

24. Eliot, *Selected Essays,* pp. 130–131.

25. Marjorie Levinson, *Wordsworth's Great Period Poems* (Cambridge: Cambridge University Press, 1986), p. 57.

26. Stevens, *Palm at the End of the Mind,* p. 218.

27. Christopher Ricks, "The Pursuit of Metaphor," in Alvin Kernan, editor, *What's Happened to the Humanities?* (Princeton: Princeton University Press, 1997), p. 194.

28. Stevens, *Palm at the End of the Mind,* p. 368.

Chapter 4: The Practice of Reading

1. I. A. Richards, *Speculative Instruments* (Chicago: University of Chicago Press, 1955), p. 63.

2. D. W. Harding, *Experience into Words* (Cambridge: Cambridge University Press, 1982 reprint), p. 99.

3. Ibid., pp. 181–182.

4. Helen Gardner, *The Business of Criticism* (Oxford: Clarendon, 1959), pp. 59–60.

5. F. R. Leavis, *Education and the University: A Sketch for an 'English School,* rev. ed. (London: Chatto and Windus, 1948), p. 116.

6. Ibid., pp. 123–124.

7. Ibid., p. 124.

8. William Empson, *Seven Types of Ambiguity* (New York: New Directions, 1955), pp. 59–60.

9. William Empson, *Argufying,* edited by John Haffenden (Iowa City: University of Iowa Press, 1991), p. 108.

10. Leavis, *Education and the University,* p. 68.

11. Ibid., p. 69.

12. John Guillory, *Cultural Capital: The Problem of Literary Canon Formation* (Chicago: University of Chicago Press, 1993), p. 156.

13. *Shakespeare Studies,* edited by J. Leeds Barroll (New York: Burt Franklin, 1975) 8:255–277.

14. John Russell Brown, editor, *Focus on "Macbeth"* (London: Routledge and Kegan Paul, 1982), pp. 189–209.

15. Terry Eagleton, *William Shakespeare* (Oxford: Basil Blackwell, 1986), pp. 1–2.

16. Madelon Gohlke, " 'I wooed thee with my sword': Shakespeare's Tragic Paradigms," in Murray M. Schwartz and Coppelia Kahn, editors, *Representing Shakespeare: New Psychoanalytic Essays* (Baltimore: Johns Hopkins, University Press, 1980), p. 176.

17. Jonathan Goldberg, "Speculations: *Macbeth* and Source," in Jean E. Howard and

Marion F. O'Connor, editors, *Shakespeare Reproduced: The Text in History and Ideology* (New York: Methuen, 1987), pp. 259–260.

18. Janet Adelman, "'Born of Woman': Fantasies of Maternal Power in *Macbeth*," in Marjorie Garber, *Cannibals, Witches, and Divorce: Estranging the Renaissance* (Baltimore: Johns Hopkins University Press, 1987), pp. 90–121.

19. Janet Adelman, *Suffocating Mothers: Fantasies of Maternal Origin in Shakespeare's Plays: "Hamlet" to "The Tempest"* (New York: Routledge, 1992), pp. 130, 146.

20. Geoffrey Hill, "Style and Faith," *Times Literary Supplement*, December 27, 1991, p. 4.

21. Eagleton, *William Shakespeare*, p. 3.

22. L. C. Knights, *Some Shakespearean Themes* (Stanford: Stanford University Press, 1959), p. 141.

23. Lisa Jardine, *Still Harping on Daughters: Women and Drama in the Age of Shakespeare* (Sussex: Harvester, 1983), pp. 94–95, 97.

24. Catherine Belsey, *The Subject of Tragedy* (London: Methuen, 1985), p. 51.

25. Stanley Cavell, "Macbeth Appalled (II)," *Raritan* 12, no. 3 (Winter 1992):2.

26. Maurice Blanchot, *The Gaze of Orpheus*, translated by Lydia Davis (Barrytown, N.Y.: Station Hill Press, 1981), p. 93.

27. Jorie Graham, *Region of Unlikeness* (New York: Ecco, 1991), pp. 120–121.

28. Matei Calinescu, *Rereading* (New Haven: Yale University Press, 1993), p. 265.

29. Walter Benjamin, *Illuminations*, translated by Harry Zohn (New York: Schocken, 1969), p. 256.

30. Peter L. Berger and Thomas Luckmann, *The Social Construction of Reality: A Treatise in the Sociology of Knowledge* (New York: Doubleday, 1966), p. 1.

31. Michel Serres, *Hermes: Literature, Science, Philosophy,* edited by Josué V. Harari and David F. Bell (Baltimore: Johns Hopkins University Press, 1992 reprint), p. 106.

32. John Guillory, *Cultural Capital: The Problem of Literary Canon Formation* (Chicago: University of Chicago Press, 1993), p. 35.

33. Paul de Man, *Blindness and Insight: Essays in the Rhetoric of Contemporary Criticism* rev. 2nd ed. (Minneapolis: University of Minnesota Press, 1983), p. 17.

34. Quoted in Frank Kermode, *The Genesis of Secrecy: On the Interpretation of Narrative* (Cambridge, Mass.: Harvard University Press, 1979) p. xi.

35. J. Hillis Miller, *Theory Now and Then* (Durham: Duke University Press, 1991), p. 391.

36. Edward Corbett, "Literature and Composition: Allies or Rivals in the Classroom?" in Winifred Bryan Horner, editor, *Composition and Literature* (Chicago: University of Chicago Press, 1983), p. 180.

37. Wlad Godzich, *The Culture of Literacy* (Cambridge, Mass.: Harvard University Press, 1994), p. 5.

38. Guillory, *Cultural Capital*, pp. 79–80.

39. Pierre Bourdieu, *Language and Symbolic Power,* translated by Gino Raymond and Matthew Adamson, edited by John B. Thompson (Cambridge, Mass.: Harvard University Press, 1991), p. 66.

40. Peter Brooks, "Aesthetics and Ideology: What Happened to Poetics?" *Critical Inquiry* 20, no. 3 (Spring 1994):509–523. George Levine, editor, *Aesthetics and Ideology* (New Brunswick: Rutgers University Press, 1994), p. 15.

41. Levine, *Aesthetics and Ideology,* p. 17.

Chapter 5: What Is Interpretation?

1. Hans-Georg Gadamer, *Truth and Method* (London: Sheed and Ward, 1985 reprint), p. 278.

2. Susan Noakes, "Gracious Words: Luke's Jesus and the Reading of Sacred Poetry at the Beginning of the Christian Era," in Jonathan Boyarin, editor, *The Ethnography of Reading* (Berkeley: University of California Press, 1993), p. 46.

3. Wallace Stevens, *The Palm at the End of the Mind,* edited by Holly Stevens (New York: Vintage, 1972), p. 386.

4. Ibid., p. 292.

5. Wallace Stevens, *Letters,* edited by Holly Stevens (Berkeley: University of California Press, 1996), p. 781. Letter of June 11, 1953.

6. W. B. Yeats, *Collected Poems* (New York: Macmillan, 1952), p. 322.

7. W. B. Yeats, *Explorations* (London: Macmillan, 1962), p. 451.

8. Gadamer, *Truth and Method,* p. 356.

9. F. W. Bateson, "The Function of Criticism at the Present Time," *Essays in Criticism* 8, no. 1 (January 1953):14.

10. Andrew Marvell, *The Complete English Poems,* edited by Elizabeth Story Donno (New York: St. Martin's, 1974), p. 103.

11. Ibid., p. 259.

12. *The Oxford Authors: Alexander Pope,* edited by Pat Rogers (Oxford: Oxford University Press, 1993), p. 544.

13. Bateson, "Function of Criticism," p. 15.

14. Ibid., p. 18.

15. F. R. Leavis, "The Responsible Critic or the Function of Criticism at Any Time," in *A Selection from Scrutiny,* compiled by F. R. Leavis (Cambridge: Cambridge University Press, 1968), 2:284.

16. Ibid., p. 285.

17. Ibid., p. 287.

18. Bateson, "Function of Criticism," pp. 15–16.

19. *Oxford Authors: Alexander Pope,* p. 544n.

20. F. W. Bateson, "The Responsible Critic: Reply," in *A Selection from Scrutiny,* 2:306.

21. Leavis, "Responsible Critic," p. 290.

22. Ibid., p. 290.

23. Ibid., p. 311.

24. Ibid., p. 312.

25. Ibid.

26. Ibid., p. 295.

27. Bateson, "Responsible Critic: Reply," p. 307.

28. Ibid., p. 307.

29. Cf. my *England, Their England: Commentaries on English Language and Literature* (New York: Knopf, 1988), pp. 332–350.

30. Michel de Certeau, *The Practice of Everyday Life*, translated by Steven Rendall (Berkeley: University of California Press, 1988), p. 172.

31. Quoted in Walter Benjamin, *Illuminations*, translated by Harry Zohn (New York: Harcourt, Brace & World, 1955), pp. 89–90.

32. Ibid., p. 90.

33. T. S. Eliot, *Selected Prose*, edited by Frank Kermode (New York: Harcourt Brace Jovanovich, 1975), p. 110.

34. Ibid.

35. William Morris, *The Defence of Guenevere and Other Poems* (London: De La More Press, 1904), p. 190.

36. Elizabeth Sewell, *The Field of Nonsense* (London: Chatto and Windus, 1952), pp. 17, 21, 47, 129, 144.

37. Helen Vendler, *The Music of What Happens: Poems, Poets, Critics* (Cambridge, Mass.: Harvard University Press, 1988), p. 1.

38. Ibid., p. 2.

39. Guy Davenport, *Every Force Evolves a Form* (San Francisco: North Point, 1987), p. ix.

Chapter 6: Doing Things with Words

1. *Harvard Magazine*, September–October 1982.

2. Paul de Man, *The Resistance to Theory* (Minneapolis: University of Minnesota Press, 1986), p. 24.

3. Ibid., pp. 45foll.

4. Fredric Jameson, "Wallace Stevens," *New Orleans Review* 11 (1984):19.

5. Jacques Derrida, *Writing and Difference*, translated by Alan Bass (Chicago: University of Chicago Press, 1978), p. 291.

6. Antonio Gramsci, *The Modern Prince and Other Writings* (New York: International Publishers, 1967), p. 64.

7. Fredric Jameson, "Wyndham Lewis as Futurist," *Hudson Review*, July 1973, p. 318.

8. Fredric Jameson, *The Political Unconscious* (Ithaca: Cornell University Press, 1981), p. 238.

9. Ibid., p. 212.

10. I. A. Richards, "Fifteen Lines from Landor," *Criterion* 12, no. 48 (April 1933): 369–370.

11. Derrida, *Writing and Difference*, p. 292.

12. Richard Macksey and Eugenio Donato, editors, *The Languages of Criticism and the Sciences of Man: The Structuralist Controversy* (Baltimore: Johns Hopkins University Press, 1970), p. 291.

13. Roland Barthes, *S/Z,* translated by Richard Miller (London: Jonathan Cape, 1975), p. 5.

14. De Man, *Resistance to Theory,* p. 23.

15. Marjorie Levinson, "Back to the Future: Wordsworth's New Historicism," *South Atlantic Quarterly* 88, no. 3 (Summer 1989):652.

16. M. H. Bakhtin, *The Dialogic Imagination,* translated by Carly Emerson and Michael Holquist (Austin: University of Texas Press, 1981), p. 259.

17. Emmanuel Levinas, "The Other in Proust," in *The Levinas Reader,* edited by Sean Hand (Oxford: Basil Blackwell, 1989), p. 164.

18. Roland Barthes, *The Pleasure of the Text,* translated by Richard Miller (New York: Hill and Wang, 1975), p. 62.

Chapter 7: Orality, Literacy, and Their Discontents

1. W. B. Yeats, *Collected Poems,* edited by Richard J. Finneran (New York: Collier Macmillan, 1989), p. 154.

2. Quoted in Stanley Cavell, *A Pitch of Philosophy: Autobiographical Exercises* (Cambridge, Mass.: Harvard University Press, 1994), p. 119.

3. Brian Stock, *Listening for the Text: On the Uses of the Past* (Baltimore: Johns Hopkins University Press, 1990), p. 4.

4. Hannah Arendt, *The Human Condition* (Chicago: University of Chicago Press, 1958), p. 4.

5. Eric A. Havelock, *Preface to Plato,* pp. 197–233.

6. Cavell, *Pitch of Philosophy,* p. 79.

7. Stock, *Listening for the Text,* p. 46.

8. Michel de Certeau, *The Writing of History,* translated by Tom Conley (New York: Columbia University Press, 1988), pp. 183–184.

9. Michel de Certeau, *The Practice of Everyday Life,* translated by Steven Rendall (Berkeley: University of California Press, 1984), p. 146.

10. Derek Attridge, *Peculiar Language: Literature as Difference from the Renaissance to James Joyce* (Ithaca: Cornell University Press, 1988), p. 161.

11. W. B. Yeats, *Explorations* (London: Macmillan, 1962), pp. 206–207, 209.

12. John B. Thompson, editor, *Hermeneutics and the Human Sciences* (London: Cambridge University Press, 1981), p. 152.

13. Claude Lévi-Strauss, *Tristes Tropiques,* translated by John and Doreen Weightman (New York: Atheneum, 1974), p. 299.

14. Cf. Michael Warner, *The Letters of the Republic: Publication and the Public Sphere in Eighteenth-Century America* (Cambridge, Mass.: Harvard University Press, 1990).

15. De Certeau, *Practice of Everyday Life*, p. xviii.

16. Stanley Cavell, *Conditions Handsome and Unhandsome: The Constitution of Emersonian Perfectionism* (Chicago: University of Chicago Press, 1990), p. 37.

Chapter 8: Murray Krieger Versus Paul de Man

Epigraph: Wallace Stevens, *The Palm at the End of the Mind* (New York: Vintage, 1972), p. 95.

1. Paul de Man, *Romanticism and Contemporary Criticism: The Gauss Seminars and Other Papers*, edited by E. S. Burt, Kevin Newmark, and Andrzej Warminski (Baltimore: Johns Hopkins University Press, 1993), pp. 181–187.

2. Morton W. Bloomfield, editor, *Allegory, Myth, and Symbol* (Cambridge, Mass.: Harvard University Press, 1981), pp. 1–22. Murray Krieger, *Words About Words About Words: Theory, Criticism, and the Literary Text* (Baltimore: Johns Hopkins University Press, 1988), pp. 271–288.

3. Murray Krieger, *A Reopening of Closure: Organicism Against Itself* (New York: Columbia University Press, 1989), pp. 40–41.

4. *The Collected Works of Samuel Taylor Coleridge: Lay Sermons*, edited by R. J. White (London: Routledge & Kegan Paul; Princeton: Bollingen Series 75, Princeton University Press, 1972), p. 30.

5. Krieger, *Words About Words About Words*, p. 276.

6. Paul de Man, *Blindness and Insight: Essays in the Rhetoric of Contemporary Criticism*, rev. 2nd ed. (Minneapolis: University of Minnesota Press, 1983), pp. 206–207.

7. Krieger, *Words About Words About Words*, p. 285.

8. Ibid., pp. 287–288.

9. De Man, *Blindness and Insight*, p. 13.

10. De Man, *Romanticism and Contemporary Criticism*, p. 182.

11. Paul de Man, *The Resistance to Theory* (Minneapolis: University of Minnesota Press, 1993), pp. 27–53.

12. Ibid., p. 185.

13. De Man, *Romanticism and Contemporary Criticism*, pp. 186–187.

14. William Hazlitt quoted in David Bromwich, *Hazlitt: The Mind of a Critic* (New York: Oxford University Press, 1983), p. 385.

15. Bromwich, *Hazlitt;* p. 386.

16. De Man, *Resistance to Theory*, p. 50.

17. De Man, *Romanticism and Contemporary Criticism*, p. 187.

18. De Man, *Blindness and Insight*, pp. 16–17.

19. De Man, *Romanticism and Contemporary Criticism*, pp. 9, 12–13.

20. Walter Benjamin, *The Origin of German Tragic Drama*, translated by John Osborne (London: NLB, 1977), pp. 166, 178.

21. Giambattista Vico, *The New Science* (New York: Doubleday, 1961), p. 87. Quoted in

Cynthia Chase, *Decomposing Figures: Rhetorical Readings in the Romantic Tradition* (Baltimore: Johns Hopkins University Press, 1986), p. 215.

22. De Man, *Resistance to Theory,* pp. 36, 48, 45.

23. Ibid., pp. 49–50.

24. Krieger, *Words About Words About Words,* p. 271.

25. Kenneth Burke, *A Grammar of Motives* (Cleveland: World Publishing, 1962), p. 447.

26. Kenneth Burke, *Counter-Statement* (Chicago: University of Chicago Press, 1957 reprint), p. 31.

27. Helen Vendler, *The Odes of John Keats* (Cambridge, Mass.: Harvard University Press, 1983), p. 95.

28. Krieger, *Words About Words About Words,* p. 286.

29. Arthur Symons, *The Symbolist Movement in Literature* (New York: E. P. Dutton, 1958 reprint), pp. 2–3.

30. David Lloyd, *Anomalous States: Irish Writing and the Post-Colonial Moment* (Durham: Duke University Press, 1993), p. 85.

31. Ibid., pp. 70–71.

Chapter 9: What Happens in *Othello*

1. John Peale Bishop, *Collected Poems* (New York: Scribner, 1948), pp. 5–6.

2. T. S. Eliot, *Selected Essays* (London: Faber and Faber, 1963 reprint), p. 129.

3. Ibid., p. 131.

4. Ibid., p. 68.

5. Wallace Stevens, *Collected Poems* (London: Faber and Faber, 1955), p. 173.

6. *Othello,* edited by M. R. Ridley (Arden Edition) (London: Methuen, 1958), pp. 12–13.

7. Eliot, *Selected Essays,* p. 326.

8. Ibid., p. 327.

9. Hilda M. Hulme, *Explorations in Shakespeare's Language: Some Problems of Lexical Meaning in the Dramatic Text* (New York: Barnes and Noble, 1963), pp. 124–125.

10. Cf. Eldred D. Jones, *The Elizabethan Image of Africa* (Charlottesville: University Press of Virginia: Folger Shakespeare Library, 1971), pp. 21–30.

11. Sigmund Freud, *The Interpretation of Dreams,* in *Standard Edition of the Complete Psychological Works of Sigmund Freud,* edited by James Strachey et al. (London: Hogarth Press, 1953–74), 5:511.

12. André Gide, *The Counterfeiters, with Journal of "The Counterfeiters,"* the novel translated by Dorothy Bussy, the journal by Justin O'Brien (New York: Knopf, 1959 reprint), p. 363.

13. Stephen Greenblatt, *Renaissance Self-Fashioning: From More to Shakespeare* (Chicago: University of Chicago Press, 1980), p. 228.

14. Ibid., p. 230.

15. Ibid.

16. Ibid., p. 233.

17. James Joyce, *Ulysses*, edited by Hans Walter Gabler et al. (New York: Garland, 1984), 1:457.

18. Cf. Eamon Grennan, "The Women's Voices in *Othello*: Speech, Song, Silence," *Shakespeare Quarterly*, Autumn 1987, p. 281.

Chapter 10: Reading *Gulliver's Travels*

Epigraph: James Joyce, *Ulysses: A Critical and Synoptic Edition*, edited by Hans Walter Gabler et al. (New York: Garland, 1984), 1:81.

1. Jonathan Swift, *Correspondence*, edited by Harold Williams (Oxford: Clarendon, 1963), 3:182.

2. Ibid., 3:179. Letter of November 5, 1726.

3. Northrop Frye, "The Four Forms of Prose Fiction," *Hudson Review*, Winter 1950, 588–589.

4. Hugh Kenner, *Joyce's Voices* (Berkeley: University of California Press, 1978), p. 4.

5. Jonathan Swift, *Gulliver's Travels*, edited by Herbert Davis (Oxford: Basil Blackwell, 1959), p. 107.

6. John Locke, *An Essay Concerning Human Understanding*, edited by P. H. Nidditch (Oxford: Clarendon, 1975). The numbers refer to book, chapter, and section of the *Essay*, respectively.

7. Jonathan Swift, *Irish Tracts, 1720–1723*, edited by Herbert Davis (Oxford: Basil Blackwell, 1968), p. 150.

8. W. B. Yeats, *The Poems*, edited by Daniel Albright (London: Dent, 1994), p. 260.

9. Quoted in Charles Taylor, *Sources of the Self: The Making of the Modern Identity* (Cambridge, Mass.: Harvard University Press, 1989), p. 251.

10. Swift, *Irish Tracts*, p. 151.

11. Christopher Ricks, *Tennyson: A Selected Edition* (Berkeley: University of California Press, 1989), pp. 584–590.

12. Swift, *Gulliver's Travels*, p. 267.

13. Abram Tertz (Andrei Sinyavsky), *A Voice from the Chorus*, translated by Kyril Fitzlyon and Max Hayward (New York: Farrar, Straus and Giroux, 1976), p. 22.

14. Peter L. Berger and Thomas Luckmann, *The Social Construction of Reality: A Treatise in the Sociology of Knowledge* (New York: Doubleday, 1966), p. 1.

Chapter 11: On a Word in Wordsworth

1. William Wordsworth, *The Prelude or Growth of a Poet's Mind*, edited by Ernest de Selincourt, 2nd rev. ed. by Helen Darbishire (Oxford: Clarendon, 1959), pp. 158–160.

2. Ibid., pp. 639–640. This version is also published, and the manuscript reproduced, in *The Prelude, 1798–1799*, edited by Stephen Parrish (Ithaca: Cornell University Press, 1977), pp. 86–87.

3. William Wordsworth, *Lyrical Ballads and Other Poems, 1797–1800*, edited by James Butler and Karen Green (Ithaca: Cornell University Press, 1992), pp. 139–141.

4. *Wordsworth's Literary Criticism*, edited by W. J. B. Owen (London: Routledge & Kegan Paul, 1974), pp. 184, 190.

5. *Collected Letters of Samuel Taylor Coleridge: Volume 1, 1785–1800*, edited by Earl Leslie Griggs (Oxford:Clarendon, 1956), pp. 266–267.

6. Samuel Taylor Coleridge, *Biographia Literaria*, edited by James Engell and W. Jackson Bate (Princeton: Princeton University Press, 1983), 2:106.

7. Geoffrey H. Hartman, *Wordsworth's Poetry, 1787–1814* (New Haven: Yale University Press, new edition 1971), p. 19.

8. Ibid., p. 103.

9. Ibid. The lines are from John Milton *Paradise Lost*, IV.139–142.

10. Samuel Taylor Coleridge, *Logic*, edited by J. R. de J. Jackson (Princeton: Princeton University Press, 1981), pp. 242–243.

11. *Wordsworth's Literary Criticism*, pp. 180–181. The passages quoted are Virgil, *Eclogues* I.75–76: "I shall not, as I lie in the green cavern, see you again hanging from the bushy rock." Shakespeare, *King Lear*, IV.vi.15–16, and Milton, *Paradise Lost*, II.636–643.

12. *The Prelude, 1798–1799*, edited by Stephen Parrish, I.57–59, p. 44.

13. *Wordsworth's Literary Criticism*, pp. 123–124.

14. *Poetry and Prose of William Blake*, edited by Geoffrey Keynes (New York: Random House, 1927), pp. 1024–1025.

15. Hartman, *Wordsworth's Poetry*, p. xi.

16. Ibid., p. 350.

17. Milton, *Paradise Lost*, V.853–864.

18. Ibid., VIII.277–279.

19. "'Heaven and Earth in Wordsworth and Hölderlin" and "Time and History in Wordsworth" are published in the posthumous Paul de Man, *Romanticism and Contemporary Criticism*, edited by E. S. Burt, Kevin Newmark, and Andrzej Warminski (Baltimore: Johns Hopkins University Press, 1993), pp. 137–146, 74–94. "Wordsworth and Hölderlin" is published in Paul de Man, *The Rhetoric of Romanticism* (New York: Columbia University Press, 1984), pp. 47–65.

20. William Wordsworth and Samuel Taylor Coleridge, *Lyrical Ballads, 1798*, edited by W. J. B. Owen (London: Oxford University Press, 1967), p. 167.

21. De Man, *Romanticism and Contemporary Criticism*, p. 78.

22. Ibid., p. 144.

23. Ibid., p. 93.

24. Ibid., pp. 99, 93–94.

25. Ibid., p. 146.

26. De Man, *Rhetoric of Romanticism*, p. 54.

27. De Man, *Romanticism and Contemporary Criticism*, p. 88.

28. Robert Frost, *Selected Poems* (New York: Holt, Rinehart and Winston, 1963), pp. 224–225.

29. Aldous Huxley, *Collected Essays* (New York: Harper and Row, 1958), p. 3.

30. Frost, *Selected Poems*, p. 78.

31. Jean-Joseph Goux, *Symbolic Economies: After Marx and Freud*, translated by Jennifer Curtiss Gage (Ithaca: Cornell University Press, 1990), p. 187.

Chapter 12: The Antinomian Pater

1. Walter Pater, *The Renaissance: Studies in Art and Poetry: The 1893 Text*, edited by Donald L. Hill (Berkeley: University of California Press, 1980), p. 1.

2. Ibid., p. 19.

3. Ibid.

4. W. B. Yeats, *Essays and Introductions* (London: Macmillan, 1961), p. 192.

5. Cf. E. P. Thompson, *Witness against the Beast: William Blake and the Moral Law* (New York: New Press, 1993), p. 10.

6. W. J. B. Owen, editor, *Wordsworth's Literary Criticism* (London: Routledge & Kegan Paul, 1974), p. 124.

7. Pater, *Renaissance*, p. 2.

8. Ibid., pp. 20–21.

9. Ibid., p. 5.

10. Ibid., p. 6.

11. Ibid., p. 213.

12. Walter Pater, *Miscellaneous Studies* (London: Macmillan, 1895), p. 248.

13. Thomas Carlyle, *The French Revolution* (Oxford: Oxford University Press, 1989 reprint), p. 294.

14. Johann Fichte, *Science of Knowledge (Wissenschaftslehre) with the First and Second Introductions*, edited and translated by Peter Heath and John Lachs (New York: Appleton-Century-Crofts, 1970), pp. 69, 99.

15. *The Popular Works of Johann Gottlieb Fichte*, translated by William Smith (London, 1889), 1:210–211, 284–285. Quoted in Gerald Monsman, "Pater, Hopkins, and Fichte's Ideal Student," *South Atlantic Quarterly* 70 (1971):371.

16. Pater, *Miscellaneous Studies*, p. 251.

17. Ibid., p. 61.

18. Pater, *Renaissance*, p. 152.

19. Ibid., pp. 175–176.

20. Ibid., pp. 174–175.

21. Pater, *Miscellaneous Studies*, p. 253.

22. Ibid., p. 254.

23. W. B. Yeats, *The Poems: A New Edition,* edited by Richard J. Finneran (London: Macmillan, 1984), pp. 134–135.

24. Edward Thomas, *Walter Pater: A Critical Study* (London: Martin Secker, 1913), p. 79.

25. Pater, *Renaissance,* p. 185.

26. Ibid., p. 43.

27. William Morris, *Selected Poems,* edited by Pater Faulkner (Manchester: Carcanet, 1992), p. 88.

28. John Lucas, *England and Englishness: Ideas of Nationhood in English Poetry, 1688–1900* (London: Hogarth, 1990), p. 202.

29. [Pater], "Poems by William Morris," *Westminster Review* 24, n.s. (October 1868):300.

30. Ibid.

31. Ibid., p. 305.

32. Ibid., p. 306.

33. Ibid., p. 302.

34. Ibid.

Chapter 13: On a Chapter of *Ulysses*

1. Hugh Kenner, *Joyce's Voices* (Berkeley: University of California Press, 1978), p. 17.

2. James Joyce, *Letters,* vol. 1, edited by Stuart Gilbert (New York: Viking, 1966), p. 135, Letter of January 3, 1920.

3. Homer, *The Odyssey,* translated by A. T. Murray (Cambridge, Mass.: Harvard University Press, 1976), 1:225 (VI, lines 241–245).

4. Margot Norris, "Modernism, Myth, and Desire in 'Nausicaa,'" *James Joyce Quarterly* 26, no. 1 (Fall 1988):37–50.

5. Line references are to James Joyce, *Ulysses,* 3 vols., edited by Hans Walter Gabler with Wolfhard Steppe and Claus Melchior (New York: Garland, 1984).

6. James Joyce, *A Portrait of the Artist as a Young Man,* edited by Hans Walter Gabler with Walter Hettche (New York: Garland, 1993), p. 81.

7. Kenner, *Joyce's Voices,* p. 18.

8. Henry James, *The Wings of the Dove,* edited by J. Donald Crowley and Richard A. Hocks (New York: W. W. Norton, 1978), p. 23.

9. Kenner, *Joyce's Voices,* p. 19.

10. Norris, "Modernism, Myth, and Desire in 'Nausicaa,'" p. 39.

11. Fritz Senn, *Joyce's Dislocutions: Essays on Reading as Translation,* edited by John Paul Riquelme (Baltimore: Johns Hopkins University Press, 1984), p. 185.

12. Jules de Gaultier, *Bovarysm,* translated by Gerald M. Spring (New York: Philosophical Library, 1970), p. 4.

13. René Girard, *Deceit, Desire, and the Novel: Self and Other in Literary Structure,* translated by Yvonne Freccero (Baltimore: Johns Hopkins University Press, 1965), p. 73.

14. Renato Poggioli, "Tragedy or Romance? A Reading of the Paolo and Francesca Episode in Dante's *Inferno*" *PMLA* 72 (June 1957):315–358.

15. Senn, *Joyce's Dislocutions,* p. 174.

16. Ibid., pp. 185–186.

17. Quoted in Saul Friedlander, "On Kitsch," *Salmagundi,* nos. 85–86 (Winter–Spring 1990):8.

18. Norris, "Modernism, Myth, and Desire in 'Nausicaa,'" p. 49.

19. John Carlos Rowe, "Modern Art and the Invention of Postmodern Capital," *American Quarterly* 39, no. 1 (Spring 1987):160.

20. Ibid., p. 156.

Chapter 14: Yeats: The New Political Issue

1. Three versions called "Annunciation" and one called "Leda and the Swan" are given in W. B. Yeats, *Memoirs,* transcribed and edited by Denis Donoghue (London: Macmillan, 1972), pp. 272–275.

2. R. F. Foster, *Paddy and Mr. Punch: Connections in Irish and English History* (London: Allen Lane, 1993), p. 220.

3. Conor Cruise O'Brien, "Passion and Cunning: An Essay on the Politics of W. B. Yeats," in A. Norman Jeffares and K. G. W. Cross, editors, *In Excited Reverie: A Centenary Tribute to W. B. Yeats, 1865–1939* (New York: Macmillan, 1965), p. 218.

4. Ibid., p. 237.

5. Ibid., p. 257.

6. Ibid., p. 224.

7. Peter Alt and Russell K. Alspach, editors, *The Variorum Edition of the Poems of W. B. Yeats* (New York: Macmillan, 1957), p. 828.

8. O'Brien, "Passion and Cunning," pp. 274–275.

9. W. B. Yeats, *A Vision* (New York: Macmillan, 1956), p. 268.

10. Leo Spitzer, "On Yeats's Poem 'Leda and the Swan,'" *Modern Philology* 51, no. 4, (May 1954):271–276.

11. W. B. Yeats, *Collected Poems* (New York: Macmillan, 1952), p. 185.

12. Ibid., p. 124.

13. Giorgio Melchiori, *The Whole Mystery of Art: Pattern into Poetry in the Work of W. B. Yeats* (New York: Macmillan, 1961), pp. 73–163.

14. Edward W. Said, "Yeats and Decolonization," in *Nationalism, Colonialism, and Literature* (Minneapolis: University of Minnesota Press, 1990), p. 90.

15. Seamus Deane, *Celtic Revivals* (London: Faber and Faber, 1985), p. 49.

16. David Lloyd, *Anomalous States: Irish Writing and the Post-Colonial Moment* (Dublin: Lilliput, 1993), p. 74.

17. Declan Kiberd, *Inventing Ireland* (Cambridge, Mass.: Harvard University Press, 1995), p. 330.

18. Ibid., pp. 314–315.

19. Karl Mannheim, *Ideology and Utopia* (New York: Harcourt, Brace and Company, 1936), p. 34.

20. Tom Garvin, *1922: The Birth of Irish Democracy* (New York: St. Martin's, 1996), pp. 169foll.

21. T. S. Eliot, *The Sacred Wood* (London: Methuen, 1960), pp. viii–x.

22. Lloyd, *Anomalous States*, p. 59.

23. Ibid., p. 69.

24. Ibid.

25. Ibid., p. 72.

26. Ibid., p. 74.

27. Paul de Man, *The Rhetoric of Romanticism* (New York: Columbia University Press, 1984), p. 201.

28. Ibid., p. 194.

29. Ibid., p. 197.

30. Yeats, *Collected Poems*, p. 275.

31. De Man, *Rhetoric of Romanticism*, pp. 139–140.

32. Cf. Ian Fletcher, *W. B. Yeats and His Contemporaries* (New York: St. Martin's, 1987), pp. 220–251.

33. W. B. Yeats, *Variorum Edition of the Plays*, edited by Russell K. Alspach (London: Macmillan, 1966), p. 789.

34. De Man, *Rhetoric of Romanticism*, p. 140.

35. Ezra Pound, *The Cantos* (New York: New Directions, 1948), p. 106.

36. Donald Davie, *Ezra Pound: Poet as Sculptor* (New York: Oxford University Press, 1964), p. 173.

37. Hugh Kenner, *The Poetry of Ezra Pound* (London: Faber and Faber, 1951), p. 210.

38. Davie, *Ezra Pound*, p. 174.

39. Lloyd, *Anomalous States*, p. 79.

40. Fredric Jameson, "Wyndham Lewis as Futurist," *Hudson Review*, July 1973, p. 298.

41. R. P. Blackmur, *A Primer of Ignorance*, edited by Joseph Frank (New York: Harcourt, Brace and World, 1967), p. 58.

Chapter 15: Teaching *Blood Meridian*

1. Cormac McCarthy, *The Orchard Keeper* (New York: Random House, 1965), p. 246.

2. Cormac McCarthy, *Outer Dark* (New York: Random House, 1968), p. 236.

3. Cormac McCarthy, *Child of God* (New York: Random House, 1973), p. 23.

4. Ibid., p. 103.

5. Alexis de Tocqueville, *Democracy in America*, edited by J. P. Mayer (New York: Doubleday, 1969), p. 468.

6. Sigmund Freud, *The Interpretation of Dreams*, in *Standard Edition of the Complete*

Psychological Works of Sigmund Freud, edited by James Strachey et al. (London: Hogarth, 1953–1974), 5:511.

7. McCarthy, *Child of God,* p. 138.

8. McCarthy, *Orchard Keeper,* p. 88.

9. Svetlana Alpers, *The Art of Describing: Dutch Art in the Seventeenth Century* (Chicago: University of Chicago Press, 1983), p. xix.

10. Cormac McCarthy, *Suttree* (New York: Random House, 1979), pp. 385–386.

11. Ibid., p. 414.

12. Ibid., p. 129.

13. Cf. John Emil Sepich, " 'What kind of indians was them?': Some Historical Sources in Cormac McCarthy's *Blood Meridian,*" in Edwin T. Arnold and Dianne C. Luce, editors, *Perspectives on Cormac McCarthy* (Jackson: University Press of Mississippi, 1993), pp. 121–141.

14. Northrop Frye, "The Four Forms of Prose Fiction," *Hudson Review* 2, Winter 1950, p. 586.

15. Ibid., p. 584.

16. Cormac McCarthy, *Blood Meridian or The Evening Redness in the West* (New York: Random House, 1985), p. 172.

17. Ibid., p. 173.

18. Ibid., p. 247.

19. Erich Auerbach, *Mimesis: The Representation of Reality in Western Literature,* translated by Willard Trask (Princeton: Princeton University Press, 1953), pp. 3–4.

20. McCarthy, *Blood Meridian,* p. 72.

21. Friedrich Nietzsche, *The Birth of Tragedy* and *The Genealogy of Morals,* translated by Francis Golffing (New York: Doubleday, 1956), p. 29.

22. McCarthy, *Blood Meridian,* pp. 297–298.

23. Samuel E. Chamberlain, *My Confession* (Lincoln: University of Nebraska Press, 1987 reprint), pp. 271–272. Quoted in Sepich, "What kind of indians was them?" pp. 125–126.

24. McCarthy, *Blood Meridian,* p. 198.

25. Ibid., p. 250.

26. Ibid., p. 299.

27. Ibid., p. 307.

28. Ibid., p. 328.

29. Ibid., p. 327.

30. Ibid., p. 333.

31. Nietzsche, *Birth of Tragedy* and *The Genealogy of Morals,* p. 42.

32. McCarthy, *Blood Meridian,* p. 335.

33. Cf. Leo Daughtery, "Gravers False and True: *Blood Meridian* as Gnostic Tragedy," in Arnold and Luce, *Perspectives on Cormac McCarthy,* pp. 157–172.

34. McCarthy, *Blood Meridian,* p. 237.

35. Cf. Daughterty, "Gravers False and True," pp. 157–172.

36. McCarthy, *Blood Meridian,* p. 109.

37. Cormac McCarthy, *All the Pretty Horses* (New York: Knopf, 1992), p. 60.

38. Lionel Trilling, *Beyond Culture: Essays on Literature and Learning* (New York: Viking, 1965), pp. 19, 30.

Index

Lucian, 167

Luckmann, Thomas, 72–73, 185

"Lycidas" (Milton), 69

Lyotard, Jean-François, 22, 273

Macbeth, 57–78

"*Macbeth* and Witchcraft" (Stallybrass), 65

Macfarlane, Alan, 64

Macherey, Pierre, 49

MacNeice, Louis, 238

Madame Bovary (Flaubert), 45–46, 47–48, 224–25

"Magi, The" (Yeats), 242

"Man and the Echo" (Yeats), 248

Manchurian Candidate, The (Condon), 181

Mandeville, Sir John, 181

Mann, Thomas, 101

Mannheim, Karl, 246

"Man with the Blue Guitar" (Stevens), 146, 156

Marcuse, Herbert, 78

"Marina" (Eliot), 145

Marius the Epicurean (Pater), 219

Marvell, Andrew, 85–87

Marx, Karl, 23, 185

Marxist Criticism, 100

Maturin, Charles, 237

Mauron, Charles, 103

McCarthy, Cormac, 259–77

McLuhan, Marshall, 114

"Meditations in Time of Civil War" (Yeats), 250

Melchiori, Giorgio, 241, 242–43

Melmoth the Wanderer (Maturin), 237

Menippean satire, 167

Metaphor, 134, 138

Mill, John Stuart, 196

Miller, J. Hillis, 75, 107

Milton, John, 69, 191, 195, 197–98

Mimesis (Auerbach), 267

Miscellaneous Studies (Pater), 208

Mitchell, W. J. T., 96

Monsman, Gerald, 211

Morality: *Gulliver's Travels* and, 179–81; and McCarthy, 260–77; and Pater, 212

More, Henry, 179

Morris, William, 94–95, 217–21

Morton, A. L., 206

"Most of It, The" (Frost), 201–4

Muldoon, Paul, 248

Murphy, William Martin, 238

Music, 9–10

"Music of Poetry, The" (Eliot), 94–95

My Confession (Chamberlain), 263–64, 269–70

Myth, 8, 127, 138, 224; historicized, 264; and Yeats, 240–41

Nabokov, Vladimir, 156

Nationalism, 244, 249

Nature, 195–204. *See also* Human nature

Negative Dialectics (Adorno), 5

New Critics, 3–4, 5–9, 63–64, 78, 103

New Historicism, 100–101

New Thematics, 64–68, 72–73

Nietzsche, Friedrich, 23, 104, 268, 273, 277

Night Battles: Witchcraft and Agrarian Cults in the Sixteenth and Seventeenth Centuries (Ginzburg), 64

"Nineteen Hundred and Nineteen" (Yeats), 247

Nonsense, 94–96

Norris, Margot, 229, 231–32

Norton Anthology of Literature by Women, The, 35

Notes of a Son and Brother, 6–7

"Notes Toward a Supreme Fiction" (Stevens), 53